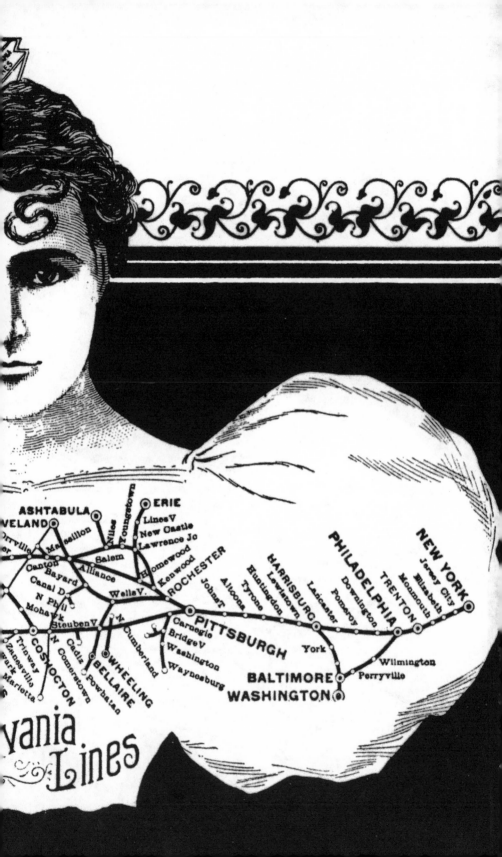

Women, the Railroad,

and the Rise of Public

Home

Domesticity

on the Rails

AMY G. RICHTER

The University of North Carolina Press

Chapel Hill & London

Publication of this work was aided by a generous
grant from the Z. Smith Reynolds Foundation.

Set in Filosofia and Didot types
by Tseng Information Systems, Inc.
Manufactured in the United States of America

The paper in this book meets the guidelines for
permanence and durability of the Committee on
Production Guidelines for Book Longevity of the
Council on Library Resources.

Library of Congress Cataloging-in-Publication Data
Richter, Amy G.
Home on the rails : women, the railroad, and the rise
of public domesticity / by Amy G. Richter.
    p. cm. — (Gender and American culture)
Includes bibliographical references and index.
ISBN 0-8078-2926-9 (cloth : alk. paper) —
ISBN 0-8078-5591-x (pbk. : alk. paper)
1. Railroads—United States—History—19th century.
2. Railroads—Social aspects—United States—History—
19th century. 3. Sex role—United States—History—19th
century. 4. Women—United States—History—19th
century. I. Title. II. Gender & American culture.
HE2751.R534 2005
303.48'32'097309034—dc22   2004016552

A portion of this work appeared earlier, in somewhat
different form, as "At Home Aboard: The American Railroad
and the Changing Ideal of Public Domesticity," in *Gender
and Landscape: Renegotiating the Moral Landscape*, ed. Lorraine
Dowler, Josephine Carubia, and Bonj Szczygiel (London:
Routledge, 2004), and is reprinted here with permission.

cloth   09 08 07 06 05   5 4 3 2 1
paper   09 08 07 06 05   5 4 3 2 1

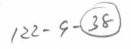

122- 9 - 38

To Simon,

and

in memory of

his grandfather,

Sidney Richter

SUMMER EXCURSION ROUTES
Pennsylvania Railroad

CONTENTS

ILLUSTRATIONS

ACKNOWLEDGMENTS

Grants, fellowships, and awards have provided me with more than financial support; they have served as a source of encouragement and validation. At Clark University, I am grateful to the History Department for a Hillery Research Award and to the Higgins School for the Humanities for a Faculty Research Grant. The Lerner-Scott dissertation award from the Organization of American Historians gave me faith that my dissertation could someday become a book. At the dissertation stage, I received an Albert J. Beveridge Grant from the American Historical Association; a Predoctoral Fellowship from the National Museum of American History, Smithsonian Institution; a Hagley-Winterthur Arts and Industries Fellowship; and a Prize Teaching Fellowship and Penfield Fellowship from the History Department at New York University. I would never have reached the dissertation stage had it not been for a Margaret Brown Fellowship and a teaching assistantship from NYU.

Material support and encouragement can get a scholar only so far; she needs to get her hands on good evidence. Looking for women in railroad sources and the railroad in women's sources was often slow going. I am thankful for the patience, knowledge, and inventiveness of librarians, archivists, and curators at the following institutions: Archives Center, National Museum of American History; Beinecke Library, Yale University; Bobst Library, New York University; Brooklyn Public Library; Butler Library, Columbia University; Goddard Library, Clark University; Hagley Library; Law Library, New York University; Library of Congress; New York Public Library; Newberry Library; Photo and Transportation Divisions, National Museum of American History; and Winterthur Library. Special thanks to John Fleckner, Lynne Joshi, Richard McKinstry, Michael Nash, Craig Orr, Shannon Perich, Gail Stanislaw, Neville Thompson, Dot Wiggins, and William Withuhn.

This project began as a seminar paper in my first year of graduate school at New York University. From that first paper, Thomas Bender has supported this project and me. He is a wonderful mentor—accessible, engaged, and committed. He delights in his students' successes and tells reassuring stories when things go wrong. I do not have words to convey my gratitude or admiration. Susan Ware's careful reading of the dissertation helped me clarify my thinking, and her commitment to her own scholarship has served as an example. Martha Hodes, Walter Johnson, Darline Levy, Molly Nolan, Catharine Stimpson, and Marilyn Young read my work at this early stage and made suggestions for the future. I continued to consult their comments while transforming the dissertation into a book and hope I have done them justice.

This book also reflects the influence of friends, commentators, co-presenters, and audiences who read or listened to papers and presentations based on this project. I am grateful to Richard John and the Newberry Seminar on Technology, Politics, and Culture for providing me with a wonderful forum in which to present the research that appears in Chapter 6. I also thank Dan Bender, Terry Bouton, Cynthia Brandimarte, Anna Clark, Catherine Cocks, Patricia Cline Cohen, Lorraine Dowler, Amy Froide, Roger Horowitz, Meg Jacobs, Walter Johnson, Sarah Judson, David Nasaw, Scott Nelson, Joseph Panetta, Mark Pendergrast, Paul Ropp, Roy Rosenzweig, Daphne Spain, and Mark Tebeau for sharing their work and offering comments on mine.

In graduate school I learned that it pays to have smart and kind people read one's work. This study has benefited from many such readers over the years. Among the first were Dan Bender, Terry Collins, Cindy Derrow, Greg Robinson, Joan Saab, and the members of Tom Bender's dissertation seminar. Among the last was Bob Roe, who kept asking for one more crack at the manuscript. His skill as an editor is rivaled only by his generosity as a friend. I am also grateful to Catherine Cocks, Pete Daniel, Charlie McGovern, and Barbara Clark Smith, who read early chapter drafts during my time at the NMAH. At key moments in my progress, Susan Porter Benson, Daniel Horowitz, and Rosalind Rosenberg read my work, and their enthusiasm for the project energized me. The same is true of my colleagues at Clark University.

Kate Torrey has been the ideal editor—critical, smart, and supportive. I am especially thankful that she got my manuscript into the hands of Eileen Boris, whose comments were both detailed and expansive; she not only improved the book but inspired me with her commitment to an unknown junior scholar. Jane Dailey also read the manuscript for the University of North Carolina Press, pushing me to expand my research and fine-tune my argument. H. Roger Grant generously read a late draft and saved me from making several embarrassing errors in railroad history. At UNCP, Kathleen Ketterman, Gina Mahalek, and Ron Maner's hard work made the final stages of this project run smoothly (special thanks to Gina for suggesting the title). I am also grateful to Liz Gray for copyediting the manuscript.

Friends and family have sustained me with their interest and enthusiasm for my project. They have provided distraction when needed and motivation when it was lacking. Leslie and Scott offered a place to stay; Thea gave me time to write when I needed it most; Janet and Jerry nourished me with bread, cupcakes, and questions; my mother, Adele, loved me enough for two.

There would be no book without my husband, Jim. Again and again, he reminds me that it is a privilege to have work that I love. Whenever I hesitate, he pushes me forward—to Washington, to Worcester, or back to the computer. Our son, Simon, is lucky to have him as a dad. His confidence gives me courage and enriches my life—public and private.

HOME ON THE RAILS

INTRODUCTION

"Look at the map." With these words the Pennsylvania Railroad invited travelers to contemplate its routes: New York City to Toledo, Chicago to Washington, D.C., Pittsburgh to Cincinnati. . . . The choices seemed limitless; the permutations mesmerized. Dazzled by the intricacies of the Pennsylvania's lines, the viewer might have missed the larger picture: the routes were printed on the torso of a woman—right across the bodice and balloon sleeves of her dress, her expression serious and her eyes dark. The message, perhaps unintended, is significant; during the nineteenth century, railroads and women appeared to have little in common. Indeed, within the cultural values of the day, the ideals of the railroad stood in opposition to those of "respectable" womanhood. The first represented Victorian hopes of commercial, technological, and national progress; the second embodied a realm of moral and emotional rejuvenation beyond the reach of such social change.[1] Yet, as the Pennsylvania's "railroad poster girl" suggests, despite their cultural distinctiveness, women and the railroad share a history. To see it, though, we must train our eyes to take in both at the same time. To that end, this study considers women on trains as the key to a different map, one charting the changing terrain of nineteenth-century public culture.[2]

To see women and the railroad together demands a recasting of railroad history and historiography—a shift away from technological innovation and economic indicators.[3] Railroads have long been understood as places of masculine power—of industrial labor, technological development, business innovation, and political debate. But if trains, as traditionally depicted, were "masculine" because of the power of their engines and the courage of their engineers, they were "feminine" because of the domesticity of their parlor cars and the refinement of their female passengers.[4] In the summer of 1869, *Godey's Lady's Book* made this point in an editorial celebrating the

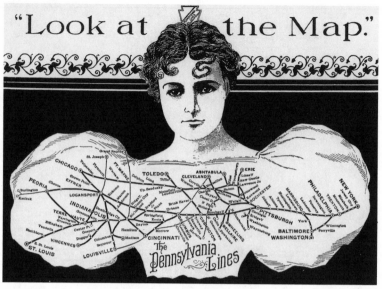

"Look at the Map" (no date). Courtesy of the Warshaw Collection of Business Americana—Railroads, Archives Center, National Museum of American History, Behring Center, Smithsonian Institution.

completion of the transcontinental railroad. Praising this new "wonder of the world," the author reminded readers, "This great work was begun, carried on and completed by men only. No woman has laid a rail: no woman has made a survey. The muscular force and the intellectual guidance have come alike from men." Nonetheless, the author did not portray the railroad as an exclusively male endeavor. Instead *Godey's*, the champion of woman's "true sphere," made a case for femininity's place in the history of the railroad, suggesting a connection between women, commercial life, and national identity: "The great works of modern civilization, the Pacific Railway, for example, are chiefly made in the interest of those humane and peaceful employments in which the feminine element is so prominent; for the advancement of trade, the intercourse of friends, the binding together of the nation."[5]

Simply put, talking about women and the railroad was, and is, a way to talk about larger cultural changes.[6] A cursory survey of illustrations of railroad life confirms the presence of women and the importance of femininity aboard the trains. As expected, images of gentlemanly conductors, brave engineers, and attentive porters convey the

"The Train is Coming." Even a fashion plate noted the train's presence in women's lives and underscored that the separate spheres gained meaning through proximity rather than isolation. From Godey's Lady's Book, May 1850. Courtesy of the Winterthur Library, Printed Book and Periodical Collection.

familiar variety of masculine types associated with the railroad. More startling, however, is the portrayal of women. Lucius Beebe's celebratory *Mr. Pullman's Elegant Palace Car*, for example, contains numerous images of white female passengers flouting conventions of appropriate feminine conduct—an older woman pulling on the conductor's signal with her umbrella, a lone female passenger combing out her hairpiece in plain sight, an attractive woman turned away from her traveling companion to meet the viewer's gaze. Other images depict women carrying themselves in public with the same decorum and air of domestic propriety with which they oversaw their own parlors. Here they tend to children, converse with gentlemen, and even sing hymns.[7] These contrasting portrayals point to a tension in Victorian public culture: aboard the trains, ladies were not always "ladylike," yet the trains were depicted as public spaces in which women could maintain their respectability beyond the home. In these images, women are both the markers of unsettling cultural change and the means of stabilizing such transformation.[8]

The railroad did not single-handedly transform the American economy or remake American public life and culture. It was, however, both site and symbol producing experiences and stories about historical change in general and the reorganization of Victorian culture in particular. For nineteenth-century Americans, the railroad was the apotheosis of their age—the ultimate realization of Victorian faith in hard work, discipline, order, and national progress. According to Daniel Walker Howe, American Victorianism was a system of values that "exercised a kind of hegemony" for most of the nineteenth century. It celebrated nationalism, discipline, rationality, efficiency, didacticism, and morality—values that were projected onto the railroad.[9] The railroad's development was typical of changes elsewhere—rationalization, industrialization, urbanization—yet special in its ability to concentrate the impact of those changes within a small space.[10] (More than one hundred years later, Michel Foucault would wonder at the "extraordinary" nature of the train and contemplate its power as a cultural symbol: "It is something through which one goes, it is also something by means of which one can go from one point to another, and then it is also something that goes by.")[11] For these reasons, nineteenth-century journalists, travelers, and poets used it as shorthand for social diversity, national integration, technological innovation, and corporate organization.

Because the railroad stood for contemporary life in all its ambiguous guises, popular depictions of it reveal American Victorianism in a state of contradiction and transition.[12] Although nineteenth-century travelers touted the railroad as an example of rational business practice or technical order, they experienced it as complicated and unruly. Many passengers boarded trains with the belief that they were entering a space with the power to remake them and all of society. A sense of newness—of modernity itself—inspired them to seek meaning and impose order, as they traveled between one realm of experience and another.[13] Michel de Certeau suggests the timelessness of this phenomenon when he writes that the experience of railway travel "is necessary for the birth, . . . of unknown landscapes and the strange fables of our private stories."[14] In crafting their railroad stories, passengers and railroad companies used Victorian values to meet the challenges of large-scale social disorientation. In the words of Marshall Berman, they attempted "to become subjects as well as objects of modernization, to get a grip on the modern world and make themselves at home in it."[15]

The nature of the railroad sparked such cultural adaptation. Scholars of the American South have, for example, pointed to the railroad as an important site of contact and struggle between whites and blacks at the close of the nineteenth century. These railroad stories offer some of the earliest and starkest examples of a much larger effort to create, impose, and resist new racial identities.[16] In them, the railroad takes on significance because of its modern qualities—as a commercial space subject to the demands of the market, as a mobile space carrying people beyond local controls and knowledge, as a small and intimate space challenging notions of what constituted respectable contact among strangers, as a socially diverse and fluid space capable of blurring the lines of class and caste. These qualities of railroad travel inspired white southerners to reinvent the signs of whiteness and blackness in the form of Jim Crow segregation. As W. E. B. Du Bois famously explained, for many whites an African American was quite simply someone "who must ride Jim Crow in Georgia."[17]

The renegotiation and imposition of racial identities comprised only one effort to stabilize social and cultural change on the trains; gender too was central to attempts to come to terms with the new experiences of public life in the cars. Mid-nineteenth-century Victorianism divided the world into two distinct and gendered realms.

The presence of women aboard the trains revealed that the boundary between the two spheres was permeable. A traveler might sit for hours elbow-to-elbow with another passenger; she ate and slept among strangers. How could she maintain her privacy—the basis of her respectability—under such circumstances? Did she, in fact, have any claim to privacy in such a public space? The railroad's ability to juxtapose social complexity and corporate rationalization complicated matters by further confounding the distinction between public and private activities and behavior. To what extent were the railroads public? They were privately owned and managed yet at times had been subsidized with government funds and were increasingly regulated to serve the "public interest."[18] By repeatedly redrawing the line between private and public, often connoting multiple definitions of each ideal, the railroad and its female passengers challenged the separate spheres ideal that defined Victorian gender roles.

This book revisits the debate over separate spheres in order to argue that the rearrangement of public and private stood at the center of the transition from Victorian to modern American culture for both women and men. Since the 1960s, historians have used the concept of separate spheres to interpret the lives of women.[19] Some women's historians have defined it as an oppressive set of cultural norms that confined women to the home and limited their destinies. Other scholars have interpreted the private sphere as a women's domain—a nurturing alternative to the public world of men, a catalyst for gender consciousness and the emergence of feminism. Still others have studied distinct feminized "publics" operating alongside the male bourgeois public sphere described by Jürgen Habermas.[20] Some have argued that women's "domestication" of public life was subversive and enabled women to influence a number of social and political issues.[21] This last group describes white middle-class women's involvement in family decision making, voluntary associations, and the consumer marketplace. It also chronicles working-class and African American women's presence in the public concerns of politics and the economy. Most scholars now agree that the boundary between the two spheres was permeable and that "private" values exerted a powerful influence upon "public" activities.[22] Indeed, some suggest that the line between public and private has become so blurry that the dichotomy has lost all explanatory power.[23]

the line between public and private

Finding femininity in a setting steeped in the values of manly achievement offers an opportunity to reconsider the separate spheres ideal as an agent of cultural change. Using separate spheres to describe a broad array of transformations, scholars have created a historical narrative in which women are forever entering public life but are never quite public actors beside men.[24] Recasting the railroad as a "women's space," this study places the female and male spheres side by side.[25] Tracing the changing values encoded in one very important domesticated public space as they moved away from Victorian notions of self-restraint and moral responsibility toward a consumer ethos of individual comfort, it shows not only that public life changed the experiences and opportunities of women, but that women were part of the fundamental transformation of Victorian public culture. When women boarded railroad cars they entered cultural conversations about social difference, racial dominance, and order. Significantly, they contributed a cultural vocabulary for remaking public life ("domesticity") without shattering the belief that it was an unruly realm best left to white men. Nonetheless, women—white and black, wealthy and working-class—were part of a contested and messy Victorian public culture in the throes of remaking itself.[26]

Nineteenth-century railroad car designs, company rule books, etiquette manuals, popular fiction, jokes, and even legal rulings reveal a variety of people imposing the separate spheres ideal on the rails, with white women travelers serving as the justification for the inclusion of domestic trappings. As the private (in the form of domesticated accommodations, special spaces reserved for ladies and their escorts, a wide array of services and courtesies) became more prevalent in public, the meaning of the private shifted. Originally considered a moral haven from the competitive world of business, the private sphere came to connote comfort, convenience, and social respectability. Morality had been perceived as the special domain of women, but comfort, convenience, and respectability were not. And so, the domestication of public life transformed the railroad from a place of risk and social mixing to a setting in which both men and women sought to insulate themselves from social contact. Victorian Americans' reliance on gender difference to mask the often discomforting divisions of class and race fueled the emergence of a mixed-sex public in which both women and men bought goods and services to insulate themselves from the experiences of true social diversity.

For a culture steeped in the ideal of separate spheres—as American Victorianism was—this was a striking innovation, like deciding night were day or winter summer. If home was the site of comfort and womanly influence sequestered from the competitive, diverse, and morally suspect world of men, how could someone expect to feel "at home" in public? In the confined spaces of the railroad, women and men renegotiated the boundary between private and public. They shaped public life to their will, reimagining it as a realm of moral and physical comfort, transplanting the values and expectations of the private/feminine home onto the public/manly world on rails. To be sure strikes and interracial violence, social diversity and danger challenged this new domesticated ideal, but the vision of a homelike public took on growing importance with the emergence of America's consumer culture—in hotel lobbies, department stores, photographers' studios, theaters, and even public parks.[27] By the opening decade of the twentieth century, these spaces comprised a hybrid sphere—a social and cultural realm shared by women and men, where deference, privilege, and comfort were determined through commercial rather than personal relationships. In other words, the midcentury understanding of public life as uncertain, dangerous, and masculine was replaced with a modern ideal of "public domesticity"—a vision of an orderly, comfortable, and safe realm that, while not feminized, was no longer solely masculine. This larger transformation is revealed in stark relief aboard the railroad.

The opening chapters of this study establish the historical connections between women, the railroad, and the public culture of late-nineteenth-century America. They demonstrate the value of studying women and the railroad together. Key words of women's history (separate spheres, domesticity, lady) impart new meaning when joined with those of business history (rationalization) or African American history (segregation), all of which were used to interpret and order public life. Chapter 1 places the railroad in cultural context by examining popular railroad narratives. Chapter 2 considers the railroad's place in the lives of nineteenth-century women by providing a composite travel narrative constructed from women's diaries, letters, and advice manuals. Chapter 3 considers the changing meaning of domesticity on the rails and traces the implications for public life. Focusing on the emergence of specialty cars (sleeping cars, dining cars, parlor cars) in the 1860s and 1870s, this chapter argues that public domesticity was not simply an attempt to make women "at home" in public, but a contested ideal tied to new commercial values and the articulation of social difference.

The next three chapters examine the shifting terrain of public and private as revealed in depictions of the "lady," the "gentleman," and the "New Woman." Although the first two figures are often associated with the ideals of Victorian propriety and the last with the bold strivings of modern womanhood, all three were trying to answer the same question: How can public life accommodate the presence of women? Women's entry into public life neither emancipated them from the private sphere nor produced a public uplifted or purified by womanly influence. Instead, altered gender ideals and a revised notion of public and private permitted American culture to move from Victorian restraint to modernity without abandoning the notion of separate spheres. In many respects the idealized modern woman who stepped off a train in the 1920s was a capable public actor. Yet, despite her fitness for the public realm, she continued to carry the baggage of private values. More important, the public culture she encountered was not the same as that imagined or experienced by her mid-nineteenth-century predecessors; no longer perceived as an unwieldy sphere of diversity and anonymity, the public defined by the cars had been domesticated for both women and men.

Tracking the public culture of the railroad provides insights into the complex and contradictory ways Victorian Americans accommodated the anonymity, social diversity, and technological uncertainty of modern life. It builds upon and challenges existing scholarship on identity and public spaces; the meaning of the home in Victorian culture and its relation to more public domains; the relationship between modernity and novel configurations of sex, racial, and class segregation; and the interaction between gender and technology, including changing ideals of femininity. Charting connections—between business practices and domestic life, between the language of law and the vocabulary of Victorian etiquette, between the demands of "masculine" technology and popular depictions of "feminine" ideals—encourages (even demands) a more nuanced exploration of the gendered nature of culture, both private and public, at the end of the nineteenth century. What emerges is new map of the shifting boundary between private and public and a gendered understanding of the passage from Victorian to modern American culture. We must bring the "poster girl" out from behind the map; she is the key.

# Narrative Lines

RAILROAD STORIES IN
VICTORIAN CULTURE

Writing during the 1870s, Charles Francis Adams was perhaps the first to note the railroad's usefulness to cultural historians. Adams, an economist and historian, spent much of his career as an advocate of railroad regulation, serving on the Massachusetts Board of Railroad Commissioners and as president of the Union Pacific Railroad. Despite his commitment to the importance of facts and figures in matters of railroad administration, he began his book *The Railroads: Their Origin and Problems* with a cultural consideration of his subject. Before turning to the challenges of regulating the railroads, he looked back to the railroad's origin and observed that "the honest wonder" it inspired had left a legacy of considerable intellectual value. The suddenness and enormity of the railroad's impact were, in Adams's estimation, even more dramatic than the discovery of America. The "engine and its sequence, the railroad, . . . burst rather than stole or crept upon the world," while Columbus and his crew alone witnessed their spectacular discovery in 1492. Countless spectators greeted the railroad "with a full realizing sense that something great and momentous was impending."[1] From its invention, the railroad reshaped the landscape and transformed daily life. It operated as agent, site, and metaphor for both the gradual and far-reaching processes—acceleration, expansion, industrialization, integration, migration—that were remaking American life. By opening his study in this manner, Adams acknowledged the railroad not only as a business enterprise to be quantified and regulated but also as a site for emotion, uncertainty, and cultural change.

During the nineteenth century, everyone seemed to have a railroad story. People—famous and unknown—watched, participated in, and commented upon the many transformations wrought by the railroad. Victorian Americans produced a rich body of narratives—personal, cultural, commercial, legal—all intended, like Adams's figures and regulations, to order the new experiences of railroad travel. By drawing a wide variety of ordinary people into a debate about the path of progress, the railroad inspired a lively and contradictory record. Railroad promoters told stories of efficiency, speed, and national cohesion; to them the railroad was an agent of progress—a teacher of democracy, a social and moral benefactor of the common man, an instrument of commerce, and the means of fulfilling America's manifest destiny. To its detractors, the railroad was, at best, an unnecessary invention rendered redundant by the growing number of canals; at worst, the handiwork of the devil, defiling the countryside, endangering women and children, and undermining American morals.[2] The spectacular, participatory, and controversial nature of the railroad's arrival enhanced its cultural significance. As Adams observed, "Every day people watched the gradual development of the thing, and actually took part in it. . . . There is consequently an element of human nature surrounding it. . . . To their [contemporary] descriptions time has only lent a new freshness."[3]

[handwritten margin note: Art, River – bire canal and moral decline]

Descriptions of the railroad remained "fresh" throughout the nineteenth century because the railroad underwent its own transformations—its arrival was both sudden and gradual; its development characterized by tremendous raw potential and constant refinement. Because of the dual nature of its development—from trains of mounted stage coaches pulled by steam locomotives in the 1830s to the fully integrated lines of ten to fifteen cars a mere forty years later—the railroad was forever new to nineteenth-century travelers and commentators. The novelty of rattling along during the early days of rail travel in an open car at the rate of ten miles per hour and inhaling coal soot did not prepare one for the experience a few decades later of having dinner at a beautifully set table and looking out the window as the scenery passed at forty miles an hour.[4] The innovations in railroad design and car architecture during the nineteenth century were almost dizzying in their variety as designers, engineers, and railroad companies met the demand for separate ladies' cars, classed accommodations, and specialty cars offering sleeping, dining, and parlor settings.[5]

The extension of track mileage similarly reflected the suddenness of the railroad's impact and the importance of more gradual fine-tuning. In 1826, John Stevens operated the first steam locomotive to run on tracks in the United States—a locomotive of his own design on a circular track in the yard of his New Jersey home. Less than a decade later, in 1835, there were 1,098 miles of railroad track in the United States. By 1850, the figure stood at 9,021 miles and, in just five years, fueled by the California gold rush and a new congressional policy of land grants, more than doubled to 18,374 miles. In the ten years following the end of the Civil War, track mileage doubled again from 35,085 miles in 1865 to 74,096 in 1875.[6] This impressive growth, however, failed to transform significantly the movement of goods and people. The early rail lines connected existing commercial centers, and by 1850 only a few hundred of the 9,021 miles of track lay outside the Atlantic and Gulf seaboard states. Moreover, much of the new track built during the 1830s and 1840s consisted of individual short lines, frequently single-tracked and of differing gauges. Despite the convenience these new railroads offered some passengers and shippers, each operated on its own timetable, making connections between lines difficult. (Even the timetables were unreliable, giving rise to the popular expression "to lie like a timetable.")[7]

Throughout the century, technological and business innovations coordinated the expansion of track mileage and the planning of schedules, as some lines were abandoned and others knit together into an integrated system. Through such gradual but significant adjustments, the railroad became a familiar part of American life while still connoting innovation. Even as Adams praised the railroad's ties to the past, Walt Whitman hailed the locomotive as the essence of his age, "type of the modern—emblem of motion and power—pulse of the continent." Whitman's locomotive, with its "train of cars, behind, obedient, merrily flowing," seemed to capture the full range of social, technological, and business developments that characterized the moment.[8] Whitman celebrated the modern railroad as consolidation and coordination enabled companies like the New York Central and the Pennsylvania Railroad to provide faster and more direct travel. The meeting of the Central Pacific and Union Pacific at Promontory Summit, Utah, in 1869 ushered in a new era of mobility as the North American continent was opened up to an increasing number of railway passengers.[9] The celebration of the famous "golden spike" uniting the two lines was emblematic of the importance of the railroad to American progress. As the haphazard proliferation of railroad lines gave way to system building, the railroads established themselves as the country's first "modern business enterprises."[10]

Rail passengers now encountered the benefits of complex administrative coordination as well as the monopolistic tendencies under which such coordination thrived. By the turn of the century, one could travel from New York to Chicago in twenty hours without changing cars. (During the 1850s the same journey would have taken over three days and involved several different rail lines.) The institution of standard gauge and standard time in the 1880s helped fulfill the railroad's promises of speed, efficiency, and national integration.[11] The 1880s and 1890s witnessed the standardization of basic railroad equipment — automatic couplers, air brakes, and block signals. In 1892, the power of the railroad companies and the need for standardization of rates and fares was reflected in the Populists' call for nationalization of the railroads.

While the railroad was a vital site for developing methods of standardization, integrating distant towns and small depots into a growing national network, the cars were also a part of an expanding sphere of anonymous social relations associated with the nineteenth-century city.[12] In fiction and nonfiction, cities and railroads revealed themselves as chaotic sites characterized by unpredictable encounters with strangers.[13] Theodore Dreiser portrayed the promise and threat of the unknown city by first presenting his protagonist Carrie Meeber on a train headed for Chicago. Published in 1900, *Sister Carrie* tells of a young woman's transformation within an urban world of strangers, and the railroad serves as the site where that process begins. Confidence men, dangerous strangers, and unknown benefactors lurked in cities and on railroad cars.[14] Both settings encouraged contact among strangers of different classes and races and demanded deciphering to ensure safe passage. Yet even as the social life of the railroad mirrored that of cities, train travel differed from urban life and created a distinctive milieu: only rail travel demanded the constant and simultaneous negotiation of both urban social disorder and the systematic ordering associated with the rise of larger business enterprises and managerial capitalism. In this way, the railroad stood squarely at the crossroad of the major social, business, cultural, and technological changes remaking national life during the second half of the nineteenth century.

 No wonder then that Americans told so many railroad stories; it seemed as though everyone and everything was "aboard." In 1886, a brakeman recalled a single train transporting "a corpse in the baggage car and a bridal party in the Pullman, . . . over a hundred going to the court at Winona, one murderer, two horse thieves and a post-office robber, two secret societies, and besides all this a couple of bright little girls."[15] Similar (albeit less colorful) lists appear with an almost overwhelming frequency in a wide range of sources, as travelers claimed that a train trip "reflected the comprehensive scope of our national life during the closing days of the nineteenth century."[16] Or that "a railroad is a microcosm, a trip thereon is an epitome of life."[17] Yet another traveler proclaimed the railroad car "the epitome of the United States" and praised its ability to reduce "the whole game of national life" to "the dimensions of a drawing-room."[18] And Whitman lauded the interstate railroad lines as "the most typical and representative things in the United States."[19]

This metaphor of the railroad as nineteenth-century microcosm operated as a self-fulfilling prophecy, encouraging passengers to view the railroad and contemporary life as reflections of each other. Narratives about the railroad were recorded in diaries, newspapers, respectable family periodicals, volumes of jokes and anecdotes, etiquette manuals, children's books, and even lullabies.[20] In 1880, the passenger department of the Chicago, Rock Island & Pacific Railway published a small volume of Christmas stories for its young passengers.[21] One story, entitled "Santa Claus' New Team," portrayed an aging Santa complaining of cold weather, fatigue, and the burden of delivering toys. Finding his traditional method of toy delivery wanting, St. Nick replaces his team of reindeer with a locomotive. This story might be interpreted as a marketing ploy, evidence of the growing specialization and sophistication of railroad management and promotion. Railroads were revising the nature of Santa's fame—moving vast amounts of freight and sustaining the urban emporia that celebrated Christmas in a dazzling array of lights and consumer goods. By the end of the century, Santa Claus, once a sentimental character of Victorian home life, was a celebrity reflecting the values of a lively consumer culture.[22] It is only fitting then that the railroads used him in their promotions. But within the context of other contemporary writings on the railroad, this brief, humorous story takes on broader meaning, fueling the belief that no one—not even Santa Claus—could escape the influence of the trains.

Such narratives implicitly connected the railroad to the remaking of not only national but also everyday life. They expanded and amplified the impact of the railroad, bringing stories of travel to audiences beyond the confines of the cars and rails; passengers, in turn, carried these stories with them onto the trains and saw their experiences through these narratives. Experience and narrative each imparted meaning to the other, and together gave the railroad its cultural standing. William Dean Howells's 1872 novel *Their Wedding Journey* cleverly made use of this interaction. Echoing other popular accounts of newlyweds in the cars, Howells told the story of Basil and Isabel March as they traveled to Niagara on their honeymoon tour. Throughout the journey, Isabel seeks to elude the notice of other travelers; she does not wish to be identified as a newlywed and checks every public display of affection between herself and Basil for fear of being associated with those who "sleep on each other's shoulders on every railroad train." While seeking to avoid the gaze of others, Isabel engages in the popular pastime of identifying newlyweds abroad and proclaims their conduct "outrageous, . . . scandalous, . . . really infamous." Despite her protestations and vigilance, Isabel ultimately gives in to the monotony of rail travel and wakes "to find her head resting tenderly upon her husband's shoulder."[23] Ironically, Howells's novel heightened the visibility of honeymooners on the trains. According to a travel writer in 1897, "the bridal couple, with showers of rice coming from every source, are ever present [aboard the trains], and objects of marked interest since the advent of Mr. Howells's 'Wedding Journey.'"[24]

Both "Santa Claus' New Team" and *Their Wedding Journey* depict a world of expanded demands and increasingly complex social negotiations: How can Santa possibly deliver toys to so many children? How can Isabel March withstand the gaze of so many strangers and still enjoy her honeymoon? These seemingly unrelated (and silly) questions underscore the cultural significance of railroad narratives. Even as both stories suggest that the railroad has opened up a larger and more challenging social sphere, they celebrate order; Santa and Isabel both encounter new demands—geographic expansion, social diversity, intimacy with strangers—but, in the end, prove themselves part of the world the railroads have created. Both narratives assert the triumph of order aboard the rails: Santa delivers his toys more efficiently; Isabel is a typical honeymooner after all.

When people told railroad stories they were trying to discern patterns not only on the rails but in the larger world epitomized by this drawing room–sized microcosm. Like timetables and business plans, railroad narratives were part of a larger effort to create order amid sweeping historical change. The stories organized the experiences of rail travel, sorting them into familiar categories and circulating them among readers. Despite their number and variety, when taken together, nineteenth-century railroad stories convey wide-ranging preoccupations with the nature of American national life, the influence of new commercial relationships, and the shifting boundary between private and public life. By examining these themes, it is possible to map the railroad's various narrative lines, to trace their meandering (often circular) routes, and to chart their common destinations.

By the latter half of the nineteenth century, travelers spoke of the railroad as a national space. For many white Americans railroad cars served as settings to celebrate or lament the social arrangements of their heterogeneous democracy. Some Victorians viewed the mixed social life of the cars as evidence of a uniquely American love of togetherness. An 1870 article on "American Railway Traveling," for example, declared that "the American, gregarious by nature and by education, . . . seeks his comfort in the greatest number with whom he can associate."[25] The article favorably contrasted the American open coach with the European compartment car. The latter, marked by clear divisions of class, accommodated only a small number of passengers who were locked into their car and required to remain seated for the duration of their journey. The large American coach, with its broad central aisle, rows upon rows of seats, and heterogeneous passengers, encouraged interaction and mobility and sustained many Americans' sense of themselves as members of a classless society. This belief in the diversity and equality of the traveling public was a vital part of many railroad narratives and remained such an important part of railroad lore that many white passengers clung to it even in the era of specialty cars and racial segregation.

It is tempting to dismiss such praise of the American open coach as

Early American Open Coach Car (c. 1830s). From "Railway Passenger Travel," Scribner's Magazine, *September 1888. Courtesy of the New York University Libraries.*

overblown expressions of Victorian nationalism and unreliable measures of American exceptionalism, but the development of the American railroad differed from that of Europe in important ways. The low capitalization and the terrific rate of development in the United States yielded lines constructed of light tracks, and the lightweight open car was better suited to these tracks. The open coach was also cheaper to build and could carry more fares than the European carriage car. The material conditions of American railroad development produced a unique technological form that in turn sustained nationalistic sentiment. Rather than responding to the increased needs of an industrializing nation, as in England, the American railroad was part of the early stages of the country's industrialization.[26] In most of the country, the railroad not only facilitated travel but created it. Moving across North America the railroad created a national space in which Americans both experienced and articulated their distinctiveness from Europe.[27]

It is not surprising then that railroad stories repeatedly considered the nature and status of the United States' national life. Two types of American railway journeys in particular captured the popular imagination and dominated writings about the railroad: the passage from the country to the city and from the city to the impressive scenery of the American landscape.[28] In both journeys, the railroad, in the phrase of the day, "annihilated time and space." This movement of people mirrored the railroad's rapid movement of freight, linking vast regions in a network of mass production and distribution of goods.[29] Such mobility—from rural to urban, from urban to wild—fostered the commingling of city, country, and wilderness. Railroads carrying mail, newspapers, catalogs, and goods broke down the isolation of "island communities" and drew them into a larger national consciousness.[30] Francis Lynde, author of popular railroad fiction, had one of his protagonists observe that "the railway civilizing process is much the same the country over" and that those brought in contact with the railroads "lose their identity as sectional types."[31]

For passengers from rural communities a train journey carried them beyond local knowledge and drew them into the orbit of urban life. A story from 1896 tells of a traveling salesman painting a picture of urban sophistication for a "pretty girl" with whom he finds himself traveling. Discovering that the woman has never been to New York City, the salesman "draws a very graphic picture 'of the only town in the country.' She is charmed—nay, fascinated. Perhaps he invites her to have a little lunch on the train. . . . Her heart is no longer in the country town. It is traveling at the rate of forty miles an hour and beating very fast."[32] Like Dreiser's more famous Sister Carrie, this young woman and other such passengers could contemplate "the great city, bound more closely by these very trains" and ask themselves, "what, pray, is a few hours—a few hundred miles?"[33] In a matter of moments the distance between urban and rural could be erased.

Conversely, a long-distance journey from the city introduced urbanites to the expansive North American landscape. This journey, too, revealed the lure of the unfamiliar and the loosening of local ties. "I never felt as if I was out of doors before," was a common exclamation as Easterners viewed for the first time the grandeur of the trans-Mississippi West.[34] The barriers between city and country, North and South, East and West collapsed under the railroad's wheels.[35] Within the cars, regional distinction yielded to an imagined connection to the nation. In 1903, M. G. Cunniff reported on "the comforts of railroad travel" in the pages of *World's Work* and noted the crosscurrents of American travelers. "Thousands of Chicago people . . . visit the Rocky Mountains, but thousands of mountain dwellers in New Hampshire and Vermont pack excursion trains to Boston."[36]

The mobility provided by the railroads sustained a new narrative of American civilization as not only unified but balanced.[37] David Nye notes that nineteenth-century Americans celebrated both "the biggest waterfall" and "the longest railway bridge." According to Nye, "natural places and great public works became icons of American greatness."[38] The railroad brought these two visions of the sublime into closer relation with each other and, in the eyes of many Victorian Americans, heightened the greatness of their nation.[39] The engineering achievements of the railroad inspired a sense of pride in American technology and its triumph over the landscape. Guidebooks depicted with equal enthusiasm the wonder of the landscape and the feats of technology that made them accessible. The image of tracks reaching to the horizon or climbing to staggering heights made concrete the Victorian faith in limitless national progress.

Despite accelerating the pace of daily life and introducing new dangers, the railroad offered release from modern anxieties. By delivering passengers quickly to the beauty of nature, the railroad provided an antidote to the enervating forces it seemed to embody. The landscape soothed the harried nerves of a technologically advanced civilization and offered rejuvenation. In the words of an 1884 guidebook, Americans needed escape "from the toil and vexations of business, the wear and grind, and the routine of usual avocations." The railroad enabled them "to gain new vigor by simple contact with nature, breathing the air, using the diet, seeing the sights, and hearing the sounds of the country."[40] While celebrating the power of new technology, Americans implicitly acknowledged its danger to individuals.[41] The reciprocity between technology and nature, national progress and rejuvenation was hailed as the unique achievement of the nineteenth-century railroad and, by extension, American civilization. Or so it seemed.

As the railroad set the nation in motion and knit the country more tightly together, it demanded that passengers contemplate the relationships that would sustain a national society. The end of the Civil War and the trend toward the consolidation and coordination of smaller lines created greater opportunities for individuals—especially middle-class individuals—to take long trips and to move beyond their everyday associations into a complex social world.[42] The mix of classes and regional types celebrated in so many railroad stories failed in others to create a well-ordered society. Many narratives conveyed discomfort with diversity by ridiculing rural people. An 1899 anecdote entitled "One of Those Sleeping Car Yarns" described passengers traveling from Indiana to Niagara Falls on a reduced excursion rate. The travelers "were of the raw, blue jeans type, many of whom were crossing the border of their state for the first time, and the few who patronized the sleepers were getting their first taste of [railroad] luxuries." During the journey, an elderly couple mistakes the air brake cord for a clothesline and hangs "all of their wearing apparel, including boots and shoes, on it."[43] The weight of the clothing eventually stretches the cord, sets the air brakes, and brings the train to a jarring halt. An observer of railway types writing just two years earlier noted that "Uncle Rube and his 'first trip on the kyars'" was becoming a figure of the past, but mocked the immigrant traveler who insisted upon bringing his "little odd cap, queer looking sack, his lunch of sausage."[44]

Rather than portraying the railroad as unifying the nation, such accounts underscored how travel exacerbated the differences that divided Americans. In popular and personal accounts, rail passengers described the cars as places to meet people they saw as different. Respectable ladies might travel beside women and men of a different class, race, or region. In a smoking car, businessmen from New York City could rub shoulders with country doctors or farmers. As previously noted, everyone—northern and southern, urban and rural, immigrant and native-born, black and white—seemed to be aboard the trains.[45] Under such circumstances, the celebrated and democratic large American coach often failed to satisfy Victorian notions of propriety and the importance of privacy. According to one practitioner of the "art of travel," American railroad cars were especially inhospitable to "the temperament which prefers retirement, freedom from intrusion, dislikes the burden of seeing other people come and go, and is wearied by having its attention constantly attracted by crying children, or newspaper boys, or by many diverse objects."[46]

The problem was not only the diversity of the traveling public but the anonymity of the people aboard. Set free from the watchful eyes of small communities, uncertain of the identities and status of those around them, passengers often flouted the rules of conduct. Enumerating the "rules for travelers" in 1885, one railroad observer joked that rudeness itself had become a rule when he proclaimed that "the traveler who has never before been 20 miles from home is permitted to sit in one seat and put his feet on the other."[47] More than a de-

"A Kiss in the Dark," Currier & Ives (1881). Depicting the moment when the car emerges from a tunnel, this image plays upon the anonymity of railroad car life and suggests how moral uncertainty, social danger, and racial confusion merged in popular railroad stories. Under the cover of the tunnel's darkness, one man (front left) takes out his bottle of liquor and another man (front right) turns to kiss the woman nearest him. The smiles and laughter of several other passengers reflect not only that the men have been caught but that the railroad Romeo has mistakenly kissed an African American woman. Courtesy of the Library of Congress, LC-USZ62-1382.

cade earlier, an article in *Putnam's Magazine* called for "some simple code of railway-traveling . . . by which such [conduct] could easily be regulated." [48] As they contemplated the world of strangers in the cars, passengers struggled to create social order and define new rules of common conduct.

Story after story portrayed the railroad as an unruly world where strangers mixed freely and innocent confusion or well-crafted duplicity thrived. Conductors warned off three-card monte players and lamented the professional costs of mistaking a village alderman for an "impecunious passenger." [49] A couple of drummers might take pity on a poor blind man selling berries only to discover that he "was the most successful 'bunco steerer' and gambler in town." [50] Could one know for sure that the sickly old man in need of a seat was a war hero and not some "wretched specimen" with a second-class ticket? [51] Amid such uncertainty, a woman seeking to maintain her respectability and avoid insult was well advised to keep her eye on the neatly dressed college student sitting behind her; despite his fine appearance, stories, songs, and poems suggested that he would try to steal a kiss as the train passed through a tunnel.[52]

In some accounts, showing kindness to the right stranger led to a felicitous and financially enriching marriage; in others, trusting the wrong person led to lost dignity, property, or worse. For example, in "An Incident of Travel," Isabel Winchester asks her cousin Fitz James Eustace to surrender his seat to an elderly man. When he refuses, Isabel gives up her seat. The train soon arrives in Boston and is met with a great celebration—a public welcome for General John Sutherton, hero of the Mexican War. Of course, the old man is General Sutherton. The next day Isabel and Fitz James receive two invitations to a ball honoring the general. At the ball, the general thanks Isabel again, praises her for respecting the aged, and introduces her to his son, Alfred Sutherton, a successful Boston businessman. Eventually, Isabel and Alfred marry, and Fitz James, long his cousin's suitor, is thrown aside.[53] A popular song, by contrast, described the pitfalls of kindness to strangers. In "The Charming Young Widow I Met on the Train," a sympathetic passenger loses his watch, purse, ticket, and gold pencil-case to a confidence woman.[54] In both accounts, the railroad is an extreme incarnation of public life, challenging individuals to evaluate their fellow passengers and to match wits with strangers.

Could the railroad companies smooth over the conflicts and confusions that emerged from diversity in the cars? Although the railroads remained privately owned they were inextricably tied to the public interest and subject to judicial authority that increasingly demanded the companies maintain order. By the 1860s American courts had created a body of rulings obligating railroad companies to promote the welfare of their customers and the public in general. Known as the common law of common carriers, these decisions argued that the railroads were quasi-public businesses because they provided services to the public. The courts therefore could exercise their authority over the railroads on behalf of the public.[55] Built with private capital, the American railroads benefited from public aid in the form of land grants, loans, and liberal credit. By 1871, the year Congress discontinued land grants, the government had given 158,293,377 acres of public land to railroads or to individual states to subsidize railroad construction. Such government involvement both reflected and fostered a belief that the railroads served the American public.[56] Under the common law, railroads were required to carry any passenger who offered to pay the established fare and were obligated to provide equal service to customers. But the law did allow exceptions. Railroads could exclude individuals of known "bad character," people who carried contagious disease, or persons intending to harm the railroad or its passengers. Finally, as a common carrier, a railroad had the right and obligation to establish reasonable rules to guarantee the physical well-being, comfort, and convenience of its passengers. In order to withstand legal scrutiny, these rules needed to be made known to the public and enforced consistently. If the railroad met these two criteria, it could legally eject passengers for failure to comply with its rules.

By establishing the public interest in the railroad, the law of common carriers made railroad companies responsible for policing the cars, and they took charge of the unruliness and uncertainty of public life. But as business enterprises in a competitive marketplace, railroads also needed to act in their own commercial interest. A safe and well-policed space would attract passengers and encourage repeat patronage, but how could companies control passengers without alienating them?[57] What rules were appropriate and enforceable within a space that was both commercial and public? During the 1870s and 1880s, as farmers and politicians struggled to regulate the railroad companies, the companies themselves sought to regulate the conduct of passengers. For example, the courts ruled that passengers had a right "to protection from drunken and disorderly persons, and from ruffians in general," and if rail companies failed to "use 'due diligence' for the protection of peaceable passengers," they would be held liable.[58] As early as the mid-1860s, railroad companies instructed their workers to prevent passengers from endangering themselves or from being hurt by other passengers. The wording of the employee rule book of the Indianapolis and Madison Rail Road captured the delicacy of this task: "In the event of any Passenger being drunk or disorderly, to the annoyance of others, [trainmen] must use all gentle means to stop the nuisance."[59] Even a public nuisance needed to be reprimanded gently because he too was a paying customer.

Over the second half of the nineteenth century, as railroad companies developed sophisticated means for exerting control over the social environment, railroad managers and passengers struggled to reconcile the emerging commercial culture with older Victorian notions of self-control.[60] In the cars Victorians confronted the failure of self-control to organize public life and the courts ceded to corporate authorities the responsibility for that failure.[61] If passengers viewed railroad cars as public spaces of diversity and social confusion, railroad companies and entrepreneurs needed to minimize the chaos of car life. The commercial relationship between company and passenger took on greater importance relative to that between individual passengers, and railroad staff and services intervened to smooth over rough spots.

An 1871 anecdote reflected this shift. In "Money vs. Husband" the commercial bond between passenger and railroad company takes precedence over the marital bond between husband and wife; professional and commercial concerns win out over personal connections. A woman traveling on the Vermont & Massachusetts Railway takes her seat and the train pulls away from the station. She runs to the back window and sees her husband, who had been delayed buying tickets, chasing the train. The woman begs the conductor to stop the train, but he refuses. The wife explains, "I'm starting on a journey and can't get along without my husband." The conductor is unmoved. Finally the woman reveals that she has no money and cannot pay her fare. Now the conductor stops the train: "Moral—Money will stop a train of cars much quicker than husbands." Despite the humorous tone and the implied sympathy for the unattended woman, the anecdote's narrator offers the moral with no irony and advises the husband to "attend to his business better next time."[62]

In the final decades of the nineteenth century, railroad companies increasingly tempered the starkness of their business demands with amenities. As the organization and reach of the new corporate railroad systems grew, so did the efficiency and quality of service aboard the rails. The amenities of travel proliferated during the 1870s and 1880s as companies added specialty and extra-fare cars to their trains. By the 1890s, the passenger departments of railroad lines enthusiastically promoted their cars' comforts and raised passenger expectations. Rail company brochures extolled the amenities available aboard their lines. Perhaps the most visible service was that provided by black porters: this reframed the social diversity of rail travel by staging a set performance of racial inequality in the cars. In addition, many companies addressed the challenges of diversity by organizing "personally conducted tours" with guides to see to the logistics of tickets, baggage, and sightseeing. Rather than an uncertain public space in which individuals struggled to establish their relationship to strangers, the cars emerge here as an increasingly privatized and commercial space where passengers "owned" their seat, section, or even car for the duration of their journey and remained aloof from the vagaries of public life.[63]

In 1903, a travel writer boasted that "a citizen may enter a railroad ticket-office, have a vacation spot picked out for him, have a boarding place secured and a guide chosen. All he has to do is to name the sort of fish he wishes to catch—the railroad will bring him most comfortably to the fish."[64] Or as conductor Charles B. George noted, "It all seems a simple matter to be a traveler," passing "from the care of one corporation to another, until he has been in charge of perhaps half a dozen companies."[65] In this narrative, the unruly and heterogeneous life of the cars was replaced with a fantasy of consumerism and service. If the first narrative portrays the cars as a city on rails, the latter conjures up a department store moving through the landscape. Both narratives coexisted well into the twentieth century.

Like other narrative lines considered here, the narrative of the cars as a consumer haven traveled in contradictory directions. Some passengers embraced the comforts of railroad travel and marveled at their growing sophistication. For such travelers there was no stronger evidence of America's greatness as a modern civilization. More comfortable seats, better food, and attentive service from polite porters and conductors freed passengers from petty concerns, inspired good conduct, and returned civility to the rail travel experience. Companies increasingly guaranteed uniformity of service along their routes, establishing the railroads as conduits for a shared culture, subsuming regional differences in standardized service.[66] But the same amenities and services that heralded the nation's most recent triumph carried a taint of luxury, overindulgence, and dependence antithetical to American notions of republican virtue. Writing in 1895, E. W. Sanborn complained that the attentive service of the railroad companies took power from passengers and undermined the system of checks and balances provided in the U.S. Constitution. The founding fathers "had no knowledge of the railroad . . . Much less could they imagine palaces rolling through the land on wheels."[67] As the railroad companies confronted the burden of regulating commercial public space, travelers like Sanborn considered the gains and losses inherent in such an arrangement. At the heart of this reckoning lay the shifting relationship between private and public—the separate spheres that gave meaning to Victorian notions of respectability.

〰️ As corporate managers and strategists used the railroad's dual nature as a private institution in the public service to recast railroads as increasingly private spaces owned by passengers for the duration of their journey, passengers too used the ambiguities of the experience to exert their own sense of control over social interactions. During a railroad journey, a traveler easily observed her fellow passengers in what Howells described as humanity's "habitual moods of vacancy and tiresomeness."[68] Another passenger marveled at the "perfect intimacy which comes from a total lack of acquaintance," and praised "the intimacy of strangeness." He noted, "strangers find a certain comfort in confiding to other strangers details of their inner lives, which they would go to infinite pains to conceal from a friend or relative."[69] Or, as retired conductor Charles B. George explained in his 1888 autobiography, "Perhaps no other place furnishes a better opportunity than the train does for the study of human nature." According to George, "the mask that is worn so successfully in church and society is dropped . . . without reserve." After forty years of railroad work, he could readily enumerate the varied species of travelers—the selfish passenger, the timid traveler, the inveterate questioner, among others.[70] Lulled into a sense of privacy by the overwhelming anonymity of rail travel, passengers revealed their "true selves" in public.

Many travelers and railroad employees embraced this quirk of rail travel to rationalize and order their experiences aboard. Nearly a decade after George's autobiography, an article entitled "Types of Railroad Travelers" echoed his observation that the railroad provided an ideal setting for classifying human beings into social types: "During a twelve-month [period] nearly every person is at one time or another upon a railroad train, and to the student of types this furnishes a favorable opportunity for observation."[71] Among those identified were: "the bridal couple," "the sleepy man in the corner," "the traveling man," "the sedate business man," and "the young lady writing letters." The brief characterization of each suggests that these figures were familiar to readers. And, in fact, a wide array of magazines, railway guidebooks, and promotional publications were already encouraging passengers to fix the identity of their traveling companions by such discernible characteristics.[72] An 1884 book playfully drew children into this process, implying that anyone who traveled by rail, even a child, would recognize these common railway types. It asked, "Do you see that great big, red-faced, fat man, who has two seats to himself, and who looks as if he were an alderman, and never did anything but eat?" The story also identified "the thin gentleman who sits behind him, and the strong-minded lady with the umbrella, who is on the other side of the car."[73] The fat man was the inconsiderate traveler who opens the window and exposes his fellow passengers to a draft; the thin man, the sickly passenger who catches pneumonia; and the lady, the demanding passenger who requires the conductor's constant attention. The constricted space of the railroad car and the social contacts incidental to long-distance travel seemed to render life in the cars manageable by permitting observation and creating bonds among passengers.

Again underscoring that the cars were characterized by both anonymity and intimacy, many stories expressed discomfort with the mingling of public and private aboard the rails. A recurring narrative conveyed a sense of social confusion by portraying individuals in the throes of personal tragedy during travel. In these accounts, the depiction of private emotion amid an unknowing public represented the unique challenge of social life in the cars. In the words of one contemporary observer: "How many are hastening on a death message! . . . There, a young husband and his babe—the mother sleeping in the baggage car. Perhaps the young sister, wife or brother is brought back from the sunny South or West, where they went a few months before to fight the stern battle against consumption. Life's most pathetic incidents are mingled one way or another with the tide of railway travel."[74] Such observations emphasized both the importance and public invisibility of the private context for travel. Death and illness found their way into many railroad stories in order to make this point. Howells even had his newlyweds interrupt their honeymoon to share a few moments with an invalid they meet in a station waiting room.[75] Similarly, songs like "The Baby on the Train" and "In the Baggage Coach Ahead" told of railway travelers disturbed by an infant's cries. In each song, when the passengers reprimand the father and instruct him to take the baby to his mother for consolation, the father explains that she lies dead in the baggage car. In both songs, a family's tragedy moves the passengers to tears and reveals the pettiness of their complaints.[76] But how were they to know? Is a crying baby a nuisance or an object of sympathy? Such stories suggested that at any moment aboard the train public life could collide with private needs.

By assailing the foundational cultural boundary between private and public life so openly, the cars presented travelers with an unfamiliar social environment. The separation of private and public into distinct spheres shaped Victorian notions of proper conduct and deemed the activities and postures of private life inappropriate for public display. When abroad, one was to be both well groomed and well mannered. The preparation for such public display took place in the private spaces of the home. But passengers' private moments played themselves out in public. From one's seat in the back of a railway car, one could view, unobserved, the private dramas of strangers: "The young man who kissed his hand from the back platform, and the girl he left behind waving her 'kerchief in response. . . . The young mother with a child in her arms, whose lips were still moist with the father's parting kiss."[77] Such scenes suggest that while the nineteenth-century cult of domesticity celebrated the domestic sphere as a safe and well-ordered sanctuary from the competitive and uncertain public life of industrializing America, the seemingly separate spheres of private and public life continued to collide in the cars.

In response to these conditions, many railroad narratives reflected anxiety over prolonged periods of confinement with a heterogeneous group of strangers. The same "intimacy of strangeness" that fostered an ideal setting for studying human nature exacerbated the problems of social interaction in the cars. On the one hand, the cars were depicted as sites ripe for public display of intimacy; on the other hand, the public atmosphere and demands of the cars interfered with the intimacies of marriage and courting. A nineteenth-century anecdote book, for example, tells the story of five college men traveling home from a vacation. The conductor enters their car and says, "Well, boys, in the next car there is as lovin' a pair as it ever was my lot to see. They are going . . . to get married, and now if you can have any fun over it, just pitch in." The boys have their fun by convincing the woman that her fiancé is already married. They enter the couple's car and greet the man, "Why, Jones, what the deuce are you doing with this girl?" The fiancé insists his name is Harper, but each man addresses him as Jones and asks after his wife and children until the woman is finally convinced that her fiancé is a married man and father.[78] The story suggests how easily public life on the rails could call identity into question and transform even loved ones into strangers.

The inconvenient and frequently embarrassing collapse of the divide between public and private found its way into the descriptions of common railway types—one of the main narrative devices for creating social order on board. Writing in 1874, the journalist Benjamin Franklin Taylor praised the cars as a site of observation even as he expressed concern for propriety, property, and privacy—all of which seemed threatened by the collapsed social distance of the cars. Among the types described was the "Railway Hog," who gave offense by forsaking appropriate public conduct in the name of private comfort. The Railway Hog was "the man who takes two seats, turns them *vis-a-vis*, and makes a letter X of himself, so as to keep them all." In this awkward manner, he claimed public space for his private advantage and took more than was rightfully his. "Meanwhile, women old enough to be his mother pass feebly along the crowded car, vainly seeking a seat, but he gives them a threatening grunt, and they timidly look the other way." Taylor also mocked "the Bouncers," readily identified by their tendency to "discuss private affairs in a public manner." Such travelers, usually young girls traveling in pairs, remained unaware that their fellow passengers could hear them chattering on in a manner as loud "as a scarlet vest and a saffron neck-tie." The Bouncers openly gave themselves over to private concerns and activities while in public. According to Taylor, "by-and-by they fall to fixing their back-hair, smoothing their eyebrows with a licked finger, and making other preparations." In short, the Bouncers failed to conform to the conventions of public presentation and instead forced their private selves upon strangers.[79]

Is there a moral to all these railroad stories? No single narrative best reflects the railroad's impact on American life. Nor do the varied narratives produce a clear chronology—from danger to security or from confidence to doubt. Railroad narratives cannot report the meaning or direction of historical change, but they do reveal persistent cultural tensions. The forging of a national space and culture, the challenges of an expanding consumer ethos, and the relationship between public and private life—these three themes emerge repeatedly from the body of late-nineteenth-century railroad narratives. The railroad's historical significance resides in these cultural narratives and themes as much as in measures of track mileage and freight tonnage. Narratives and numbers, as Charles Adams noted, are ultimately two different vocabularies for representing and ordering the experiences of modernity created by and encapsulated in late-nineteenth-century rail travel.

According to these stories, the railroad stood poised between national progress and dissolution, between prudent consumption and enslaving luxury, between private and public. Surprisingly, then, at the end of the nineteenth century the railroad occupied a cultural space similar to that of a figure little identified with the rails—the idealized Victorian woman. The next chapter establishes the similarities between these unlikely cultural analogues and places women within the railroad's narrative lines.

When Spheres Collide

WOMEN TRAVELERS, RESPECTABILITY,
AND LIFE IN THE CARS

A book of railway anecdotes published in 1871 asked readers, "Why is a fine woman like a locomotive?" The answer: "Because she draws a train after her, scatters the sparks, and transports the males."[1] Many such jokes circulated in the popular literature of the nineteenth century. Visual puns playing on trains of ladies' dresses and trains of railway cars adorned sheet music and provided the punch line for cartoons. The juxtaposition of women and railroads fueled this humor, since railroads were routinely identified as masculine endeavors. In December of 1868, *Harper's Bazar* printed a cartoon of a man and woman walking beside a train track. The woman's dress flows in a long train of fabric that dominates the image. The caption quotes the "Fair Creature's" observation that "The Train is very much Behind, isn't it, Dear?" The woman's exaggerated costume is inappropriate in this setting and suggests that only one type of train belongs here. Women, such jokes implied, were out of place among the powerful machines that propelled so much of America's industrial and commercial life.[2] Yet even as jokes and cartoons asserted that women were out of place among the trains, they depicted women in these spaces alongside men. Whether joking, fretting, or scolding, popular railroad narratives portrayed "decent" women as part of life in the cars.

The women who boarded the trains during the second half of the nineteenth century shared cultural assumptions that they simultaneously upheld and challenged. Most clung to the conventions of "respectable" womanhood as defined by the ideology of separate spheres —the network of Victorian social and cultural assumptions that associated women with domestic values and social deference. The separate spheres ideal masked class and racial divisions by crossing the

"The Train is very much Behind." From Harper's Bazar, *12 December 1868.*
Courtesy of the Winterthur Library, Printed Book and Periodical Collection.

boundaries of the American class structure and transcending racial lines. A working-class immigrant could learn from a ten-cent pamphlet the same rules of etiquette that an African American woman read as part of her education at normal school or that a white middle-class woman read in a beautifully bound etiquette manual. Following these rules, all might consider themselves "respectable" within Victorian social conventions.[3] The diversity of women embracing this ideal highlighted the social power of gender within Victorian culture, complicated notions of class and racial difference, and eventually transformed the separate spheres ideal itself.

And so, the same improbable pairing that made Victorian Americans laugh reflects a complex process of historical change, as a respectable woman's place expanded to include the railroad. Travel accounts by women and popular writings about women travelers reveal the cultural tensions and accommodations that emerged when men and women shared the same public spaces. Like so many other railroad stories, narratives of women passengers capture the contradictions of their historical moment: women are portrayed as both marginal and yet central to the stories told about this late-nineteenth-century "world on wheels." In a railway journey, a Victorian woman struggled to maintain her respectability as she traveled back and forth among an almost domestic ideal of privacy, an expanded network of

"Big Four Two-Step" (1897) offers another play on the lady's train. Courtesy of the DeVincent Collection of Illustrated Sheet Music, Archives Center, National Museum of American History, Behring Center, Smithsonian Institution.

polite society, and, finally, a public world of social differences, new experiences, risks, and possibilities. She charted a cultural voyage in which she conformed to—and at the same time revised—the cultural prescriptions defining her as a creature of the private sphere.[4] In so doing, she helped redraw America's cultural map.

There was nothing implicitly subversive in a woman's decision to travel.[5] Because both Victorian men and women believed that the ideal woman was domestic and private, women in public used the conventions of the private sphere to demonstrate their respectability at every turn, even when these expressions proved unsuitable for public life. Many women towed their gendered and domestic identities into public as a matter of course, not as a disguise or social wedge. Once in public, however, women did much more than merely uphold the cultural and social status quo. In so far as the demands, skills, and opportunities of public and commercial life were perceived as inconsistent with the conventions of feminine respectability, travelers' claiming the responsibilities and privileges of Victorian womanhood demanded considerable cultural innovation and negotiation. By asserting the values and conventions of Victorian womanhood in public, women widened the gap between social prescription and experience and guaranteed that those values and conventions would become both the agents and objects of cultural change.

Instead of attempting to free themselves from their domestic roles and responsibilities, many nineteenth-century women traveled in order to meet the demands of the private sphere. Often a woman's first experiences as a wife took place within the confined and public spaces of a railroad car. A honeymoon trip was in many respects a journey to, rather than away from, domesticity. It provided, in the words of one advice manual, "escape [from] the prying eyes of friends and relatives" so that husband and wife could acquire "that more intimate knowledge of each other's character so essential to their future happiness."[6] Despite their distance from family and neighbors, the newlywed couple remained a subject of intense scrutiny. In the railway car, under the watchful eyes of her fellow passengers, a young bride first tried on her role as wife. Confined with strangers for hours at a time, she attempted to balance new marital intimacy with appropriate public conduct. Finding the perfect balance proved difficult often enough that etiquette books warned that "couples who may evince a silly affection by overfondling of each other in public make themselves appear extremely ridiculous to all who may see them."[7] Humorists, by contrast, ridiculed those who erred in the direction of stiff propriety by behaving like "old married people or cousins, as they sit demurely in the cars."[8]

Once married, many women continued to travel by rail in the

company of their husbands. They traveled because their husbands wanted or needed their wives with them as they met their professional responsibilities. Aboard trains, women and men tended to frame women's experiences in domestic terms and highlight the activities that confirmed this interpretation. When members of the Boston Board of Trade undertook the "first through entire train" excursion from Boston to San Francisco in 1870, almost half the passengers were women, but most were noted in the passenger list as "and wife."[9] Throughout the trip, the members of the board complimented their female companions for their attempts to add beauty and homey touches to the train. When railroad engineer John J. Thomas planned a railroad journey from Selma, Alabama, to Chicago to attend a convention of the Brotherhood of Locomotive Engineers in 1887, he simply told his wife Frances that he "wanted to go, adding that [they] would take a sleeper and have a nice comfortable trip." Although hesitant about riding in a sleeper, Frances agreed to travel with John and "enjoyed it so much, that in all our trips after that she asked about a sleeper the first thing."[10] The inclusion of wives in such excursions seems to have been taken for granted, and Frances accompanied John to all subsequent conventions.

Women frequently took to the rails for the maintenance of extended family networks, often traveling great distances alone to visit relatives. Between 1879 and 1898, Meta Du Pont Coleman traveled annually from her home in Louisville, Kentucky, to her grandmother's home in Wilmington, Delaware. In a letter to her grandmother reporting her safe arrival in Louisville, Coleman boasted, "I hope the two postals have reached you, and that you will realize how easy it is to travel alone."[11] Coleman's correspondence reveals the intricate web of familial connections that tempered the apparent freedom of women's traveling alone. Flanked by relatives at the beginning and end of a journey, women supplemented family surveillance during their travels by writing letters, reporting on their progress and safety. Coleman sent these reports even when it was inconvenient to do so. In one of many letters to her grandmother, Coleman wrote, "I fortunately got your postal written just a moment before the train moved off. I rushed to the door and asked the porter if he would mail it for me."[12] Traveling from one home to another, Coleman never lost sight of her family obligations. During a station stop, for example, Coleman shopped for a napkin ring for one relative and bought a book on sewing recommended by her aunt. Later in life, she traveled by train with her children, and her identity as a proud mother permeated her experiences. Writing to her husband in August of 1890, she expressed her wish "that you could have seen the baby on the train." Reporting that the baby "did not cry once" and that the other passengers admired his behavior, she asked her husband, "Don't you think we are blessed with such a good baby?"[13] For Coleman, travel emphasized and strengthened her ties to family.

Even women who traveled to escape domesticity often sought only a temporary reprieve. Traveling with family members for a brief tour of Yellowstone Park or taking a journey alone to improve her health, a woman traveler understood that her trip was finite.[14] Many expected a return to their usual way of life. Anna Brackett presented an extreme example of such travel to the readers of *Harper's Monthly* in 1891. Writing on the dangers of nervous exhaustion, she described a friend so worn out from maintaining a comfortable home that she took a six-hour train ride just to have time for herself. Brackett quoted her friend's explanation for her choice: "It is such a comfort not to have the fireman come in to ask whether he shall put any more coal on the fire, and the engineer pulls his throttle valve without looking to see if I signal him; and even if the train runs off the track, it is none of my business, and I am sure that it is not my fault, and nobody will think of blaming me for it." And so renewed by her six-hour journey, "she comes back the next day ready to go to work again."[15]

These honeymooners, wives, kin, and tourists moved about in public within prescribed Victorian gender roles.[16] They did not perceive themselves—nor were they widely perceived by others—as transgressing the conventions of respectable womanhood. But to say that women were accepted on the trains is not to claim that they moved about on the same terms as men. As suggested by their reasons for travel, women continued to stand for and enact private values. Aboard the trains, they were subject to dual expectations: to maintain their private roles and to learn and conform to the rules governing much of public life. The flexible, unstable relationship between domestic and public life pushed respectable women to play a complicated part: sometimes they retreated into the protected privacy that was the traditional right of their sex; at others, they developed the new social and commercial skills needed to navigate in public.

The continued association of Victorian women with their private roles even when in public is apparent in popular anecdotes. In an 1896 article on child rearing, Mary Cadwalader Jones included a story in which a woman approaches the ticket window of a busy railroad station. After waiting in line, "she gets to the window [and] she [asks] a number of questions, take[s] some time to make up her mind, more to find her money, and perhaps, after she has passed on come[s] back again for supplementary information."[17] Another story described an older woman buying her ticket in a crowded depot. As the trains are about to depart and passengers rush to purchase tickets, she makes conversation with the clerk. She remains oblivious to the needs of the other travelers anxious to buy their tickets and make their trains. When the clerk asks for her destination, she eagerly replies that she is visiting her daughter, rather than responding with a station name. The exasperated ticket clerk finally reprimands her with a "now, look here, my good woman."[18] Other anecdotes made similar observations—women pestering conductors with questions, falsely accusing porters of taking money they themselves had misplaced, or annoying fellow passengers by claiming too many seats and carrying too much luggage.

These anecdotes reflect the persistent belief that women were ill-suited for commercial public life. In June 1881, the *Spice Mill* reported, "For once in the history of the Union depot its roof has sheltered a woman who knew just where she wanted to go, the train she wanted to take, the hour for departure, the fare, and the time of arrival."[19] According to Jones, such a creature was an anomaly: "The mass of their sex do not show that they have much sense of discipline or responsibility outside their own households, unless it is forced on them by the necessities of business life." She concluded that women lacked the appropriate honor for public life. A man's honor, she explained, was concerned "in all his doings, whether for business or pleasure; but with a woman it is not so far-reaching, being commonly taken to mean only the virtue of chastity."[20] According to Jones and other popular accounts, women were too accustomed to the protection and insulation of the private sphere and therefore were generally not fitted to the demands of commercial transactions.[21]

Life on the trains, moreover, seemed likely to rob women of the limited honor they did possess. Many stories emphasized the vulnerability of a woman's virtue and again gave credence to the notion that women were incapable of navigating public life, but with a slightly different spin. Women appeared in fiction, newspaper accounts, and railroad exposés as the preferred victims of unscrupulous men. Often, the lines between romance, insult, and some sketchily drawn sexual victimization blurred, but all such stories justified women's confinement in the home, reminding readers that in public men lured women into inappropriate familiarity and thereby compromised their virtue. At best, an overly intimate conversation or display of affection drew the attention of fellow passengers and marked a woman as silly, inexperienced, flirtatious, or simply rude. At worst, it led to theft or even greater victimization.

In 1877 the *New York Times* warned against "nomadic flirtations" on trains and expressed its wish "that young ladies will shun the conversation and pea-nuts of strangers, lest they should find themselves entertaining pickpockets unawares."[22] Many stories of female vulnerability began quite innocently with a male traveler offering some small courtesy. One knowing conductor described what he called "The Magazine Route," in which a man offers a woman a magazine and returns later to see if she has enjoyed it. "The love diplomat," as the conductor called him, then invites her to share a meal in the dining car, where he treats and they share a bottle of wine. The ultimate victimization presumably takes place after they arrive at their final destination and leave the train together.[23] The cautionary tales of the pickpocket and love diplomat warned women that the anonymity of the trains endangered them because it freed men from the fetters of their reputations and tempted women to compromise their own.

Popular depictions of traveling salesmen combined concerns about the spread of commercial interactions with anxieties about women's virtue. The skills that made good commercial men—an outgoing personality, the ability to anticipate the needs or desires of others, a broad knowledge of the pleasures and discomforts of travel— were equally suited to taking advantage of inexperienced female travelers and compromising their reputations. In the opening pages of *Sister Carrie*, Theodore Dreiser described the method of one of the best-known traveling salesman ever to talk up a lone woman in the cars. Charles H. Drouet, according to Dreiser, was always ready to assist a woman traveling alone and "if some seemingly vulnerable object appeared he was all attention—to pass the compliments of the day, to lead the way to the parlor car, carrying her grip, or, failing that to take a seat next to her with the hope of being able to court her to her destination." [24]

Many salesmen considered such conduct a matter of professional pride. They presented themselves as defenders of women and children—as the most gentlemanly of gentlemen. Sharing their commercial knowledge, helping mothers traveling with irritable children, or passing the time with stories of the big cities they had seen, drummers saw themselves gladly compensating women for the hardships of railroad travel. These contrasting depictions of the commercial traveler encapsulate two of the themes that dominated popular accounts of women traveling by rail: in the salesman, women encountered the contradictory demands that they acquire commercial knowledge yet conform to the Victorian ideals of female virtue and dependence. [25]

Portrayed as lacking the skills necessary for successful commercial or public interactions, women considered respectable by Victorian standards were, nonetheless, out in public. One female traveler, recalling the days before her journey, confessed, "If there was any one particular thing that I had always had a horror of, it was traveling, and especially traveling alone." She recalled that "the fatigue and deprivations of travel—the attention to baggage, tickets, changes, et cetera," appalled her. "Any enjoyment which involved an hour's ride on the cars, or the finding of a new locality, even in the familiar city of New York," she concluded was just "not worth the trouble." [26] The trouble women experienced when traveling was indeed considerable; it involved not only attention to the type of details enumerated by this hesitant traveler but also constant recognition and renegotiation of the roles and expectations that shaped a woman's public reception. In spite of these difficulties, this woman decided to travel. She and other female travelers mastered more than timetables, ticket coupons, and baggage checks. Once in the cars, they overcame the challenges of finding a suitable seat, establishing their relationship to the train staff and fellow passengers, as well as passing the time until reaching their station without incident. Victorian assumptions about woman's virtue influenced the performance of all these tasks.

A woman's negotiation of public life began at home when she decided what to pack and how to dress for her journey. Good preparation could mitigate the fears and troubles that accompanied a woman on her journey and help recreate the protections of the private sphere. For an extended rail journey, a woman carried an oilskin bag that held her sponge, soap, and towel as well as brushes for hair, teeth, and nails.[27] In her carpet bag she was advised to pack a shawl, night clothes, and clean linen, including collars, cuffs, gloves, and hand-kerchiefs. Etiquette books advised the traveler to store away in a trunk everything that she would not need until her final destination and check it for the duration of the trip. Although long-distance trains made twenty-minute stops for meals, such stops were irregular and the rush to order, eat, and reboard so great that etiquette books and guidebooks also advised women to bring elaborately packed lunch baskets.[28]

Sparing women the crush at trackside restaurants, the lunch bas-ket offered them exemption from one of the more unruly elements of train travel. Observing a number of lunch baskets in the cars between San Francisco and Lake Tahoe, Lucy Bird wrote, "they gave the car the look of conveying a great picnic party." [29] A well-stocked basket could last for many days. During a trip from Boston to California in 1876 Jennie Kimball and her companions filled their basket with "cold beef and some tongue and . . . pickles, and jellies, and canned fruits, and mustards and sauces . . . plenty of bread, and a pat of fresh butter and some doughnuts to go with Coffee and a bit of cake . . . a package of Tea, some sugar, condensed milk . . . a new shiny tin tea-pot and a big mug." [30] Despite the advantages of taking along one's food, only women were advised to carry baskets. According to an article on "the art of travel," men risked their dignity when they did so, "but if there is a woman in the party, the luncheon-basket could be made to ap-pear as hers, and the escort might enjoy it, even if under protest." [31] Women were permitted, even encouraged, to take precautions against the inconveniences of public travel, yet men were instructed to en-dure these inconveniences as a matter of honor.

Once bags and basket were packed, the appropriate traveling out-fit—balancing convenience and propriety—had to be selected. Again, etiquette books provided explicit instructions. The recommended costume mirrored a respectable woman's street attire: simple, un-adorned, muted in tone, with a veil to minimize eye contact. Women were to avoid velvet because it attracted dust and silk because it at-tracted attention. Instead they were advised to choose durable fabrics: merino or alpaca in winter, gingham or linen in summer. Thick-soled

Advertisement for Wilson Packing Company's cooked meats (trade card, no date). The couple enjoys a peaceful lunch aboard while other travelers rush about outside the train window. Note the sign reading "20 Minutes for Refreshments." Author's collection.

boots and an underskirt or petticoat with a pocket for money completed a woman's traveling costume. The message of such an outfit was clear: a well-mannered woman strove to be inconspicuous. She sought to insulate herself from the rudeness of others and, more important, identified herself as polite and genteel. In the words of one etiquette book, "A quiet unpretending dress, and dignified demeanor, will insure for a lady respect though she travel alone from Maine to Florida." [32] By her costume, a female traveler conveyed awareness that she had passed beyond the moral and physical protection of the home into a new realm where she would need to take responsibility for her safety.

The instructions regarding a woman's traveling costume emphasized the importance of maintaining one's privacy, but the oilskin bag in which she packed sponge, soap, towel, and assorted brushes alerted the female traveler that, especially if she were traveling long distances, she would need to perform some usually private acts in public. The public intimacy of washing and dressing on the cars heightened the need for a woman to protect herself from over-familiarity and simultaneously made it difficult for her to do so. Benjamin Taylor, writing for the *New York Examiner and Chronicle* during the summer of 1873, captured the resultant discomfort and surprise when these

"Traveling Dress for Lady" on the figure on the right.
From Godey's Lady's Book, *August 1886. Courtesy of*
the Winterthur Library, Printed Book and Periodical
Collection.

private acts became public. Surveying the car after a night of travel, Taylor noticed a heap of clothes "shaped like an egg" occupying one of the seats. Slowly the egg "hatched" and a "drowsy piece of woman-hood" emerged. Apparently she had "slept in her head but not in her hair," and as Taylor watches she carefully attaches, "arranges and sorts out curls and ringlets. . . . She washes her face with a handkerchief, rights her collar, shakes out the creases, tosses the little hat upon the top of all things, and is ready for breakfast." [33] The lady, when compelled to apply her public face in public, became a subject of ridicule rather than respect.

An Englishman traveling in the United States in 1867 admired the American women so well accustomed to "the publicity of their system of railway traveling." Traveling in the South, he praised the many married women who slept comfortably under the watchful eyes of strangers, "each laying her head on her husband's shoulder for a pillow." In the morning the same ladies "appeared all to have with them brushes and combs and towels and soap" as they set about their toilette in the car.[34] Women described these arrangements in a less positive light, often complaining about the wait for the ladies' dressing room and washroom. Caroline Dall reported that one day while traveling on the Rock Island Railroad "thirty-three women and children and two men used our [the women's] dressing room."[35] Once inside, many women found an uncomfortable room "so small that you can barely turn around in it." Several noted that their elaborate clothes were difficult to manage in tight spaces. Eliza Clendenin and her companion "had an awful time this morning getting dressed, but after a fierce struggle we succeeded." Cornelia Adair complained bitterly about the inconveniences women faced on the train. She described the difficulty of dressing, undressing, and washing and was shocked to see "ladies with their hair down and in their dressing-gowns walking quietly down the centre of the car from their section to the washroom, through rows of half-dressed men."[36]

Even a comfortable lavatory could generate complaints, because it encouraged the ladies inside to forget those who were still waiting. Laments about the many ladies who spent a "half hour in an elaborate arrangement of their bangs while some poor wretch is waiting for the chance of washing her hands after the long, black journey" was further evidence that women did not know how to get along in public.[37] Indeed this problem seems to have been so widespread that etiquette books and railroad car designers sought to regulate it. John A. Ruth admonished readers of *Decorum: A Practical Treatise on Etiquette and Dress of the Best American Society* that "ladies in traveling should scrupulously avoid monopolizing, to the exclusion of others, whatever conveniences are provided for their use." According to Ruth, "Mr. Pullman, the inventor of the palace car, was asked why there were no locks or bolts upon the ladies' dressing-rooms. He replied that 'if these were furnished, but two or three ladies in a sleeping car would be able to avail themselves of the conveniences, for these would lock themselves in and perform their toiletts [*sic*] at their leisure.'"[38]

One could hardly blame women for monopolizing the dressing rooms. By conveying the right message with her clothes and carriage, a woman could travel within an almost private envelope of male protection and free herself from other responsibilities of public life; or so the etiquette books promised. If accompanied by male friends, family, or an arranged escort, these companions could easily perform small acts of kindness—helping a woman up the steep step onto the train, finding her a comfortable seat, opening or closing windows as needed—and by doing so keep strange men at a distance. In July 1886, Ida B. Wells traveled from Memphis to Kansas City and noted that her traveling companions helped smooth over the bumps of rail travel. "We had the most pleasant trip. . . . The gentlemen were attentive and kind, and my first experience with a sleeper [car] was by no means unpleasant." She even suggested that male protection could, on occasion, insulate black women from the slights of racism. At St. Louis, she recalled, "they put us in a dingy old car that was very unpleasant, but thanks to Dr. Burchett we at last secured a very pleasant place in a chair car."[39]

Wells's experience highlights the role of gentlemanly companions, but what about women who traveled "unattended"? These women needed to decipher and adhere to seemingly contradictory social prescriptions only hinted at in Wells's account. On the one hand, the hardships of travel emphasized women's dependence on men; on the other, the omnipresent threat to women's respectability demanded that they avoid the wrong men at all costs. Etiquette books warned women to avoid overfamiliarity with strange—especially male—passengers. Florence Hartley suggested that women traveling alone find "a seat next to another lady, or near an elderly gentleman."[40] Young men should be avoided. In *The Behavior Book*, Eliza Leslie advised readers that "if a gentleman of whom you know nothing, endeavors to get into conversation with you, turn away and make no reply." Women who avoided improper company would attract the sympathy and respect of gentlemen eager to help and protect them. Leslie explained, "Travelling in America, ladies frequently meet with little civilities from gentlemen, so delicately offered, that to refuse them would be rude."[41] This advice begs the question of how a woman could know from whom she was accepting these "little civilities." Which male behavior was threatening and which chivalrous? Which feminine response was prudent and which rude? The only definitive advice from the etiquette books was that too much familiarity was dangerous and "that no *gentleman* will be guilty of such familiarity."[42]

Despite these ambiguous rules, women gained confidence and a sense of security from their own good conduct. Many black women believed that their polite behavior could provide them with protection during travel. As Anna Julia Cooper noted in 1892, "The Black Woman of the South has to do considerable traveling in this country, often unattended. She thinks she is quiet and unobtrusive in her manner, simple and inconspicuous in her dress, and can see no reason why in any chance assemblage of ladies, or even a promiscuous gathering of ordinarily well-bred and dignified individuals, she should be signaled out for any marked consideration."[43] Too often, however, such hopes were dashed, and white women were much more likely than black women to describe strange males as either nonthreatening presences or eager protectors. Caroline Dall delighted in being "the only lady" in her "fine car" traveling from Salt Lake City in November 1880. In nearly seven months of travel she reported only one instance of threatening male behavior "that could possibly give a woman annoyance."[44] Julia Shubrick wrote to her daughter about a "plain looking man" who offered to "attend to anything for me . . . and saved me much trouble."[45] During her extensive travels, Lillian Leland was similarly "touched by the gentle consideration of men."[46]

White women travelers often used the language of etiquette to describe their interactions with the male train staff, repeatedly describing conductors and porters as "gentlemanly" or "civil" and the assistance provided as "courtesy." When women did not receive the service they desired they dismissed the staff as "discourteous" and "rude." This vocabulary reveals a continued reliance upon the values and behaviors of polite society in commercial situations—a belief that women deserved courtesy from the conductors and porters primarily because they were ladies and only secondarily because they were passengers who had paid for particular services or accommodations. These expectations were not always met. Dall was sorely disappointed when "for the first time, I found myself commanding neither attention nor respect on the ground of simple womanhood." She noted that the porters frequently paid more attention to male passengers who tipped generously than to women traveling alone.[47] Men, more familiar with the importance and ways of tipping, could pay for the attentions that women like Dall felt were the rights of their sex.

Anna Julia Cooper also described the limits of courtesy among the railroad staff. The "gentlemanly and efficient railroad conductors," while eager to anticipate and meet the needs of white women, "deliberately fold their arms and turn round when the Black Woman's turn came to alight." Yet unlike Dall and other white women, Cooper did not dismiss such treatment as rude. When a conductor sent her to the Jim Crow car she "could not take it for want of courtesy on the conductor's part."[48] Where white women saw politeness, Cooper saw a marketplace from which she and other black women were increasingly excluded. Nonetheless, Cooper and other black women held on to the ideal of a polite public realm that would include them—a realm informed by what Frances Ellen Watkins Harper called "true politeness." According to Harper, "True politeness is broadly inclusive; false politeness narrowly exclusive."[49] Noting this distinction, black women hoped to foster a polite public culture in which they would be welcomed.

⁓ Although women travelers invoked the values of the private sphere and were at times circumscribed by them during travel, they also moved beyond them, mastering some of the rules and behaviors of public life. Despite the jokes at their expense, many women had successful commercial exchanges and increased their knowledge of the railroad network. Meta Coleman described to her grandmother "a very pleasant evening at the depot." She proudly recounted that she "checked my trunk, bought tickets and '*chinned*' the man at the Bureau of Information." She then borrowed an umbrella from the checkroom boy, ran some errands, and returned to the depot, where she took her supper.[50] Caroline Dall's account of her trip through Colorado, Utah, and California reveals a high level of sophistication in her ability to evaluate the various railroad services and amenities. When she first contemplated traveling from Washington, D.C., to California she "thought I might as well start for the moon." Early in her journey, however, she confidently offered advice to other "ladies travelling alone" about the relative advantages of drawing-room cars, Pullman cars, silver palace cars, and hotel cars.[51] Even Julia Shubrick, who had needed a stranger's assistance to travel from Syracuse to Albany, later wrote to her cousin Mary about how easy it would be to travel from New York to Lenox, Massachusetts. Shubrick had already gathered "all the advertisements &c." and determined that Mary could easily "go from New York to Bridgeport Con in the steam boat, from there she takes the cars on the Housatonic Rail road and reaches Lenox for tea." Surely, if Mary "is well enough to entertain *French beaus*," Shubrick concluded, "she ought to be able to go to Lenox."[52]

Women also acquired considerable skill in scrutinizing strangers — an ability commonly associated with the flaneur of urban sketches.[53] Proscribed from freely roaming the city streets, where such skills were cultivated, women in the cars studied their fellow passengers and tried to make sense of them. Jennie Kimball noted that public observation was "quite an *art*," as she settled into the car at Omaha and confronted the moment "when . . . we must look about and see who our neighbors are."[54] Mary Frances Armstrong encouraged such observation in an etiquette book written for use in the classrooms of the Hampton Normal and Agricultural Institute. In the section headed "Manners of the Road," Armstrong advised her African American students to "be observant of all about you. A great deal can be learned on a journey, not only of geography, but of human nature and social customs." Armstrong, emphasizing the importance of good conduct to the status of blacks in general and Hampton students in particular, told the story of a young girl traveling a short distance alone by rail. She "amused herself for some time by watching the ways of people in the same car, and seeing one very pleasant, modest looking young lady, not far off, resolved that she would take her for a model all the way." By watching the lady, the girl learned to store her satchel, fold her shawl, take up only one seat, and offer the empty seat next to her to a fellow passenger in need of a place. Careful observation of strangers could teach young women how to act in public.[55]

Observing other passengers was one of the chief amusements of railroad travel. Unlike fleeting encounters with strangers on city streets, life in the cars provided an opportunity for extended observation. Traveling west from Minneapolis, Eliza Clendenin was happy to "have the excitement of a dude to watch us and we to watch him." She mentioned "the dude" several times in her diary, noting that one morning he "donned most of his apparel in the aisle," and on another occasion engaged in some "very peculiar antics."[56] Some women entertained themselves by listening to the conversations around them. Meta Coleman passed the time between trains eavesdropping on a humorous disagreement between a husband and wife; she later recounted it to her grandmother in considerable detail.[57] Another woman wrote that her journey "would have been very stupid if it had not been for two gentlemen that sat across the car from me. One of them was very old, and from half past four until we reached New Albany at eight he told the other about [his experiences in] the Indian war with Tecumseh."[58] Tetia Moss recalled that during her journey to Stroudsbourg she was "obliged to content myself with human nature displayed before me."[59] Making the most of a similar opportunity, Lillian Leland confided in her diary that "I have leisure to observe my fellow passengers" and described them at great length, including not only her first impressions, but also descriptions of their behavior. She affirmed her skill as an accurate reader of men and women as she knowingly identified "one of these women" as "a type I have seen more than once."[60]

The more women observed fellow passengers, the more likely they were to break the etiquette rules that advised them to abstain from conversation with strangers. Anna Dickinson wrote of her "firm conviction that the *only* people who travel are queer people, or worse," and she therefore made it her policy to "never talk in the cars." Having stated this policy in no uncertain terms, Dickinson soon revealed that "now and again I have broken the rule of car silence to my content, or profit, or amusement as the case may be." Much as etiquette books advised women to avoid ungentlemanly men but encouraged them to accept the courtesies of gentlemen, the seeming contradiction between Dickinson's policy of silence and her subsequent behavior emphasizes a belief that women could tell whom they were dealing with on the train. Dickinson never spoke to "queer" people but saw no danger in befriending a young woman traveling by herself.[61] Why should she? Etiquette books encouraged older women to offer protection and companionship to "other ladies younger or less experienced."[62]

Louisa du Pont wrote her mother: "About six I took an observation of my fellow passengers. All were men but two. One of which was a poor unfortunate, with two wee kids, and the other a girl of about my age. The latter was evidently a lady. . . . She was travelling alone and seemed rather lonely. After looking at her a while, and putting her down in my mind as a Virginian, I got up and went over and talked to her." [63]

Etiquette books recommended that acquaintances made in the cars should terminate at the end of journey.[64] Ironically, this advice may have heightened the confidences shared by female passengers. After a long journey on the Northern Pacific Railroad, Lillian Leland observed that "one night in a sleeper does not stir up one's social instincts as two or three days and nights do." Long-term confinement with strangers bred a peculiar kind of intimacy and encouraged self-revelation. In Leland's words: "How confidential people grow after thirty-six hours in a Pullman car. And how one will be drawn into frank acquaintanceship after enjoying for twenty-four hours that solitude only to be found in a crowd." Leland supported this observation by summarizing a conversation with a young girl who described to her "the exact kind of man she wanted to marry and the particular amount of affection she would require from him." In between destinations, with the opportunity to reflect on their lives, women turned to strangers to mull over their dreams and fears. Anna Dickinson found herself offering advice to a young woman trying to decide between marrying or lecturing on behalf of women. Again confirming that travel did not necessarily mean a flight from domesticity, Dickinson, herself a lecturer on behalf of woman's suffrage, encouraged the young woman to become a *"home-maker."* [65]

Women broke "the rule of car silence" with men as well. The courtesies a man could offer a woman sometimes led to extended conversations. Caroline Dall recalled a day spent with "three gentlemen from Cincinnati . . . [who] got me a campstool, set me out in the rear platform, told me stories, and gathered me flowers all day." There is no suggestion of impropriety; she seems simply to have enjoyed the attention and the company that made "the day [pass] like a festival."[66] Meta Coleman told her grandmother about "taking supper and promenading with an unknown man in Cincin[nati] last night." The content and tone of Coleman's letter, as well as her willingness to share the incident with her grandmother suggest that some young women had faith enough in their skills of observation to stretch the rules that defined appropriate female conduct. Although trying to provoke her grandmother, she was ultimately reassuring. After describing how the acquaintance began, Coleman displayed her skills in learning about and evaluating strangers. She reported that the man was from Pittsburgh, that they had common acquaintances in both Pittsburgh and Louisville, and that "he was a very good looking man, that is to say he had a nice face, free from beard, and his age might have been anywhere from thirty to forty-five." Only after conveying all this information did Coleman inform her grandmother that he was a married man, joking that "my hopes were blighted." She concluded by saying that she had "found him a perfect gentleman in every respect, but could not find out his name." [67]

Much of the observation women engaged in on the train focused on identifying people who were like them in order to find safe companionship. The "queer" people were to be quickly identified and ignored. Despite this, women also experienced the railroad car as a site for observing strangers they perceived as different from themselves. From the car windows, women saw Indians and contemplated the lifestyle of Mormons. Although not exactly the freewheeling democratic spaces depicted by railroad enthusiasts, the cars afforded many women a more expansive and diverse public with which they could interact. White women traveled in the cars with African Americans, Britons, Chinese, Highlanders, Indians, and Irish, as well as emigrants traveling west or returning to the East. Up until the early 1890s, black women travelers would have traveled with whites of all classes. Frances Ellen Watkins Harper, traveling as a lecturer in 1867, was frequently drawn into conversation. Despite her nonchalant tone, her experiences underscore that women were truly in public on the cars. Describing one encounter, she wrote, "Last week I had a small congregation of listeners in the cars where I sat. I got in conversation with a former slave dealer, and we had rather an exciting time." Even though she was "traveling alone," Harper did not "show any signs of fear." [68]

Despite the rules of etiquette, the protection of male companions, or even their own desires to remain insulated from those around them, women on the cars interacted to varying degrees with strangers unlike themselves. Women remarked on these differences in a variety of ways. Lucy Bird casually mentioned that the smoking car of her train was filled with Chinese men.[69] Louisa du Pont described two "fat colored parsons that got on in Philadelphia [and] came as far as Washington," but suggested that they were familiar and nonthreatening types. She wrote her mother that the two men "talked Conference Meeting all the way down, and refreshed their eloquence by frequent nips from a black bottle, that had very much the odor of Dr. Strawbridge's general cure all." By depicting the parsons as humorous stereotypes, du Pont confirmed that she was worldly enough to be in on the joke, reasserting white supremacy while sharing public spaces with African Americans.[70]

Many white women described the Indians who gathered at western railway stations, and carefully evaluated their observations against popular depictions in photographs and literature.[71] Lillian Leland noted that the men she observed at the depot "do not suggest the dime novel brave of our childish fancy."[72] Martha Lawrence conveyed her disappointment when she wrote her aunt and uncle that "the wigwams look just like the pictures of them look only they [the pictures] don't show the dirt."[73] Through such comments, women showed their keen observation and conveyed their knowledge of a world more complex than the one they usually encountered.

Observation, however, could fail women. This was, after all, the moral of popular stories about pickpockets and love-diplomats. In June 1888, Meta Coleman told her grandmother a complicated story of mistaken identity. During their honeymoon journey, Coleman and her husband met "a dreadfully horrible and sad sight." Traveling by train in Virginia, they "found a crazy woman" in their car. According to the porter, "some white man had put her on the train in Cincinnati" and friends were to meet her in Richmond. The newlyweds tended to the afflicted woman throughout the trip, and Coleman confided that "I think in the end she took me for her daughter." This tender scene was interrupted when the train arrived in Richmond and a "colored woman and man came forward to claim" the woman. Coleman was both outraged and confused. How could the railroad officials not question the black couple? What was their relationship to the afflicted woman? When the black woman claimed to be the daughter of the woman on the train, Coleman could make sense of none of it: "It was a most peculiar case for the porter said it was undoubtedly a white man that put her on the train and the woman undoubtedly looked white to me though she had a blotchy skin."[74] What was the racial identity of the woman? If the woman at the depot were truly the "crazy" woman's daughter, how could Coleman have been mistaken for her?

Although the story seems extraordinary, having one's identity called into question through contact with strangers was relatively common. Alice Dunbar-Nelson enjoyed recounting how her light complexion called racial barriers into question. Indeed, Dunbar-Nelson would have had little trouble deciphering the scene that so confounded Coleman. On one occasion, she recalled an incident involving her sister Leila and her niece Pauline. Leila's light complexion permitted her to pass as white. (Dunbar-Nelson referred to this practice as "traveling au fait.") At the end of one journey, Leila was met by the dark-skinned Pauline and greeted with a very public kiss. Imagining the meeting of mother and daughter, Dunbar-Nelson described Pauline "running up the gang plank kissing [Leila] in full view of the horrified passengers, who probably thought the brown skin young woman very impertinent to be kissing the white lady."[75] Here then is Coleman's story told from the other side of the racial divide.

The experiences of black women offer many stark examples of how seemingly stable identities were challenged when women moved into socially diverse public spaces. Relatively few African Americans traveled great distances by rail in the second half of the nineteenth century. Those who could afford to do so tended to be members of the middle class, traveling for the same reasons as white women—as part of their work for their communities, to take new teaching posts, or to attend club meetings. Black working-class women might have traveled shorter distances as part of special excursions sponsored by a church group or fraternal organization.[76] Employing the conventions of Victorian feminine respectability and aware of their visibility within the African American community and beyond, they traveled both as individuals and as representatives of their race. In 1905, Fannie Barrier Williams made the link between travel and racial uplift explicit. Writing in the *Voice of the Negro*, she noted that travel not only improved the black race through exposure to "the liberalizing influences of whatever is best and most compelling in American life," but also provided an opportunity to display improvement to one another and to whites.[77] Stephanie Shaw has argued in her study of black professional women workers that many parents and teachers encouraged young black women that they could be or do anything, and "everyone involved operated as if it were true."[78] Such faith led many black women to travel, but in the cars this belief collided with racism.

A popular anecdote mocked black women's displays of respectability on the trains. A white man traveling through Illinois asks a veiled lady if he may occupy the seat next to her. She consents, and the two travel side by side in the poorly lit car. After discussing the weather and politics the conversation takes a more personal turn, and each confides that he or she is widowed. The man grows "more affectionate in his remarks," and as his station approaches he requests the honor of a kiss. Again the lady consents. As the man lifts her veil, the conductor enters with a bright lantern and illuminates the car to reveal the "luscious lips, glistening teeth, extensive nose, white eyes, charcoal countenance, and wavy hair of a she American of African descent." The account succinctly concludes, "He did not take that kiss." Told from the standpoint of the male traveler, the story encouraged the reader to empathize with or laugh at his confusion. The lady's thoughts remain a subject of speculation. Is she confused? Are her feelings hurt? Is she amused by the confidence game she has just played? The text is silent on this issue, but the message is clear: No matter how refined, well spoken, or properly attired, a black woman could not guarantee her acceptance as a lady outside of her own community.[79]

Temporarily denied their respectable identities on the train, many black women experienced confusion, anger, and fear. Mary Church Terrell described traveling with her father in a first-class car in the 1860s. When her father left her briefly to go to the smoker, a white conductor tried to move Terrell into the second-class coach reserved for blacks. She could not understand—she "had been careful to do everything [mother] told me to do. For instance, my hands were clean and so was my face. I hadn't mussed my hair. . . . I hadn't soiled my dress a single bit. I was sitting up 'straight and proper.' Neither was I looking out of the window, resting on my knees with my feet on the seat (as I dearly loved to do). I wasn't talking loud. In short, . . . I was behaving 'like a little lady' as she told me to do."[80] Under similar circumstances, Ida B. Wells refused to leave a first-class car on the Chesapeake, Ohio & Southwestern Railroad in May of 1884. When the conductor tried to remove her physically, Wells struggled, bit the conductor, and was dragged out of the car by three white men. In her autobiography, she recalled that "they were encouraged to do this by the attitude of the white ladies and gentlemen in the car; some of them even stood on the seats so that they could get a good view and continued applauding the conductor for his brave stand."[81] Although recognized within their communities as ladies, Terrell, Wells, and many other black women were denied this identity on the train by "white ladies and gentlemen."[82]

The temporary shattering of identity could prove confusing for some female travelers, as in the case of Coleman and Terrell, or even physically dangerous as in that of Wells and many other black women. The disruption of identity could, however, push a woman to imagine a new role for herself. Separation from one's community and the relative isolation and anonymity of train travel presented women with challenges and opportunities through which they could revise their identities. Some extraordinary women were permanently transformed by the experience of train travel, while other women temporarily imagined themselves in a variety of roles. Wells's experiences on the Chesapeake, Ohio & Southwestern (and the lawsuit she initiated as a result) became the subject of her first newspaper article for a church paper in 1887. Out of this, Wells began to craft her role as a journalist and advocate for her race. Other women, especially white women, tried on identities for play. After seeing a British man behave discourteously in the cars, Lucy Bird "was so thoroughly ashamed of my countrymen and so afraid of my nationality being discovered that if anyone spoke to me, I adopted every Americanism which I could think of in reply."[83] Eliza Clendenin considered herself and her traveling companions with their luggage, walking sticks, and umbrellas and concluded, "we present quite an English appearance."[84]

Although some women expressed specific desires to take on new identities, imagining themselves as cowgirls or wealthy women in majestic parlors, others conveyed a more general sense of being remade by the landscapes revealed to them through the train's windows. Many women traveled because they and their doctors believed that a change of scenery and climate would transform them from sickly to healthy. In many cases, the thrilling and varied American landscape instilled in women a sense of power and an appreciation for change. Crossing the Rocky Mountains imparted a new type of knowledge to Anna Dickinson. In florid prose she assured her readers, "if thou hast ever breathed the elixir of this air, and felt nerve and blood thrill within thee, thou wilt long for it, many and many a time thereafter, through all thy days, as one who having known life, can never be altogether satisfied with the conditions of semi-death."[85] The desolation of this same landscape appealed to Jennie Kimball. As she traveled through Wyoming and the train ascended the Rockies, the treeless landscape of "rocks piled one upon another in the wildest confusion" filled her with "a most emphatic sense of being *alone* — alone with the maker of this wonderful creation."[86] Other women were struck by the variety of the landscapes through which they passed, amazed that one could go to sleep "under dark pines" and awake eight hours later amid the barrenness of alkali plains.[87] They delighted at high peaks and majestic gorges, at the wildness of rivers and the quiet of seemingly limitless open spaces. Again and again, they recorded wonder and a sense of pride in their ability to view unfamiliar American landscapes. Like observing Indians and Mormons or identifying strangers by type, viewing unfamiliar landscapes filled women with a sense of their own growing knowledge. In the words of Abby Woodman during her travels to the northwestern United States, what a delight to admire "such a series of lovely scenes as it is seldom one's good fortune to behold."[88]

Women readily gave credit to the invention that revealed these marvels and took pride in it, although some authorities depicted women as lacking the necessary "nerve" to face the speed and power of the trains. Abby Woodman admired not only the landscape but also "the wonderful skill and energy of man [that] had opened our way amid these wild and sublime solitudes of Nature." Women passengers praised the engineering feats that tunneled through mountains and spanned raging rivers. The Oregon & California Railroad so impressed Woodman that she described its track-work in considerable detail—how "the railroad makes the passage of the mountain, connecting the termini of two roads by a series of tacks and zigzags which measure eighteen miles in its ascent and descent of steep mountain grades."[89] Other women described with wonder the sensation of crossing an iron bridge over a deep chasm or of taking a curve at high speed and high altitude. Standing on the back platform, exposed to the elements, they thrilled not only at the scenery, but also at the sensation of speed. Alice Dunbar-Nelson had a "thrilling ride of a few minutes clinging to [the] outside of [a] Pullman."[90] For Eliza Clendenin a washed-out bridge only added to the adventure of her trip.

While traveling in Washington State she described the frequent wash-outs as "exciting" and "great fun." [91]

Sitting on the back platform or coping with a washed-out bridge, the female railroad passenger reached the furthest point of her journey away from domestic privacy through an expanded world of polite society and the new experiences afforded by technology, commercial life, and national mobility. She embraced the technological power of the train and maybe even felt herself empowered by its speed or by her own bravery. Far away from the gentility and safety of her home, comfortable with the power of the train, the female traveler here appeared free of the cultural assumptions that informed the jokes and cartoons presented at the beginning of this chapter. But women could not remain on the train's rear platform forever, and cultural journeys, unlike geographic ones, do not move linearly through time and space. A single railway journey could not transform a Victorian "True Woman" of the 1860s and 1870s into a "New Woman" of the turn of the century. Instead, cultural change proceeded unevenly.

Susie Clark's 1890 trip from Boston to San Francisco nicely encapsulates this process. Clark appreciated the train's ability to reproduce the conveniences and atmosphere of home even as it carried her to new experiences beyond the private sphere. She praised the train for making the transition from home to the world beyond almost unnoticeable. "The wrench of leaving one's native soil is scarcely felt, even though the new habitat is the width of a continent distant, and active life is resumed in a new world." Presumably this transition was eased by the polite society of the "courteous conductor" who played the role of attentive host. Despite her fondness for familiar comforts, Clark embraced the new experiences her journey presented. As her train neared the Sierra Nevada Mountains one night, she and her companions convinced a railway official to use his lantern and help them traverse "six open breezy platforms, and five cars filled with the oddest shaped sleeping human bundles, to the rear end of the long train." Once there, they clung to the brake-wheel "and thence for several miles, we were lost to all but the sublimity of this wild mountain pass."

Clark returned from her journey convinced of travel's transformative power. She pitied "the people who had not been to California" and advised readers that "if you want to be happy, healthy and wise, if you want to polish down the sharp angles of narrow selfish interest or morbid slant, if you want to grow into the image and likeness of the Creator of this beautiful world, which in all its glory is but a shadow of the *real* Home of the Soul, then—travel!" But such individual experiences did not instantly remake the cultural landscape. When the train had returned to Boston and "the 'Home agains' and 'Home sweet homes' . . . [had] all been sung," Clark looked out at the city and noticed "how unconscious it looks of our long absence or the importance of our return." [92] Despite the experiences of travel—the mastery of commercial skills, a new sense of public life, an awareness of vast landscapes, or a truer understanding of technological power—she returned to a domestic world that in many ways was unchanged.

Like Susie Clark, American culture during the last third of the nineteenth century moved beyond the circumscribed roles associated with female domesticity and transported the values of the private sphere into public. The cultural journey of women travelers recapitulates larger changes within late-nineteenth-century culture. Significantly, the three points of arrival in this female cultural journey echo the three themes that dominated the railroad narratives presented in Chapter 1—the play between public and private life, the balance between social and commercial values, the impact of technological and cultural change upon national life and identity. As women moved from the domestic sphere, traveled through an extended world of polite society and commercial relations, and finally entered a national public life of physical and technological dangers, Victorian gender roles would serve as a tool for resolving the tensions and contradictions of an American public culture in transition. Even as the ideal of separate spheres seemed to break down, notions of femininity and masculinity would create a new order.

At Home Aboard

RAILWAY TRAVEL AND THE RISE
OF PUBLIC DOMESTICITY

Miriam Leslie, departing from New York City in April of 1877, described for her readers "the charming little residence in which we found ourselves." The residence, Leslie decided, "shall be called a home, and very soon assumed the pleasant aspect of the word, as the bouquets, shawls, rugs, sofa-cushions, and various personalities of the three ladies of the party were developed and arranged upon or around a table in the center division of the car, which was to represent the general *salon*." The "little residence" Leslie described was a Wagner Palace Car. Mr. Wagner himself had provided the railroad car for Miriam Leslie's husband, journalist and publisher Frank Leslie, and the artists, writers, and photographers traveling with him to California. Mrs. Leslie and two other women completed the party. Railroads and specialty car companies had eagerly made the best accommodations available because *Frank Leslie's Illustrated Newspaper* intended to print an account of the journey. Despite this special attention, Mrs. Leslie remained in many respects typical of "respectable" women travelers—she traveled with her husband on business, carried out domestic tasks while aboard, and encountered unfamiliar people and landscapes during her journey. In her "Wagner home" Mrs. Leslie was also typical in her portrayal of trains as domestic spaces.[1]

The language of home pervaded passengers' stories of late nineteenth-century rail travel.[2] Again and again, women and men "made themselves at home" in the cars. Jennie Kimball understood that the train she and her companions had just boarded was "to be our home for some days" and quickly looked about to see "who our neighbors are."[3] Lillian Leland "look[ed] upon the once abhorred railway cars as parlors of ease."[4] Once settled on board, passengers engaged in activities usually identified with domestic leisure. According to the journalist Benjamin Franklin Taylor, the "flying drawing-room" enabled travelers to "go about in your revolving chair . . . read quietly, write comfortably, converse easily. . . . It is home adrift."[5] The train was also the site of more mundane domestic activities—a place to eat, dress, and sleep. One lady traveler lavished praise upon an 1858 sleeping car designed by S. C. Case of the Michigan Central. Traveling in Case's car, she "could almost fancy I was at home, there was such a parlor-like air about it." She enjoyed "the neat little dressing room, with all the necessary conveniences attached," and at journey's end, she "disliked to leave this huge cradle which had so gently lulled us through the night."[6] Likewise, Susie Clark praised the "trains [that] furnish every feature of a home but its usual stationary quality" and favorably compared the sleeping car's berth to her "familiar home nest."[7]

Beautiful interiors, comfortable furnishings, and well-designed amenities, however, never truly turned railroad cars into homes. The celebration of the domesticated train instead reflected the selective ways in which Victorian Americans—women and men, railroad passengers and representatives—moved qualities of private life onto the railroad and thereby amended the meaning of both home and public. They created a type of "public domesticity"—a social ideal that was neither as private as a home, nor as socially unruly as a public street. This ideal emerged in a variety of commercial settings over the course of the nineteenth century—in hotels, steamboats, department stores, photography studios.[8] At its most basic, public domesticity attempted to bring the cultural associations and behaviors of home life to bear upon social interactions among strangers, to regulate public interactions and delineate the boundary of Victorian respectability. It was a shared fantasy that sought to bring order, comfort, and familiarity to sites of rapid social and cultural change. The railroad—in so many respects the antithesis of the nineteenth-century domestic ideal—reveals the challenges, limitations, and power of public domesticity as well as the considerable cultural work Victorians did to create a home in public.

In 1875, the *New York Times* played upon the fragility of this still-emerging cultural hybrid when it mocked "the thousands of railroad trains filled with people who are enveloped in suffocating clouds of smoke and dust, and are laboring under the insane delusion that

they are actually enjoying a pleasure excursion."[9] The experiences of
female travelers attest that the train never literally became a home.
Long lines for the dressing rooms and the intrusive eyes of fellow
passengers reminded them that, no matter how comfortable or well
decorated, the cars remained public spaces. Amendment of the domestic ideal was required to imagine the train as a home. In the case of
the Leslies, their "Wagner home" was divided with a curtain to separate the sleeping area set aside for married couples from the "pleasant
Bohemia where the artists, *litterateurs* and photographers of the party
sleep and work."[10] Nonetheless, Mrs. Leslie and many other Victorians transplanted private expectations and ideals to public spaces,
and the comparison between home and train persisted.

At this time, the meaning of the ideal home also underwent a shift.
While maintaining its significance as a primary agent of moral instruction, home increasingly was a site for consumer display and the
expression of individual taste. At midcentury, Victorian homes stood
for ethical excellence and were depicted in home design and house-
keeping manuals almost exclusively in moral terms. A home might be
described as "good or bad," "honest or dishonest."[11] Moreover, the
home—especially the parlor—was expected to reflect and shape the
character of its inhabitants. This midcentury ideal of the moral home
was sustained by the belief that the proper surroundings fostered self-
discipline and gentility—what one historian has identified as the Victorian hope that "the material world . . . [would] direct people into
desired behavior."[12] Reformers and advice books preached that in the
moral home the right architectural forms and domestic goods imparted Christian values of self-restraint and order to household inhabitants. More important, the values instilled at home passed beyond the threshold and into the community. For its exponents, the
moral home exerted a civilizing influence, fostered stability and social harmony, and represented the best antidote to the disruptive
effects of westward expansion, the spread of the factory system, urban
growth, and immigration.

But by century's end, a new domestic ideal had also taken hold in
the popular imagination—one that celebrated comfort and consumption rather than self-restraint.[13] With the rise of American consumer
culture, domestic goods were more openly celebrated as reflections
of individual taste, creativity, and the ability to appreciate and afford
the best.[14] As the middle class moved out of heterogeneous cities to

more homogenized suburbs, they embraced a less structured home characterized by an open design and fewer specialized spaces. Living among people of similar social and economic class, the middle class of the late Victorian period relaxed and created homes that emphasized self-expression. This trend was fueled by the proliferation of goods, as furniture with opulent veneers permitted many to imitate the decorating habits of the wealthy and incorporate parlors into their homes.[15] If the moral home sought to bring order and stability to disorderly urban settings, the self-expressive home revealed the taste of its inhabitants. Domestic treasures previously intended to offer moral instruction also stood as evidence of superior taste and abundance; the moral home readily merged with the comfortable and self-expressive home in which domestic amenities reflected purchasing power and discernment of goods.

And so, during the second half of the nineteenth century the meanings of home abounded, blending into one another. According to the 1885 *Home Instructor* there was "no grander word in all the languages of men than that one word HOME! It is full to overflowing with rich happy meanings."[16] The shifting meaning of the Victorian home made the domestication of public life a complex and dynamic process. Travelers imagined railway cars as their temporary homes, and carried with them the cultural baggage of changing domestic meanings. The differences and tensions between the moral and the self-expressive home were played out aboard the trains. Passengers and railway companies hoped that the domesticated train could recreate the values of the moral home in public life, even as they embraced the train's luxurious interiors as sites of expressive consumption. In short, the train underwent two types of domestication. The "train as home" metaphor implied both a public space infused with the values of self-restraint usually associated with the home and also a comfortable setting that gave expression to consumer longings and the tasteful manifestation of individual purchasing power. Ultimately these two strains of domesticity produced a vision of commercial public life tempered by forms of gentility. The ideal of a public moral home, remade by the sale of domestic comforts on the train, yielded to a genteel home concerned with etiquette more than uplift.

Perhaps the greatest irony of the separate spheres ideology is that by drawing a boundary between home and the public realm,

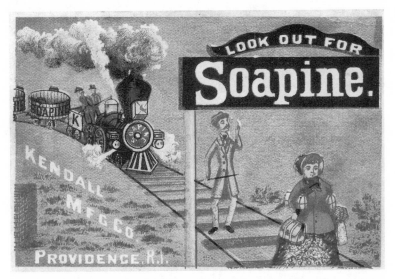

Soapine advertisement (trade card, no date) suggests the railroad's entry into the domestic sphere of women. This laundry and household cleaner is, like the railroad, depicted as a symbol of progress. Author's collection.

nineteenth-century Americans imbued the domestic sphere with powers that reached beyond its culturally defined threshold. Given the physical and social inconveniences of the early railroad cars, any comparison between the train and home (moral or self-expressive) initially appears surprising.[17] After all, as one nineteenth-century housekeeper's handbook noted, "not every place where one may sleep and eat is worthy to be called home. About home there are the ideas of comfort, repose, peace, content. Where these are wanting none can be at home."[18] Yet for the home to succeed as a haven, it needed to serve as a site for family entertainment, education, and consumer longings.[19] Like the respectable ladies who traveled by train to fulfill familial obligations, the domestic sphere easily, and almost invisibly, accommodated the very experiences that it was intended to counteract.[20] And so, even before railroad cars were rendered home-like, nineteenth-century Americans in their parlors set the stage for domesticating rail travel.

Rather than using the home as a total retreat from public life, Victorians used it as a safe setting in which to try out public experiences. Model trains, for example, brought the railroad into the heart of Victorian family life. First made out of paper cutouts and pulled by a string, these popular toys grew in their sophistication and ability to approximate rail travel. By 1896 one could purchase a brass car with track and battery for three dollars.[21] The home also served as the site of vicarious journeys for adults. As early as 1816, works like Charles Lloyd's *Travels at Home and Voyages by the Fire-side for the Instruction of Young Persons* brought the travel experience into the home. Gathered in the parlor, a family or collection of friends were encouraged to imagine themselves as part of a traveling party viewing distant scenery as they read aloud: "As we can have but little time to stay in America, we cannot describe its numerous towns minutely. . . . But we must set out and proceed hastily toward Quebec, which is yet at great distance."[22]

Lloyd's narrative predated the railroad, describing travel by boat and coach; the advent of rail travel dramatically increased the possibility for such vicarious journeys. Government survey expeditions and railroad companies frequently took photographers to document the western landscape, and these images circulated as stereographs. According to historian Louise Stevenson, "stereographs permitted viewers to take visual excursions at bargain prices to see people and places near and far from their parlors."[23] From the safety of their homes, would-be travelers viewed awe-inspiring natural wonders and distant attractions. In the words of one stereograph company, "With the stereoscope, by the fireside, one can wander through strange cities and sunny valleys, over bleak mountains, or delve among the wonderful ruins of the past."[24] In this manner, the experiences of travel placed the domestic ideal in direct conversation with the achievements of the railroad. This mingling of railroad travel and domestic entertainment may help explain why Victorian travelers carried domestic ideals with them onto trains.

Throughout the second half of the nineteenth century the exchange between home and train grew in sophistication, as parlor pursuits became more precise in the recreation of life on the rails. In 1879, Edward Wilson sought to improve the quality of homebound travel by providing detailed descriptions of sights to accompany a series of numbered stereographs and magic lantern slides. He arranged his book as a series of rail journeys through Europe and the United States. Wilson's script incorporated the hurried pace frequently experienced during rail travel—for example, informing his travel companions that their tour of Niagara would exclude "the Whirlpool rapids, and inclined plane, and the islands of the Three Sisters, and the fifty other delightful places that one could visit . . . [because they] must proceed by way of the Atlantic and Great Western Railway." Even while safely at home, the would-be tourist faced the demands of the railroad, and the timetable took precedence over the joy of sightseeing. Rather than leisurely showing his homebound tourists the natural wonders of Niagara, Wilson rushed them along "on to the far West, taking a through ticket, and not stopping until we reach Ohio." [25]

As railroad travel became more prevalent and as railroad companies grew more proficient in self-promotion, a new variety of written materials enabled the armchair traveler to supplement the domestic viewing of stereocards and to imagine a train journey. Popular magazine articles described the scenic advantages of various routes, and by the 1880s railroad companies were publishing guidebooks and brochures to tout their lines. [26] Although intended for railroad passengers to read as the scenery passed outside the car's window, these guides were equally suited to the pleasures of homebound travelers. A parlor game of the 1890s called Traveller's Tour required players to act as travel guides and display their knowledge of likely routes, station stops, and sights of interest. The player who offered the most correct information won the game. [27] Thus, equipped with guidebook and stereographs, armchair travelers turned the home parlor into a make-believe railway car for an evening's entertainment. They transformed not only sightseeing but rail travel into a domestic activity. By combining imaginary rail excursions and domestic values in the parlor, they also increased the likelihood that domestic expectations would be imposed on railroad travel.

But while the midcentury parlor could simulate the experiences of rail travel, the cars were only beginning to offer travelers the atmosphere of home. Before trains could sustain the fantasy of public domesticity, they needed to evolve. The cars of the 1830s and 1840s little resembled the restrained moral enclaves associated with the Victorian ideal of the private sphere. [28] Even if one defined a home merely in terms of its ability to provide shelter and some degree of physical comfort, the earliest railway cars were anything but homey.

Travel upon these early trains was filthy, inconvenient, and often dangerous. The cars were too warm in summer, too cold in winter, and poorly ventilated year-round. Fumes from axle lubricants mingled with smoke, dust, soot, and sparks from the locomotive to create a stifling and nauseating atmosphere. Passengers inhaled this mix as they sat upon hard, low-backed benches. Travelers seeking a little comfort paid one dollar to purchase "an upright piece of steel that would reach from the middle of the back of the head to a point below the shoulder blades. Crossing this horizontally were four other pieces of steel."[29] The device was placed between the passenger's back and the back of the seat and acted as a spring that supported his head. Jostled and jarred by uneven rails, sharp curves, and bumpy grades, travelers exposed themselves to new injuries like "railway spine" or to the dangers of derailment, which was so common that, according to one historian, some railroad tickets stipulated that "the passenger was subject to call if needed to help replace the engine or cars on the rail."[30] The best that could be said for train travel during the 1830s was that the journeys were short by nineteenth-century standards.

By the 1840s car builders had hit upon the "open car" design that would come to characterize American day coaches. Initially designed to meet the technological and financial challenges of building railroads in the United States, the open car failed to conform to the emerging Victorian domestic ideal. Unlike the British compartment car which resembled a private carriage, the American car consisted of a single large compartment with seats on either side of a center aisle. Between 1840 and 1860, these cars grew from a little under forty feet in length with an average capacity of thirty to forty passengers to fifty or sixty feet with room for fifty to sixty passengers.

The "American-style" coach embodied the unruly social interactions that distinguished the public from the private sphere. Railroad enthusiasts praised the open car for its "democratic" collection of passengers and the easy social mixing fostered by its center aisle.[31] According to one observer writing in 1870, "the American, gregarious by nature and by education . . . must have a wandering caravanserai [sic], in which eighty or a hundred persons of all classes and colors and ages are assembled together, and where he can move about in his nervous restlessness to meet friends, to make acquaintances."[32] For many travelers, the cars were too democratic. One passenger traveling from Boston to Providence in 1835 complained, "The rich and the poor, the educated and the ignorant, the polite and the vulgar, all herd together in this modern improvement in travelling. The consequence is complete amalgamation. . . . Two poor fellows, who were not much in the habit of making their toilet, squeezed me into a corner, while the hot sun drew from their garments a villainous compound of smells made up of salt fish, tar and molasses."[33]

Uncomfortable and very public, the cars of the 1840s provide a starting point for considering efforts to domesticate the train's appearance as the railroads were increasingly called upon to provide the conveniences of home. Although few people at this time spoke of trains in domestic terms, technological innovations in car design and the rail network would soon foster the early stages of domestication. During the 1830s, railroad cars reached a design plateau from which improvements could proceed. The introduction of the eight-wheel, double-truck car, for example, permitted an increase in car size, ensured a smoother motion, and resulted in fewer broken axles. Eight-wheeled cars quickly replaced earlier generations of cars that resembled stagecoaches or omnibuses mounted on four wheels.

Now that the cars were larger and more stable, car designers could pay increased attention to the comfort and decoration of their interiors. Improvements in the rail network further encouraged these efforts. As journeys of up to five hundred miles became possible, railroad companies, car designers and passengers emphasized the importance of comfort during prolonged trips. Trying to sleep in a jostling car while sitting up all night on a hard bench gave passengers a memorable—and painful—lesson in the shortcomings of railway interiors. Indeed, George Pullman was supposed to have developed his ideas for his sleeping car during an uncomfortable night of travel.[34]

By 1847 conditions had improved enough that a Frenchman traveling in the United States wrote that American railway cars "are actually houses where nothing, absolutely nothing is lacking for the necessity of life." He described a sleeping car on the Baltimore & Ohio Railroad that did indeed sound a little like a home. Unlike the open day coaches, this car reflected the specialization of space that characterized Victorian homes and was divided into several "rooms, some for men and some for women alone." The rooms each contained six beds or couches. The Frenchman conceded that "to tell you that these beds are perfectly comfortable would be a lie," but he was thankful for them nonetheless.[35] From such rudimentary beginnings, car interiors grew more elaborate and luxurious as designers and railroad companies transplanted the necessities and amenities of home life onto the cars. In addition to sleeping cars equipped with convertible berths, dressing rooms, and lavatories, they added comfortable cars with reclining chairs, parlor cars, dining cars, library cars, and even barbershops. In 1887 the invention of the vestibule reduced the violent jerking motion of car platforms and made it easier to pass safely between cars; now the entire train could be one large domestic space. A passenger willing and able to pay for his comfort could spend part of his journey reading the latest periodicals in the library car or gazing out the window of a parlor car, then eat with his family at a comfortable table in the well-stocked dining car, retire to the smoker for an evening of male camaraderie, and then pass a comfortable night's sleep in his own berth. Or in the words of the Pullman Company in 1893: "the traveler may pass from his dining-room to his sitting-room, or to his sleeping-room, as in his own home."[36]

By the 1880s, railroad companies boasted that one could "live at home" on the rails, and, together with passengers, sought to make the fantasy of a home on rails come true. In 1882, *The Pacific Tourist and Guide of Travel Across the Continent* touted the domesticity of the Pacific Railroad's Palace Cars, assuring readers that "one lives at home in the Palace Car with as much true enjoyment as in the home drawing room. . . . The little section and berth allotted to you, so neat and clean, so nicely kept becomes your home. Here you sit and read, play your games, indulge in social conversation and glee."[37] Railroad conductor Charles B. George admired the new trains of the 1880s "equipped with all the luxuries and conveniences a millionaire could desire at home."[38] The Pittsburgh, Cincinnati and St. Louis Railway informed travelers that their cars combined "not only the familiar associations of home by day, but also the comforts of one's own chamber at night."[39] Railroad professionals self-consciously embraced these domesticated trains and took pride in their efforts to make them even more like home. The Chicago, Milwaukee & St. Paul Railway's "first aim" was to "provide [the passenger with] every luxury to which one is accustomed in his home."[40] And in 1910 the Pennsylvania Railroad referred to its "Mexico Special" simply as "this comfortably appointed train-home."[41]

Despite the train's association with manliness and technological progress, railroad companies and other enthusiasts routinely embraced its more feminine and domestic elements. In advertising brochures and popular magazine articles, descriptions of sideboards and decorating styles appeared beside reports of improvements in train

Parlor car life. From "Railway Passenger Travel," Scribner's Magazine,
September 1888. Courtesy of the New York University Libraries.

speeds, bridge construction, braking mechanisms, or ventilation systems and thereby implied that the physical beauty of the cars was comparable in importance to their technological achievements. Comfortable sofas and beautiful bathroom fixtures were even discussed as
if they were technological innovations. For example, an article describing the amenities and accommodations aboard the Pennsylvania Limited appeared amid articles on pig-iron production, steam
traps, and boilers and advertisements for equipment, rolling stock,

and manufacturing services.[42] Similarly in 1853, *Scientific American* announced a new car built for the Hudson River Railroad and reported that the car was divided into compartments "furnished with a sofa, four chairs, a looking glass and a small center table"—the basic components of a home parlor.[43]

Guidebooks and railroad brochures also closely documented the luxurious amenities, offering descriptions of the fine woods, elaborate hangings, rich upholsteries, and silver-plated metal work in the best cars. One 1883 guidebook published by the Passenger Department of the Savannah, Florida and Western Railway Company boasted that the buffet in one of its sleeping cars harmonized with its surroundings to an extraordinary degree. According to the author, because "the buffet's finish, both in woodwork and marquetry, corresponds with the interior of the car, the effect is highly pleasing, suggesting in convenience and luxury an elegant sideboard in a richly appointed mansion."[44] A brochure for the Pennsylvania Railroad praised the "harmonious colors . . . snowy linen, cut glass and silver" of one of the railroad's dining cars.[45] Guidebooks and railway brochures also made note of the variety of decorating styles: some cars were decorated in an "Oriental" style and others in "Persian" or "Renaissance," and often ladies' rest rooms were decorated in a style different from the rest of the car.

The relationship between train and home extended beyond the cars into railroad stations. Stations, so often celebrated as gateways to already great cities or as the beginnings of urban greatness for cities on the rise, were also being recast as public homes. A traveler writing in 1871 complained that American railroad stations were too public, that anyone—even those without a ticket—could enter. "Let the stations be closed to this swarm of idlers, hackmen, porters, school-boys, peddlers, bad women, swindlers, pick-pockets, and conductors' 'friends.'"[46] Yet despite their resemblance to cities in the diversity of their functions, in the constant flow of strangers, in their architectural triumphs, railroad stations—both grand and modest—were increasingly praised for their domestic qualities.[47] (Indeed cities themselves were becoming more homelike with the proliferation of public domestic spaces, and railway stations were often compared to hotel lobbies and men's clubs.) As early as 1848, New Haven Station boasted "extensive Parlors . . . furnished with a profusion of rich and costly sofas, divans, chairs, ottomans, mirrors, etc."[48] Less opulent stations provided rocking chairs as a comfortable and homey touch. By the 1880s, *Lippincott's Magazine of Popular Literature and Science* spoke of the appeal of "handsome and homelike stations."[49] *World's Work* praised Boston's South Terminal Station for containing "almost everything that the traveller needs down to cradles in which the baby may be soothed."[50] Even railway man John Droege likened the station's waiting room to a "a great living room through which all the patrons must pass."[51]

Domestic comforts presented travelers with a clear symbol of progress—one that could be understood without a lot of technical knowledge. No doubt familiar domestic accents and furnishings inspired confidence by mimicking the secure environment of the home. For example, the luxury of the parlor cars, rather than simply the speed of the trains, connoted progress and convinced Americans that their trains were technologically sound. In 1885, the *New York Times* reported that the luxurious Pullman cars limited the speed of American railroads. This handicap, despite the American obsession with speed and efficiency, was a source of national pride: "The Pullman car is, of course, much more comfortable than the English carriages. . . . No one would propose to supersede it here by cars of the English pattern."[52] According to the *Chicago Times*, "In railway travel high speed is not the sole requisite; comfort and safety are equally essential conditions. More comforts and greater security to life attend everywhere, step by step, the progress of civilization."[53] A decade later the *Atlanta Constitution* explained that "the carrying of a sleeping car passenger involves the hauling of 3,000 pounds extra weight, the freight upon which at minimum rates would amount to more than the price of his berth."[54] Together the domestic train and the technological train created a single and comprehensible narrative of American progress as orderly, safe, and refined.[55]

Just as a well-appointed home was presumed to reflect the morality and character of its inhabitants, elegant trains were presumed to reflect the good character of the American people. In railway cars, the trappings of the comfortable home—the sideboards, upholstery, and paneling—imparted a sense of stability to American technological progress and communicated the values of the moral home. They offered social cues for passengers' behavior and reassurances concerning the conduct of those around them. If, as the home manuals advised, "home is the central pivot upon which depends the weal or the woe of families and communities," the home could also serve as model for national public life—if private homes built communities, public ones might be able to do the same.[56] Civility would not be sacrificed in the face of rapid social and technological change. By behaving in public as they did in private, travelers could create a public life suffused with the values of respectability.[57] In the words of *Godey's Lady's Book*: "Our public conveyances are not only schools of public instruction in ethics of etiquette, but they also testify to the high state of civilization our free institutions have reached."[58]

Victorian travelers frequently invoked the image of a long line of cars moving through the expansive western landscape to capture this sense of controlled and harmonious social progress. In so doing, they embraced the public domesticity of railway cars as both the means and the proof of their own advanced cultural development.[59] One tour company boasted that "civilization has literally rolled across the continent." Nothing confirmed this sense of pride so much as standing on the platform and looking back upon the palace car—admiring "those perfected, vestibuled trains, with their roomy, well-appointed staterooms, dining-cars and reading rooms, and [hoping] their essential features will come into common use and be within the reach of common people."[60] And even as *The Pacific Tourist* warned readers that "if ever one feels belittled, 'tis on the plains, when each individual seems but a little mite, amid the majesty of loneliness," it offered the antidote to this feeling. The domestic life of the cars—"reading, playing, conversation, making agreeable acquaintances"—counteracted the majestic loneliness of open lands and asserted the values of the advancing American civilization: "Standing at the rear of the train, and with all the doors open, there is an unobstructed view along the aisles throughout the entire length. On either side of the train are the prairies, where the eye sees nothing but wildness, and even desolation, then looking back upon this long aisle or avenue, he sees civilization and comfort and luxury. How sharp a contrast."[61] Anna Dickinson recalled standing on the rear platform and wondering at the "odd contrast" between "the steam wonder, cultured growth of brains and civilization, epitome of thought and mechanism" and "the flashes of lightening across the limitless spaces we are crossing."[62]

The "sharp" or "odd" contrast was not simply between the train and the landscape. The cars themselves embodied striking contrasts between home and public, domestic comfort and technological power, even feminine and masculine. In its ability to juxtapose these contrasts and bring them into equilibrium, the train seemed to embody all that was good about American life and civilization. Victorian travelers repeatedly expressed delight in the contrasts that proved the triumph of civilization over both threatening technology and primitive landscape. The members of the Boston Board of Trade marveled at the transcontinental train they traveled upon. They enjoyed the library cars, the Burdett organs, and the other domestic touches, but their amazement was increased by the realization that the cozy scenes of domestic life—the singing, the games of leapfrog—were being played out "all while traveling forty miles an hour." [63] Similarly, Susie Clark's pleasure in the mountain ranges, deserts, and prairies was heightened by her ability "to enjoy all this from the luxurious environment of a palace car, where choice viands are served with clock-like regularity,—what a rich experience it is." [64]

More than any other railroad man, George Mortimer Pullman was invested in and associated with the vision of a public home on rails as an agent of civilization. Born in 1831, the founder of the most influential passenger car company in the United States was raised near Lake Erie in an upwardly mobile middle-class family. His upbringing was steeped in the values of the moral home.[65] He and his family looked upon their material gains as a reflection of their hard work and religious faith and invested their financial success in their family businesses, education of their children, and improving their family home for socializing and worship. Pullman would follow this pattern throughout his life, first in Colorado and, then, on an elaborate scale in Chicago after his successes in the 1860s.[66] Both contemporary and later railroad enthusiasts have praised Pullman's vision and anointed him a great civilizer—a man who brought comfort to the rails and taught Americans the meaning of luxury.[67] The opulent decoration of his Pullman Palace Car Company's sleeping cars, hotel cars, dining cars, and parlor cars was unprecedented and reflected his commitment to domesticity and its ability to imbue public life with morality. Even his famous company town just outside of Chicago, frequently invoked as one of the worst examples of industrial paternalism, was based upon Pullman's faith in the moral home.[68]

Pullman eagerly justified the decision to spend extravagantly on elaborate car interiors—putting carpets on the floors, providing clean bed linen, decorating with costly ornamentation and upholstery. He explained, "I have always held that people are very greatly influenced by their physical surroundings, and bring [a man] into a room elegantly carpeted and furnished and the effect upon his bearing is immediate." If men behaved badly in public but were refined at home then bring the influence of home into public life; to Pullman, "the more artistic and refined the mere external surroundings, in other words, the better and more refined the man."[69] According to Pullman, in a properly designed train car the American traveler "would [not] expectorate on the surroundings and wipe his boots on the accessories." Instead the traveler would "respect [the beautiful] in a public vehicle as well as in a private home."[70] This was true of even "the roughest man."[71] Like the authors of domestic advice manuals, Pullman asserted that civility could be learned, and he designed and decorated his cars in order to educate passengers for a more harmonious public life. In Pullman's perfect world, not simply the interiors of the cars but, more important, the resulting conduct of the passengers would lend credence to the belief that civilization was literally rolling across the North American continent. His ideas gained such currency that one traveler even couched his plea for better railroad food in terms of the "educational aspect . . . the moralizing and refining influence" of the toasted sardine.[72]

The presence of women on trains seemed to confirm Pullman's vision of the railway car as a domesticated, and therefore moral, public setting. Lady travelers, many Victorians presumed, inspired self-restraint in others, and their comfort aboard proved the success of their influence.[73] This was an extension of their role in the home; they exerted their moral influence, refining and beautifying the space. An 1875 article on wives as traveling companions explained, "Home is the pleasantest place in the world, and that is not home where the wife is not."[74] Women carried the physical and moral comforts of home with them on their journeys. They tended to the lunch basket, gathered flowers to decorate the cars, or, like Miriam Leslie and her companions, arranged pillows and shawls to make the train pleasing and homey. Most important, women's ability to travel freely by train not only made the cars homelike but underscored the domesticity of American women and the superior character of American men who created a safe public setting for them.

Promotional images reinforced these gendered associations. The *Railway Age* wondered at the proliferation of domestic and feminized images used to woo travelers. How had this come about? Perhaps "some enterprising traffic manager tried the venture of advertising his line—say, for California travel—in one of the great magazines, with large type and an attractive picture of a girl or a bridal pair, seated blissfully in a luxurious car and viewing the flying summerland scenery."[75] Whatever their origin, many images in railroad brochures depicted white women at ease upon comfortable sofas as they engaged in domestic and familial pursuits. They also conveyed the domestic nature of car life by depicting female passengers tending to the needs of children, reading quietly, or sleeping in a comfortable setting that was simultaneously public and domestic. In one brochure for summer excursions on the Pennsylvania Railroad, a woman sits alone gazing out of a large curtained window, holding a small bouquet of roses. Were it not for the binoculars in her other hand and the luggage at her feet one might not notice that she was aboard a train. In a promotional illustration for the Boston & Lowell Railroad a woman sits before a window and is accompanied by a little girl who also appreciates the view.[76]

Popular fiction from the second half of the nineteenth century echoed these promotional images by portraying the train as a setting in which men and women lived out elements of domestic life. Beside anecdotes and jokes depicting the railroad as a chaotic space, women's periodicals and railroad men's magazines printed romantic stories portraying the train as a place where couples met and fell in love.[77] In many of these stories the public elements of train travel were ignored as travelers met old loves or remote acquaintances.[78] The public aspect of train life remained important to the plots, however, because it encouraged displays of respectability, reminding women to be reserved and modest and men to be respectful and gallant. In this fictional world, the railway car rivaled the home parlor as the place where a man or woman won another's heart. In several stories, couples that had failed to fall in love when at home boarded the train only to make the startling realization that they were meant to be together.

In "A Pullman Car Wooing," Gladys can bring herself to accept Jack's marriage proposal only after he has followed her onto the train from Oakland to Omaha, where she gains a new understanding of her familiar suitor.[79] In other stories, like "Floy's Journey, And What

Genteel woman traveler at home aboard. From Summer Excursion Routes,
*Pennsylvania Railroad Passenger Department, 1894. Courtesy of the Warshaw
Collection of Business Americana—Railroads, Archives Center, National
Museum of American History, Behring Center, Smithsonian Institution.*

Came of It," *For Love & Bears*, and *The Daughter of a Magnate*, women attract suitable mates by displaying their domestic skills. Tending to an orphaned boy, dressing a hunting injury, or playing a piece upon a train's piano, female protagonists made the most of their time in the cars and revealed their accomplishments to appropriately admiring male suitors.[80] Men found in the cars a setting in which they could demonstrate their worthiness as would-be husbands, showing off their professional skills, physical strength, and tender hearts. In October 1895, *Munsey's Magazine* published "On the Way North," in which a man and woman fall in love: they had met before, but had not been able to act upon their feelings for each other. Through a series of coincidences and mishaps they end up with a little boy in a runaway car. The boy mistakes the couple for his parents, calling them "Mama" and "Papa," and together this "family" faces down danger; the story ends with a mutual proclamation of love.[81] In this fictional world, men and women found romantic and domestic happiness on the rails by remaining true to the values, conduct, and gender roles deemed appropriate at home.[82]

Another common type of fictional account depicted the train as a space that brought out the most generous instincts of travelers. In these stories entire carloads of passengers were bonded into one public family as they recreated domestic pastimes or sentiments. Here the railroad car was peopled by strangers rather than acquaintances or lost loves, and the characters interacted and cooperated across class lines. In January of 1880, the *Railway Age* told a story of "Santa Claus on the Cars," in which strangers on the night express out of New York City answer the prayers of two poor children. When Maggie and Joey pray that Santa Claus finds them though they are traveling in the cars on Christmas Eve, the other passengers realize that the children's mother is too poor to buy gifts and that Santa will not visit. When the children fall asleep the passengers take up a collection and Maggie and Joey wake to find their Christmas stockings filled with "some candy, oranges and figs, and a picture book for each."[83] In other stories, strangers pass the time while snowbound by calming fellow passengers—hosting teas, telling stories, and planning and putting on recitals or tableaux.[84]

Young and old, wealthy businessmen and poor orphans, Christian ladies and troubled souls sit side by side and offer one another companionship, solace, or protection. Frequently a stranger's act of kindness breaks down social barriers and precipitates an outpouring of generosity from onlookers. For example, a man softens his heart toward a poor but devoted widow with a sick baby, or an exemplary lady offers a cup of tea and a place by the fire to an elderly peddler and thus teaches "one of those beautiful lessons which all should learn."[85] Again, with women aboard, the train proves itself a moral home capable of not only producing private happiness but fostering social harmony.

In many respects these depictions of the train as a moral enclave were fiction. Even as railroad companies, car designers, and passengers embraced the ideal of a moral home on rails, that vision was being supplanted by one of home as a site of consumer comforts and self-expression. Increasingly the ideal of being "at home aboard" implied the presence of the best amenities. Among strangers in the cars, as in a private home, the beauty and positive influence of domestic items did not always reflect the careful moral choices of the car's inhabitants but instead announced the passengers' discerning taste and ability to pay for them. The domestic touches that Pullman and others hoped would encourage self-restraint and uplift in "the roughest man" also served as an expression of a discriminating passenger's refinement. Amenities that might have permitted a sense of ease and family feeling among passengers frequently denoted economic privilege or class standing rather than impeccable moral conduct. In the end, then, Pullman passengers may have refrained from spitting on the carpets because they had paid for the privilege of riding in a beautiful car, not because they had been morally uplifted by their surroundings.

Railroad car interiors stirred up and temporarily fulfilled longings for domestic goods—even goods passengers could never dream of possessing in their own homes. One Pullman conductor confirmed the intoxicating influence of the cars' décor, especially upon passengers unfamiliar with luxury. He observed in his years of service that "all classes of people, perhaps, with the exception of millionaires, are more or less overcome by this subtle atmosphere." The impact was strongest upon those "who ride only a short distance and pay a small price." A humble grocer, for example, leaves behind "all his ordinary characteristics . . . with his apron and by merely paying 25 cents for a seat ride in a Pullman car [becomes] transformed into a grand seigneur." And women, who "at home in Cattlestown occupy a position not so immeasurably superior to the servant girl they employ . . . sweep with such a disdainful mien into a parlor car as if the very carpet ought to feel highly honored by their tread."[86]

William Dean Howells's 1876 farce *The Parlor Car* portrayed the train's ability to inflame such desires. Howells depicted a young woman traveling with her fiancé. She is most taken by the domestic elements of the train and wonders aloud whether "Mr. Pullman could be induced to sell this car?" When asked why she would like to own the car, she responds that "it's perfectly lovely, and I should like to live in it always." She imagines it "fitted up for a sort of summer-house" in the garden where her future husband could go to smoke;[87] her enjoyment of the parlor car turns into a dream of domestic consumption beyond her reach. Stephen Crane in "The Bride Comes to Yellow Sky" described a newlywed couple whose first Pullman car journey introduced them to an unfamiliar world of luxury. The couple's happy state was reflected in goods they would never own. Showing the car off to his bride, Jack Potter "had pride of an owner. He pointed out the dazzling fittings of the coach; and in truth [his wife's] eyes opened wider as she contemplated the sea-green figured velvet, the shining brass, silver, and glass, the wood that gleamed as darkly brilliant as the surface of a pool of oil."[88]

Even George Pullman, for all his faith in the moralizing influence of domestic goods, succumbed to this consumerist ethos. The writers at the *Railway Age* observed, "House decorators owe much to Mr. Pullman for the education in matters of taste which his splendid cars have given. In respect to elegance and elaborateness the Pullman cars have constantly kept in advance of the public demand, and so have proved leaders in the fine arts of building and adorning."[89] At the Chicago World's Fair in 1893, Pullman proudly claimed that his company had taught Americans to appreciate and desire tasteful homes. According to *The Story of Pullman*, which explained the company's exhibit, "from no other one source has there sprung so widely diffused an education, so general an ambition in the direction of interior decorative art, the effect of which is seen in thousands of American homes to-day." Pullman cars offered "beautiful object-lessons" and "carried [them] to the remotest regions of the country."[90] For those who could afford to purchase similar domestic amenities at home, the luxurious cars offered a decorating lesson and perhaps provided familiar surroundings. For those unable to buy at home, the additional charge of two dollars bought entry into an elaborate train car and the temporary realization of domestic splendor and ease.

The conflation of moral self-restraint with comfort and even luxury was reflected in popular images of the refined female traveler experiencing social comfort as physical comfort. Railway companies portrayed female travelers' dual nature as both moral agents of the home and consumers of domestic goods. On the one hand, women's cultural association with the self-restraint of home life made them powerful social markers of respectable public behavior aboard; on the other hand, women passengers participated in train life as enthusiastic and active consumers. Ladies' accommodations—dressing rooms, lavatories, even separate parlors and drawing rooms—received special attention from designers and were highlighted in promotional materials. In 1890, *Railway News* announced that the Pennsylvania Limited had recently provided a ladies' toilet-room equipped with "every little receptacle that the feminine heart could ask." In addition to clothes-hooks and cuff-racks, the Pennsylvania Railroad provided a "chest of cute little drawers." A decade later the Baltimore & Ohio boasted that the women's retiring rooms on their trains were "most acceptable to lady travelers" because they were "provided with dainty dressing tables with large plate glass mirrors, on each side of which are cosy corner seats." Intended as agents and markers of moral propriety, women travelers also emerged as ardent consumers of domestic goods.[91]

Unlike the fantasy of a public moral home creating social harmony and order, the consumer home proved divisive. Victorian morality, with its emphasis on uplift, reflected concerns about social division, but, despite calling attention to differences among groups, it provided a vision of society unified by shared values. The domestic amenities of travel, by contrast, separated travelers into a stratified consuming public with different types of public "homes," and by the 1890s social critics and rail promoters hesitantly acknowledged the separation of passengers along class lines.[92] The conductor Charles B. George observed with amusement "the way some people try to draw a line between themselves and their neighbors even in a palace car." George believed that they "would be glad to supplant our present democratic coach by the compartment cars of Europe."[93] An article appearing in *Scribner's Magazine* in 1894 explained that the class system on British railroads "simply amounts to this, that the passenger can get more nearly what he pays for." The author then claimed, "We have the same thing imperfectly carried out, in the United States, in the trains, the Pullman cars being the first-class."[94] An 1897 article on the art of travel noted Americans' indirect acknowledgement of class distinctions: "Abroad, carriages of the first, second, and third, and even fourth class (where you stand up) are provided, and plainly marked. Here we have the corresponding divisions without such harsh names: The Pullman is first, the day-coach second, the smoker third-class; and perhaps, a seat in the caboose of a freight train may be called fourth-class."[95]

Domestic goods denoted not only respectability but also class and, increasingly, racial difference. Breaking with earlier praise of America's classless society, the *Railway Age and Northwestern Railroader* called attention to class stratification "under other names." In 1896, the periodical noted, "the construction of sleeping, parlor and emigrant cars has practically established class distinctions among travelers no less clearly defined and even more numerous than were ever in use in England."[96] A luxurious public home informed by the forms of etiquette, not the values of morality, became the best accommodations the American train could offer. An article in the *New York Times* described without apology this genteel home on rails: "The idea of the parlor car is a place where people who wish to be treated as they know they ought to treat others while traveling can sit together by the payment of an extra fare."[97] In the parlor car, the golden rule was for sale, and only those who could afford the fee gained access. Money and consumption rather than shared morality bound these passengers together.

The separation of domestic amenities from the goals of moral uplift and social harmony was especially apparent in the conception and transformation of the cars that transported emigrants across the continent. From their beginnings in the 1850s, emigrant cars were unadorned boxcars with windows. No tasteful decoration or domestic touches sought to inspire self-restraint and refined conduct in their passengers. No upholstery fostered a sense of ease, nor did thick carpets discourage spitting on the floors. Emigrants were given bare wooden berths upon which they could place their bedding and stoves so that they could prepare their meals. Unlike first-class passengers, emigrants had neither porters nor waiters to meet their needs; instead the burdens of domestic labor traveled with them in the cars as they washed their clothes and cooked their meals.[98]

Eventually the emigrant car evolved into the tourist sleeper of the 1880s—a scaled-down version of the more luxurious and expensive sleeping cars. These cars provided bed linen and the attentions of a porter for what one brochure described as, "those who are contented with good accommodations at a lower price."[99] In 1886, one railroad observer noted, "The emigrant service of to-day, on some roads, is far in advance of first-class passenger service on many lines twenty years ago."[100] With rattan rather than upholstered seats, but at two-fifths the cost of a regular sleeper, the tourist sleepers provided an improved level of domestic comfort free of moral lessons for those unable or unwilling to pay for the best. Looking upon these improvements the old-fashioned moralists at *Godey's Lady's Book* fretted that the addition of even modest amenities removed all hardship from the long transcontinental journey. The covered wagon had "filled the great West with its self-reliant and hardy population; and perhaps it developed some fine qualities, which the [emigrant] family car, with its ease and convenience, may fail to bring out."[101] Apparently not all travelers were susceptible to the moral power of domestic comfort and required in its place the uplifting influence of hardship and struggle. Yet the rise of public comfort as a reasonable expectation circulated beyond the wealthy, as working-class tourists gained entry into their own scaled-down versions of public domesticity.

A 1903 article, "The Comforts of Railroad Travel," captured this stratified yet domestic public life. In the private car, the most exclusive, luxurious, and expensive domestic setting, the travel writer described the apotheosis of the genteel home aboard. Here, amid great luxury, the rules of genteel propriety held as "the magnate's wife is settling herself beside the broad rear plate-glass window, and the busy man is dictating letters to a stenographer beside the center table." The author beckoned the reader to "look into the second-class tourist cars of a transcontinental flyer at a prairie station" to view a more boisterous and diversified scene. Women and children mingled with single men and "whole families bound for Rocky Mountain resorts loll about on the wicker or leather seats; one or two people are heating coffee on the range at the end of the car; three or four straw-hatted men are clustered smoking on the vestibuled platforms; heads project from open windows; everybody is happy."[102] By the end of the century, the line

The interior of an immigrant sleeper offers a vision of travel stripped of domestic amenities and comfort. From "Railway Passenger Travel," Scribner's Magazine, *September 1888. Courtesy of the New York University Libraries.*

of cars moving across the continent transported a variety of groups, each in its own domestic setting instead of a single group unified by a shared appreciation of moral domestic life. Intended as an organiz-, ing and integrating force for a commercial society on the move, public domesticity both articulated and mitigated class difference.

African Americans were increasingly excluded from this market-place. Even with a first-class ticket, blacks were routinely relegated to part of the baggage car, a smoking car, or a divided-off section in a sleeper. Nor could the possession of a Pullman Car ticket consistently protect an African American traveler from racism. In Mary Church Terrell's words: "There are few ordeals more nerve-racking than the one which confronts a colored woman when she tries to secure a Pull-man reservation in the South and even in some parts of the North." [103] Some black passengers who traveled Pullman in the South were as-signed to "Lower 13," a private "drawing room" at the end of the car's twelve open sections. The drawing room could accommodate up to three passengers, and because of its expensive price was often empty.

"Interior View of Pullman Tourist Sleeper" reveals a less luxurious version of *public domesticity. From* In a Tourist Sleeper via Santa Fé Route, *Atchison, Topeka and Santa Fé Railroad, December 1892. Courtesy of the Warshaw Collection of Business Americana—Railroads, Archives Center, National Museum of American History, Behring Center, Smithsonian Institution.*

A black passenger would be given these exclusive accommodations at the lower berth fare and for the remainder of the journey be expected to stay in his drawing room, even taking his meals there.[104]

〰️ Despite the dream of a homelike public, not all passengers were made to feel at home aboard. The domestic amenities and images that sustained the possibility of a public moral home on rails provided a uniquely American vocabulary for describing increased social stratification aboard. Moreover, railroads and courts justified racial segregation in the name of comfort; the mixing of the races, they said, discomforted white passengers and endangered black travelers. (In 1903, the Texas Railroad commission even invoked white passengers' expectation of comfort to call for the exclusion of black travelers from dining cars, despite acknowledging that these accommodations were not included in the separate coach statute.)[105] In 1887 the Georgia

Railroad Company defended its new policy of racially segregated accommodations: "The difference, if any, between the white passengers' and colored passengers' cars relate to matters esthetical only, and consist in higher ornamentation and matters of that sort."[106] Despite the railroad's protests, many Americans understood that these "matters" mattered a great deal and influenced the comfort and safety of passengers by sending important cultural messages. Commenting on Georgia railroad's policy, the *Railway Age* simply noted that the Jim Crow car was "not an attractive vehicle for fastidious travelers."[107]

Yet the moral home was not entirely forgotten. The black journalist Victoria Earle Matthews imagined a different relationship between public domesticity and racial segregation. In her 1897 speech to the Annual Convention of Christian Endeavor, Matthews praised the public role of home. "It is the foundation upon which nationality rests, the pride of the citizen and the glory of the Republic." Moreover, home was the "central feature of [the black woman's] awakening." Matthews's interpretation of black womanhood and domesticity supported her condemnation of the separate car regulations. "Their entire operation tends to degrade Afro-American womanhood" and deny "her rightful position in society."[108] Matthews and many other women used the Victorian ideals of womanhood to demand their inclusion in the public home on rails. Their own sense of respectability required that they do so.

A Ladies' Place

THE RAILROAD AND THE REGENDERING
OF VICTORIAN PUBLIC LIFE

In 1854, at the age of twenty-three, Lucy Bird left England to tour the United States. In the account of her journey published two years later, *An Englishwoman in America*, she recalled in vivid detail a railway journey from Chicago to Detroit. The cars were crowded and many passengers had to stand. "According to the usages of American etiquette," Bird wrote, "the gentlemen vacated their seats in favor of the ladies, who took possession of them in a very ungracious manner." Eventually, every man but one was standing. When a woman boarded at the next station this man refused to give up his place, even after the conductor demanded, "A seat for a lady! Don't you see there's a lady wanting one?" Another male passenger shouted: "Get up for this lady!" The offending party shouted in response: "I'm an Englishman, and I tell you, I won't be brow beat by you beastly Yankees. I've paid for my seat and I mean to keep it!" Bird then watched as "two men took the culprit by the shoulders, and the others, pressing behind, impelled him to the door amid a chorus of groans and hisses, disposing of him finally by placing him in the emigrant car [and] installing the lady in the vacated seat." Greatly ashamed of her countryman's conduct, Bird passed the remainder of the ride trying to conceal her English nationality.[1]

In this account Bird proves herself a perceptive observer of the tensions that shaped so much of the United States' public life during the second half of the nineteenth century and accurately identifies many of the conflicted social and cultural arrangements that eventually transformed how American men and women interacted in public. As Bird noted, the railroads served as public sites for displaying the values of gender deference that defined polite Victorian conduct.[2] Aboard the trains, "ladies" and "gentlemen" were able to recognize each other because they conformed to an elaborate code of conduct; men were to protect women and make them comfortable in public, and women were to accept such favors without compromising their respectable status—to be grateful, but not overly familiar. Bird also showed that adherence to this code remained imperfect; some "gentlemen" failed to yield their seats freely, and some "ladies" claimed vacated places "in a very ungracious manner."

This code of conduct was central to a popular sense of "Americanness." Bird commented upon an "American etiquette," and her account acknowledged that this brand of chivalry celebrated notions of democracy even as it drew social divisions and constructed class and ethnic hierarchies: on the one hand, an unruly "chorus of groans and hisses" validated the removal of the Englishman; on the other, the Briton was placed in an emigrant car—presumably the proper setting for ungentlemanly foreigners. Moreover, Bird revealed how American notions of chivalry and gender deference conflicted with the commercial values of rail travel and the country's expanding consumer culture. The Englishman's defense was, after all, two-fold: "I am an Englishman... [and] I've paid for my seat and I mean to keep it!" During the closing decades of the century this conflict between a lady's right to deference and a passenger's right of purchase played itself out upon the rails many times.

The debate over a lady's place in public continued throughout the second half of the nineteenth century because Victorian notions of deference and visions of civility coexisted with the values of American consumerism. Clinging to their status as gentlemen, many men struggled to assert their own rights to comfort while in public. Thirty years after Lucy Bird boarded the train from Chicago to Detroit, the *Railway Age* echoed the complaints of her angry countryman: "It is unreasonable that a man should be abused and assaulted because he has selfishness enough to keep his own seat while a lady is standing. It is his own affair, and if he would rather be comfortable than gallant no one has a right to take him to task."[3] By the end of the nineteenth century the tensions between prescriptive and actual conduct, between democratic ideals and the persistence of hierarchy, between Victorian notions of respectable behavior and consumer values of comfort rearranged the Victorian public sphere into a new public culture openly fragmented by gender and race.

The lady traveler was a lightning rod for all these tensions. The presence of "respectable" women on trains heightened the need to create social order and simultaneously suggested a solution—the application of genteel gender relations. Indeed, a cursory reading of railroad narratives suggests that gender was more important than race or class in organizing Victorian public life aboard. At times, gender difference was employed to mask divisions of race and class. For example, the designated "ladies' car" was often also the first-class car and by century's end was almost exclusively for white passengers. But, of course, gender ideals could not conceal concerns about race or class and instead reflected and magnified assumptions about these social categories. The idea that gender could organize public life was, like public domesticity, a shared fantasy. Much as Victorian travelers recast railway cars as domestic spaces, they imagined that genteel conduct might be transferred from the social venues of polite society to the rails—that public life could be inhabited by "ladies" and "gentlemen" with carefully defined social obligations, that even among diverse groups of strangers clear rules of respectable conduct could hold sway.

And like the public domesticity Victorians created, this transplanting of genteel social forms and conventions to public life created a special place, both metaphorical and literal, for women in public. But as public domesticity failed to organize public life around a commitment to the moral home, so did the application of polite social forms fail to bind a diverse body of passengers into an orderly public. Intended to organize life on the rails, the Victorian categories of polite society were rearranged and the identities they were intended to protect were altered. By the close of the nineteenth century, gender difference and deference had created new social and spatial arrangements on trains. These arrangements, in turn, shaped the emerging consumer culture and fostered a commitment to a particular vision of public comfort. Nowhere was this more apparent than in the changing fate of the lady traveler. Her shifting public role suggests how seemingly static categories of gender difference operated as both agents and markers of change.[4]

At midcentury, the lady traveler was a privileged public actor—the beneficiary of male deference.[5] When not safely at home, ladies expected to move within a cocoon of genteel male attentiveness—

"A 'Limited Express,'" Currier and Ives (1884).
Courtesy of the Library of Congress, LC-USZCN4-53.

a privatized cultural space defined by an elaborate code of Victorian etiquette. Gentlemen accepted responsibility for maintaining the boundaries of this space. When a lady was present, for example, no gentleman would smoke, chew tobacco, or use foul language. Popular etiquette books included a long and detailed list of services that gentlemanly passengers should offer lady travelers. One book instructed that "when a lady, travelling alone, wishes to descend from a railway car, it is the duty of the gentleman nearest the door to assist her in alighting, even if he resumes his seat again."[6] A lady could also expect a male passenger to help her purchase a ticket and check her baggage, make her comfortable by giving up his seat, open or close the train's windows, or bring her refreshments and books during the journey. At journey's end, a gentleman might collect a lady's baggage and call a hack for her. An 1884 Currier and Ives lithograph captured the ardor with which many men took up these duties. Entitled "Limited Express/Five Seconds for Refreshments!" the lithograph shows a train stopped at a station for lunch. Women poke their heads out of each window as they wait for men to bring refreshments. On the platform, male passengers eager to get to the refreshment stand run from the train and fall in a heap, one on top of the other. Assuming responsibility for ladies' needs, men alone face the consequences of this scramble, as the female passengers remain aloof from any inconvenience or impropriety.[7]

Ladyhood entailed more than physical comfort and social pampering; it provided women with a public role as the civilizers of men. In 1910, Emily Putnam, the first dean of Barnard College, noted in her history of the lady that "the lady has established herself as the criterion of a community's civilisation."[8] According to an 1896 etiquette manual, the "small observances [of etiquette] not only conduce to the comfort of women, but they refine and do away with the rough and selfish side of man's nature, for without this refining contact with gentle womanhood, a man will never lose the innate roughness with which nature has endowed him."[9] Etiquette books repeatedly designated ladies as the markers of civilized social space both at home and in public.

A properly behaved lady in public, then, was not stepping beyond her appointed sphere. She was a public figure denoting and inspiring civility. The same 1896 social manual explained, "The height of a stage of civilization can always be measured by the amount of deference paid to woman." Another etiquette book claimed that deference to women defined polite society itself.[10] The lady's influence was both the cause of and justification for her privileged status. It legitimized her place in public and added to the quality and conduct of public life. Through contact with ladies, men learned how to conduct themselves, and even in the unruly and rude spaces of public life—especially on the streets and in the cars—women could teach and inspire men to respect the rules of polite society.[11] In the words of Walter Houghton's *American Etiquette and Rules of Politeness* (1882): "Woman is peculiarly the organizer and definer of elegant society. . . . All the nicety and elegance of polished manners must and do come through woman. . . . Worthy men strive to please and honor noble, virtuous, amiable women."[12] In short, despite the circumscribing ideology of separate spheres, ladyhood offered women an important and recognized public role.

But the lady traveler, the object of men's chivalric attentions and the marker of civilized social life, was difficult to recognize in public. According to *The Ladies' Book of Etiquette and Manual of Politeness*, "there is no situation in which a lady is more exposed than when she travels."[13] Defined by sex, class, race, and moral characteristics, the lady was vulnerable to the perceptions of others: Victorian Americans believed they knew her when they saw her. But did they? As Putnam noted in her study of the lady, this social type was "proverbial for her skill in eluding definition."[14] Many etiquette manuals held out the promise that any women could attain the outward signs of ladyhood and every man learn to act like a gentleman. The perfect lady was defined by her inner qualities—by her "good-nature, perfect courtesy, patience, punctuality, and an easy adaptation to perhaps untoward circumstances."[15] According to an 1888 etiquette manual, "refinement and nobility of character are the chief qualities that regulate giving or withholding the title of lady."[16] How could one read such qualities in a world of strangers?

Appearances were often unreliable.[17] A confidence woman might employ the social conventions of ladyhood to exploit unsuspecting victims. Allan Pinkerton (of the famed detective agency) warned that a female passenger often served as the ideal accomplice to "Palace Car Thieves." "The lady being alone, and as is generally the case, young and attractive looking, becomes the object of considerable solicitude and politeness from the conductor, who, like all of his sex, has a tender feeling for unprotected beauty." She plays upon the sympathies of the conductor and porter and, feigning a "sudden and distressing headache," distracts them while the thief goes about his business.[18] In 1865 the *American Phrenological Journal* advised bachelors that casual observation was an inadequate method of "how to tell a lady" and that "sensible men avail themselves of [phrenology]" to make such a determination.[19] Such precautions were also needed to prevent a gentleman from insulting a lady.

In the absence of a foolproof classification system, both men and women wondered whether gentlemen owed all women deference based upon their sex. In other words, were all women in public equally entitled to the protections and privileges of ladyhood? For many Americans the answer was a resounding yes. In 1867, *Godey's Lady's Book* boasted that in the United States, "men, rich, distinguished, learned, and revered rise up and offer their seats—it may be to poor, plain, uneducated persons, because they are women."[20] An 1860 etiquette book asserted that "a true gentleman . . . will assist an Irish washerwoman with her large basket or bundle over a crossing, or carry over the little charges of a distressed negro nurse, with the same gentle courtesy which he would extend toward the lady who was stepping from her private carriage."[21] A shoeworker in Lynn, Massachusetts, echoed this belief when in 1875 she wrote to the *Lynn Record* to defend her status as a lady and "to warn my young lady friends of that class of young men . . . on the eight o'clock morning train . . . who find no other employment for their time than staring at women all the way, like great idiotic, grinning country school boys."[22] This young woman saw no contradiction between her status as a worker and as a lady. For her and many others, the gendered benefits and claims of civility and respectability permeated all levels of American society.

A popular anecdote made this point by insisting that any man could be a gentleman. An Irishman offers his seat to two "well-bred and intelligent young ladies." When the ladies politely decline, the man insists, vowing, "I'd ride on the cow-catcher till New York, any time, for a smile from such *jintlemanly* ladies." The two ladies finally accept and the "Irish gentleman" exits the car amid "the cheers of those who had witnessed the affair."[23] Such stories transformed celebrations of gender deference into celebrations of America's civilized democracy.

While this inclusive vision of a multiclass, multiethnic public unified by the conventions of polite society drew upon a specific definition of ladyhood, other definitions challenged and complicated this vision. Definitions of the lady rooted in notions of aristocratic nobility depended upon exclusivity—upon, in the words of one etiquette manual, the "difference between the well-bred and ill-bred."[24] Emily Putnam succinctly described a lady "merely as the female of the favoured social class."[25] And for many Americans, wealth, education, and social position remained the ultimate guarantors of ladyhood, as money and training could frequently provide the polished manner and clothing most readily associated with ladies. Mary Church Terrell, for example, learned how to be a "little lady" before the age of five and believed that she could ensure polite treatment through her neat appearance, appropriate dress, and good posture. But, as Terrell learned, even her family's wealth and her own good conduct could not always overcome racial prejudice.[26]

Conforming to the code of middle-class etiquette and asserting that a black woman could be a lady, Terrell embodied the contradictions inherent in holding to both exclusive and inclusive definitions of ladyhood. Even the aristocratic definition of the lady based on wealth and good breeding remained contested, enabling a wide variety of women to claim the protections of ladyhood. That a white, middle-class reader of etiquette manuals, a shoeworker from Lynn, and a wealthy black woman all shared a faith in the values of Victorian ladyhood suggests not only the broad appeal of these notions but also the potential for conflict. Historian Elsa Barkley Brown has asserted that "history is everybody talking at once, multiple rhythms being played simultaneously. . . . In fact, at any given moment millions of people are talking all at once."[27] In the second half of the nineteenth century, a wide range of historical actors engaged in private and public debates about what it meant to be a lady in public. They were all taking at once and frequently offered contradictory definitions. Nonetheless, both passengers and railway companies looked to "the lady" to maintain order.

Railroad companies echoed popular etiquette manuals and explicitly inscribed gender deference upon public life, advising workers to pay special attention to the comfort of lady passengers. In the 1870s such policies were so widespread that the popular writer James D. McCabe could assure would-be lady travelers that "the employés of all the lines of travel are required by their employers to pay particular and respectful attention to ladies travelling alone."[28] A pamphlet advertising Harvey & Co.'s rail excursion to California noted that "ladies and children travelling without escort are as well cared for as though accompanied by personal friends."[29] Another travel brochure carefully "set down the experiences of four young ladies who crossed the continent unattended by male escort and met on every hand most courteous treatment and most kindly counsel and found in all their travels no one to molest them or make them afraid."[30] According to the 1893 rule book of the Pullman Palace Car Company, ladies, especially ladies traveling alone, were permitted access to the most exclusive or private accommodations and were to have their berths prepared before those of male passengers.[31] In short, rail companies cultivated the belief that the gentlemanly conduct of railway workers protected traveling ladies from the dangers associated with travel and created a hybrid space that was neither truly private nor public.

Polite assumptions about gender difference and deference even determined the layout of trains. Companies responded to the presence of women by creating a variety of separate, private, and frequently more refined accommodations specifically for ladies. As early as 1836, the Cumberland Valley Railroad Company provided a separate "ladies' compartment" in the first sleeping car operated in the United States, and two years later the Philadelphia, Wilmington &

Baltimore Railroad provided separate cars "for the accommodation of ladies and children." [32] Such spaces were privatized public sites where "decent" women could congregate and escape exposure to male passengers and the unpleasantness associated with men's smoking and tobacco chewing aboard the train. [33] Not all "decent" women traveled in ladies' cars, especially after the proliferation of specialty and Pullman cars in the 1870s created other domesticated spaces in which "respectable" women could travel comfortably alongside "respectable" men. Railroad historian August Menken has suggested that ladies' cars were limited to those lines that operated in or from the South. Court cases from the 1870s, however, confirm that ladies' cars were legally sanctioned institutions in Wisconsin and New York. [34]

These feminized public spaces, like the separate spheres ideology itself, represented a cultural ideal that loomed large in discussions of life in the cars. In the ladies' car, unaccompanied women or women traveling with their husbands or children gathered and created a presumably genteel public apart from the boisterous public of "unattended" male travelers. Under ideal circumstances the ladies' car, like the domesticated specialty cars described in the previous chapter, provided a safe haven from the rough and tumble world of strangers. Drawing upon the values of public domesticity, the gender-segregated cars not only inserted separate spheres into public life but echoed and exaggerated the gender-segregated spaces of the private home. The genteel world of polite Victorian society reconstituted itself aboard the rails.

Although designed to reflect codes of etiquette and the honorable intentions of individual railway lines, the institutionalized gender deference—especially the ladies' cars—fostered competition over the meaning, boundaries, and constituency of the "respectable" public. Gender segregation on the rails was, by necessity, a flexible system. Because many women traveled with male family members or prearranged male escorts, rail companies made special allowances for men traveling in the company of ladies. Charles Dickens noted this policy as early as 1842 in his *American Notes for General Circulation*. Traveling on the Boston & Lowell Railroad, Dickens observed that "in the ladies' car, there are a great many gentlemen who have ladies with them." [35] A story from an 1873 anecdote book encapsulated the system's inconsistencies: An "elegant lady" addresses the conductor as she boards his train, saying, "I won't go except in a ladies' car; the regulations oblige you to have one, and you *shall*." The conductor responds that he will order a ladies' car immediately but quickly adds that the lady's "baby can't go in it. . . . It must stay in the gentlemen's car; it is a *male*."[36] Rigid enforcement of gender separation proved not only impossible but ridiculous. By permitting male escorts to travel in the ladies' car with their female charges, railroads compromised the integrity of the ladies' space.

In fact, an 1869 etiquette manual advised women to bar their male escorts from "any saloon devoted exclusively to the use of ladies." According to the author, one lady's brother was another's potentially improper stranger. "Because [a man] may be her own husband, son, father, or brother does not excuse [his presence], as he cannot stand in such relation to others present."[37] Another manual complained that some men claimed the comforts of ladies' accommodations "without even the excuse of being escorts of women, preferring the purer natural and moral atmosphere of the ladies' saloon."[38] Before the widespread use of specialty cars, the association of femininity and refinement in the ladies' car left single male travelers with few means and no place to assert their own refined status. In 1865, an article in the *New York Times* found "the gentleman's smoking car" lacking: "It should be called 'the loafers' groggery,' for smoking, drinking, tobacco squirting, profanity, and gambling are indulged in to the fullest extent."[39] What were "respectable" men to do?

Men resisted the notion that they were unfit company for ladies. An 1856 article from *Holly's Railroad Advocate*, for example, attacked the ladies' car as a "barbarism" and claimed that it created a false hierarchy as "there is no more seclusion, nor safety against tobacco indecencies, where a lady journeys with married gentlemen or gallants, than where she may chance to have the company of bachelors or stray benedicts." Almost two decades later another observer of railroad life complained, "Because an inveterate chewer and squirter of tobacco has his wife with him, it does not follow that he should have any better right to the ladies' car than a well-bred gentleman who travels singly."[40] Such feelings were exacerbated by railroad policies that permitted men to ride in the ladies' car when no other seats were available; under these circumstances, companies empowered conductors to select which gentlemen were appropriate ladies' car passengers.[41] Throughout the 1860s and 1870s, faced with what they perceived as their own unjust exclusion, men increasingly questioned the belief that only women deserved genteel public settings during travel.

In 1870, *Putnam's Magazine* decried the "utter disregard paid here to the unfortunate single gentleman" and warned the prospective male traveler "that whatever his birth, rank, and station in life may be, he is here only a man, and as a man an inferior animal, who is not safely to be trusted with ladies!" No amount of money could guarantee that he would be treated well during travel, but a female traveling companion could prove an asset. The author advised that "if you really want to travel for six months in the United States, you had better marry, steal, or borrow a wife, than go alone."[42] A year later, in an article entitled "Ladies' Car Humbug," Egbert Phelps railed against the gendered institution and made a claim for the rights of the genteel male traveler. According to Phelps, "the result of excluding those without female company from the ladies' car was, as might have been expected, to reduce all the other cars of the train to a condition little better than that of a respectable pig-sty." Phelps never questioned the civilizing influence of ladies but expressed outrage that "in this democratic land" boorish men frequently travel with their wives and therefore ride in the ladies' car, while "his betters [traveling without wives] are deprived." He believed that every man, married or single, should benefit from women's presence and that this alone could create a social setting in which men could travel respectably and comfortably. Phelps, inverting chivalric assumptions, suggested that ladies could, in effect, provide protection for genteel men in public.[43]

Banished by railway company policy from the uplifting society of ladies, single male travelers frequently sought access to the ladies' car by dishonorable means. This was especially true in the days before specialty cars or if no first-class accommodations were available.[44] The journalist Benjamin Franklin Taylor considered the ladies' car "a vicious fashion [that] fosters the art of lying." Taylor described two good and honorable men, one of whom "means to study for the ministry." Both men had, nonetheless, devised elaborate pretenses for gaining access to the ladies' car.[45] A popular anecdote published in 1873 offered an account similar to Taylor's: "A clean, well-dressed man" was refused entry to a ladies' car. Rather than accept his exclusion, he "walked straight to a robust and somewhat remarkable female representative from the land of shamrock" and offered to help her with her packages. As the newly acquainted couple walked toward the ladies' car, the brakemen again tried to prevent the man's entrance. This time, however, "the man insisted that *his lady* and himself had, under the rules laid down, a right to enter."[46] The other passengers roared with laughter as the man and "his lady," with "cheeks like a cheese-rind and a nose like a piece of decayed beefsteak," entered. Less inventive men bribed conductors.[47]

Much like the lady herself, then, the ladies' cars embodied various and contradictory assumptions about gender, class, race, morality, and refinement. Europeans frequently commented on the gendered nature of American railway accommodations, noting that, unlike European travel with its variety of classed cars, American travel acknowledged only the difference between men and women. In the words of one British traveler: "Every traveler takes his place where he may fancy except that there is a car reserved for ladies and for gentlemen accompanying them."[48] By naming the most comfortable and exclusive spaces "ladies' cars," the railroads obscured divisions of class and race in favor of gender difference even as they invoked the values and standards of white middle-class gentility. On early railway lines, for example, ladies' cars often served as "first-class" cars and were frequently the only such accommodations available. For many American railroad boosters this unique arrangement was a source of pride—evidence of democracy's triumph and a popular commitment to civility. By conflating femininity and gentility while touting American democracy, the railroads enabled respectable women of various races and classes to enter the ladies' car and claim the privileges of ladyhood. But this arrangement infuriated men like Phelps, who complained that "the line cannot be drawn between the cultivated and the boor—the clean and the unclean—but only upon the basis of sex."[49] Like Phelps, many travelers asked whether ladies cars were for all women? Were working-class or black women ladies? Were men traveling alone ever deemed respectable?

During the 1880s, a variety of passengers—both male and female, black and white—asserted their claims to ride in the ladies' car. In 1877, the New York State Court heard from John M. Peck, who had been ejected from the ladies' car on the New York Central & Hudson River Railroad. Peck was traveling alone when he attempted to enter the ladies' car. The brakeman informed him that the car was reserved for ladies and their gentlemen companions. Ignoring these instructions, Peck entered, and the brakeman forcibly removed him.[50] Why

did Peck want to ride in the ladies' car? The *New York Times* specu-
lated, "Perhaps he was a ladies' man, or a fashions writer, and liked
to sit where he could see the latest styles. Perhaps he could not find
a seat by the window on the riverside in the gentleman's cars. Perhaps he liked to have his own way."[51] The reason did not matter. In
deciding Peck's case the court ruled that, although the brakeman had
been overzealous, the railway company had a legal right to set aside
a car for "females traveling alone, or with male relatives." Such an
arrangement was not simply the company's right but its obligation.
According to the court, a separate car for ladies "tended to their comfort and security, and to the preservation of good order, which it is a
duty of a carrier of passengers to be vigilant in seeking."[52] No longer a
simple matter of courtesy or commerce, a lady's comfort had become
a legal obligation.

In a similar case the court again interpreted the privileges of gender as a legal right. When a man named Bass sued after being removed
from a ladies' car on the Chicago & Northwestern Railway near Osh-
kosh in 1874, the Supreme Court of Wisconsin upheld the principles
justifying a separate car "for ladies, and for gentlemen accompanying
ladies." In *Bass v. Chicago & Northwestern Railway Company*, the court
stated that "in view of the crowds of men of all sorts and conditions
and habits constantly traveling by railroad, it appears to us to be not
only a reasonable regulation, but almost a humane duty, for railroad
companies to appropriate a car of each passenger train primarily for
women and men accompanying them." The railroad had an obligation to protect the women it had encouraged to travel: "The use of
railroads for the common carriage of passengers has not only vastly
increased travel generally, but has also specially led women to travel
without male companions. To such, the protection which is the natural instinct of manhood towards their sex is specially due by common
carriers."[53] The social conventions of polite society had moved from
the parlor to public life and found chivalrous defenders in the courts.
The *New York Times* concluded, "The Law appears to be a gentleman,
and speaks as such."[54]

Although court rulings upheld ladies' special status and mandated
gentlemanly conduct, they also revealed the ambiguities that made
systematic gender deference impossible. Proclaiming the reason-
ableness of separate ladies' spaces, the courts confronted the prob-

lems of policing their boundaries. They could provide no foolproof system for identifying ladies in public. While the court in *Bass v. Chicago & Northwestern* sanctioned ladies' cars and said that the railroad could legally exclude men unaccompanied by women, it complicated matters by claiming that "women or men accompanying women of offensive character or habits" should be barred.[55] But in *Brown v. Memphis & Charleston Railroad Co.*, the Tennessee Circuit Court ruled that bad reputation did not justify the exclusion of female passengers. Such a regulation would "put every woman purchasing a railroad ticket on trial for her virtue before the conductors as her judge. . . . It would practically exclude all sensible and sensitive women from traveling at all, no matter how virtuous, for fear they might be put into or unconsciously occupy the wrong car."[56]

On the one hand, the courts asserted that women of good character were generally endangered in public but should be able to travel without insult. The ladies' car was intended "to group women of good character on the train together, sheltered as far as practicable from annoyance and insult."[57] On the other hand, by conceding that not all women were of good character—some indeed were not "ladies"—the courts suggested that gender segregation was an inadequate mechanism for providing such shelter. Sorting passengers and preserving a separate space for "women of good character" were difficult tasks. The courts had defended the rights of ladies only to acknowledge that life in the cars made the definition and identification of true ladies difficult.

Because she rendered the problems of definition and recognition particularly acute, the black lady played an important part in the remapping of Victorian public culture's gendered boundaries.[58] According to legal historian Barbara Welke, black women brought a majority of the legal challenges to racial segregation on common carriers. More women than men brought these suits precisely because of the system of gender deference that shaped nineteenth-century rail travel. Those who brought suits against the railways tended to be young, southern, urban, middle-class, educated women who had not been enslaved.[59] These women, by identifying themselves as ladies, forged gender identities that reflected not only their race but also their moral, social, and sometimes economic status. Conforming to the behaviors and values expressed in etiquette manuals, they understood themselves as respectable black women worthy of the privileges and gender deference granted to ladies in public.

Every time an African American woman entered a railroad depot or boarded a train she needed to reconcile her identity with the gendered geography of Jim Crow. Anna Julia Cooper wondered where she belonged whenever she entered a train depot and found "two dingy little rooms with 'FOR LADIES' swinging over one and 'FOR COLORED PEOPLE' over the other."[60] Because the average southern train included only a smoking car, a first-class or ladies' car, and a sleeper, many black women asserted their public claim to respectability by demanding access to ladies' cars rather than riding in the mixed race, predominately male smoking car that the rail companies identified as suitable for all black passengers. When Ida B. Wells set out on an excursion with two friends in 1886 she noted, "We had the usual trouble about the first-class coach but we conquered."[61] By claiming the privileges white ladies routinely enjoyed, black women sought to undermine racist assumptions about black female respectability, and gained some protection from the unwanted advances of men, both white and black.[62]

Many women, like Wells, claimed their privileges knowing full well that white passengers and railway officials frequently responded with physical force—the ultimate denial of a black woman's status as a lady. In 1888 Wells boasted to the readers of the *New York Freeman* that the "typical Southern girl" possessed an impeccable character, "enriched and beautified by the setting of womanly modesty, dignity of deportment, and refinement in manners; and the whole enveloped in a casket of a sweetness of disposition, and the amiability of temperament that makes it a pleasure to be near her."[63] As recounted earlier, in 1884 Wells had boarded a first-class car on the Chesapeake, Ohio & Southwestern Railroad. The conductor attempted to eject her from the first-class accommodations and to place her instead in the smoking car. While resisting, she bit the conductor. If Wells failed to conform to the rules of "respectable" public conduct, so did those white ladies and gentlemen who cheered her forced removal.

Of all the ladies in public, African American ladies were the most scrutinized. No matter their standing in their communities, black women in the heterogeneous public of the cars had to demand recognition. Although this challenge faced all ladies in public to some degree, black ladies needed to prove their worthiness to white pas-

sengers and rail officials because the very idea of a black lady confounded whites' racist expectations. Describing the obstacles black
women faced during travel, Cooper argued that they provided the most
accurate measure of the nation's civility. "The Black Woman holds that
her femineity [sic] linked with the impossibility of popular affinity
or unexpected attraction through position and influence in her case
makes her a touchstone of American courtesy exceptionally free from
extraneous modifiers." By claiming the status of lady, a black woman
created opportunities for Americans to exercise a truer form of courtesy. There could be no ulterior motives in showing her respect. "The
man who is courteous to her is so, not because of anything he hopes
or fears or sees, but because *he is a gentleman*." [64]

During the 1870s and 1880s, the black lady's good conduct and appropriate attire served as an example both to the black community and
to white observers; for both, she embodied the potential of her race.[65]
In her 1888 etiquette manual, Mary Frances Armstrong advised the
black student body of Hampton Normal and Agricultural Institute of
the importance of being ladies and gentlemen. Good and polite conduct, according to Armstrong, reflected well not only upon individual
students but also upon the entire school.[66] In many respects, her advice mirrored that of any etiquette book directed toward a middle-
class audience. Young ladies, Armstrong noted, "must understand
that you are entitled to certain privileges by right of your sex." The section of Armstrong's book focusing on conduct during travel blandly
advised ladies to stay quiet, mind their behavior, avoid talking to
strange men, and watch their pocketbooks, echoing advice in books
for the white middle class.[67]

Armstrong's advice to male travelers, by contrast, revealed the special challenge of African American etiquette: Black men, she instructed, must "protect the womanhood of your race." She was explicit in defining the relationship between gender deference and the
protection of black ladies in public: "If you [black men] do not your-
selves show respect to the women of your own race, you will have
no right to expect such respect from other men, which is a full and
sufficient reason for you to be toward them, even more than toward
others, scrupulous and courteous in thought and deed." Armstrong
warned her students that they might not always be met courteously:
"To colored people in America the question of manners on the road
may involve at times peculiarly difficult and trying positions, and

cases where the courtesy will seem one-sided." According to Armstrong, students must, nonetheless, answer mistreatment with propriety. Only polite conduct would improve whites' treatment of blacks and expand the rights and privileges gained since emancipation.[68]

Using middle-class etiquette to serve individual and community goals, the African American lady traveler used the common language of gender deference to challenge racial segregation.[69] When Anna Williams attempted to board the ladies' car at the Rockford, Illinois, station of the Chicago & Northwestern Railway in 1870, a white railway official refused her entry and directed her to "the car set apart for and occupied mostly by men." But Williams had purchased a first-class ticket, so she pressed her claim. The brakeman again refused her entry. Williams sued and recovered a judgment of two hundred dollars. The judgment stated that she had been rudely and unfairly refused the privileges of ladyhood in a public setting and that such an insult had caused her unnecessary disgrace. Upon appeal, the verdict in Williams's favor was upheld. In *Chicago & Northwestern Railway Company v. Anna Williams*, the Illinois court ruled that Williams, "a colored woman, holding a first class ticket," should not have been barred from the ladies' car. According to the ruling, Williams "was clad in plain and decent apparel, and it is not suggested in the evidence or otherwise, that she was not a woman of good character and proper behavior."[70] The court found Anna Williams, regardless of race, to be entitled to the privileges of ladies; she carried herself well and could afford the ticket. Many white passengers and train officials failed to see what the court, in this instance, had recognized—a black woman could be a lady.[71]

Despite Williams's victory, the privileges of black lady travelers eventually lost ground in the courts. During the 1870s and 1880s the claims of black ladies were occasionally upheld in state and federal courts, but they were often overturned on appeal.[72] More important, the spread of statutory Jim Crow in the late 1880s and 1890s resolved the legal ambiguities that had enabled black women to assert that gender deference protected them from the insult and danger of riding in the predominately male, mixed-race smoker.[73] The Jim Crow car created a racially defined space for black women and men. Ironically, to uphold this separation, the courts used arguments similar to those justifying the ladies' car: Both the ladies' car and the Jim Crow car reflected a "duty . . . to provide, as far as [one] reasonably could do so, for the comfort of [one's] passengers" and were in keeping with railroads' responsibilities as common carriers.[74] The same logic that permitted railroads to sort passengers by sex supported the decision to separate passengers by race: The separation of the races, like the separation of the sexes, "may tend to prevent personal collisions and preserve peace and order."[75] The Michigan Supreme Court explained that such rules were "calculated to render transportation most comfortable and least annoying to passengers generally."[76] In the eyes of the courts, safety, order, and comfort justified racial segregation.

Although courts often demanded that they do so, rail companies provided no separate car for black ladies, and the lie of "separate but equal" left no comfortable place in which they could travel.[77] Some black women sought out the safety and genteel atmosphere of Pullman's exclusive specialty cars, but even women who could pay the surcharge for such accommodations were often denied access. One man recalled with outrage his attempt to procure a sleeping car berth for his sister who was going to enroll in a college seven hundred miles away. He could not secure these accommodations and instead "had to incur the expense of accompanying her to protect her in her smoking car journey."[78] Neither education nor money could guarantee respectable accommodations for black ladies and their gentlemen companions.

Some historians have argued that a black lady's exclusion from the privileges of gender deference served white supremacy by protecting the purity and privileges of white womanhood; in this interpretation, gender privilege becomes the ultimate marker of whiteness. Others have argued that the black lady used her gendered identity to take on a role of leadership within the black community as well as to challenge racism; here, gender privilege serves as a wedge against racism.[79] Both of these interpretations place gender in the service of racial politics, but what impact did these racial politics have upon gendered constructions like that of the lady? Black women seemed to breathe new life into traditional Victorian gender ideals and simultaneously contributed to a public debate in which those ideals were increasingly challenged. Although the consideration of gender provides insight into the processes and tensions that shaped the emergence of legalized racial segregation, black women's attempts to claim the status of ladies cannot be understood only in this context. By claiming the status and privileges of ladies in public, black women participated in and shaped a charged public discussion about the place of gender difference and deference.

At the 1899 National American Woman Suffrage Association annual meeting in Grand Rapids, Michigan, Lottie Wilson Jackson proposed a resolution: "That colored women ought not to be compelled to ride in smoking cars, and that suitable accommodations should be provided for them." During the debate that followed, Jackson explained that the dirty cars and rowdy passengers prevented black women like herself from traveling freely and limited the work that she and others could do on behalf of their race and women's suffrage. After Jackson refused a proposal that she omit the word "colored," the predominately white association rejected the resolution. Given the history of the woman's suffrage movement and its on-again, off-again ties to racist politics, the failure of Jackson's resolution may be attributed to white suffragists' unwillingness to alienate southern delegates.[80] The proposed omission of "colored," however, might also have signaled that the white delegates rightly recognized that their own status as ladies was increasingly challenged in public.[81]

While white gentlemen and black ladies sought entry into ladies' cars through the courts, a much broader debate was waged over a lady's entitlement to gentlemanly deference in public. The inability of "the lady" to create order upon the rails was reflected not only in court cases but also in the discontent of male travelers. According to one disgruntled observer, "the weary [male] traveler, who may have been sitting by his friend's side for days and nights, is unceremoniously ousted by a market-woman, who enters at some way-station, and finding him absent pleads a lady's privilege in refusing to give way to the rightful owner."[82] Rather than celebrate the inclusiveness of American civility, such complaints drew upon ethnic and regional stereotypes to make fun of women on the margins of ladyhood and further compromised the lady as a cultural ideal. They seemed to claim that even if one did know a lady when one saw her, it made no difference, since any woman could claim a lady's privileges. Men's displeasure, revealed in magazine and newspaper articles, etiquette manuals, and diaries, suggests how women's presence aboard the railroad and the assertion of ladies' privileges by a wide variety of women undermined the spirit of "American etiquette" and reshaped public culture.

At the center of these complaints was the growing belief that too many women—black and white, immigrant and native-born—acted as though male deference was their right whenever they ventured into public. For some men, once deference became a right—any woman's right—rather than a polite exchange, ladies no longer served as civilizing agents. In 1877 Albert Rhodes informed readers of the *Galaxy* that the unprecedented chivalry of the American man had made the American woman bold. She traveled unattended, safe in the knowledge that "men step forward as her protectors as if it were according to a law of State instead of a custom." In short, she claims "as a right what was only intended as a courtesy. Hence her neglect to return thanks for the seat yielded up in the car; hence the growing reluctance in the man to resign his seat."[83] Another observer fretted that "the deservedly famous chivalric attentions of our men" was making American women "less modest and sweet, more self-asserting and impatient of control."[84] An 1883 article on "courtesy in railway traveling" reported a decline in the willingness of men to offer seats to young ladies and offered a similar explanation. "Perhaps the dying out of this practice is due in a great measure to the ladies themselves. They began to look upon an act of gallantry as the concession of a right."[85]

It is no coincidence that the language of "rights" figured so prominently in this debate. As the courts spoke of "ladies' rights" to deference, comfort, and protection, the woman's suffrage movement spoke of different rights. In November 1885, the *Railway Age* printed a short piece capturing the relationship between women's rights and ladies' rights. The article reported: "At the recent women's rights convention in New York a complaint made in relation to car seats was unanimously [endorsed] by all the members of the convention. The complaint was that the seats in . . . public conveyances, were constructed entirely for the use of men, and were consequently too high for the accommodation of most women."[86] The women called for lower seats, drafted a memorial to this effect, and circulated it for signatures. Political activity demanded that women travel in public, and women used their political power to make themselves comfortable. Many men, in turn, used the language of women's rights to accuse American women of eating their cake and having it too. According to the author of "Womanhood and American Chivalry," women claimed public rights on the same terms as men even as they continued to hold on to expectations of special deference and protection. "American chivalry . . .

loves to protect, but it demands that the thing protected shall both need and acknowledge the aid afforded it."[87]

Popular writings echoed this interpretation. An 1883 etiquette book lamented that "the manners of people in public vehicles seem daily to be growing worse."[88] Another manual from 1891 encouraged ladies "to remember that fellow-passengers have rights as well as one's self."[89] The author of *The Correct Thing in Good Society* proclaimed it incorrect "for women to consider that their privileges are their rights, or to forget to bow graciously and thank courteously and *audibly* any one who may have shown them any politeness."[90] Women who failed to appreciate the services provided by men were not ladies, and periodicals and newspapers enumerated their rude acts. In May 1880, the *Railway Age* contemplated the fate of "railway manners" and concluded, "the 'unprotected female' is as liable to rudeness, imposition and neglect as is the modest, unassuming man."[91] Women took up too many seats with their bags and umbrellas; they accepted seats with no visible sign of appreciation; and when no seat was offered they would, according to one observer, "gaze around with a supercilious, disdainful stare, as if astounded by the impudence of the selfish brutes who could bury their faces in their newspapers or stare vacantly out of the window."[92] Even ladies noted the rudeness of other women. Lillian Leland admitted, "It has been my misfortune to meet some women who seem to think that a man has no kind of human right as against their selfish fancies."[93]

Unlike earlier portrayals of women travelers that emphasized their ignorance of the rules of public life, these depictions focused on deliberate rudeness. An angry male traveler described with contempt "the woman who sails through the crowded car, and brings to beside you like a monument, looks at you as if you had no business to be born without her consent, and says in a clear, incisive voice, that cuts through you like a knife, 'I know a gentleman when I see him!'" Even at seventy years old and with a case of rheumatism, what choice did the man have but to yield his seat? Exasperated, the gentleman exclaimed, "Send her to the tailor to be measured, and 'let her pass for a man!'"[94] Only then, presumably, would she feel the man's disadvantage. An account from the *San Francisco News Letter* described a similar scene: A young lady boards a car in which all the seats are taken, and when a gentleman gives up his seat she "slams down into it." The man asks, "I beg pardon?" He then makes a great show of leaning in to hear her reply. Only then does the lady "[give] up the struggle, [yell] 'Thanks!' and [leave] the car at the next crossing." [95] In 1881, the *New York Times* concluded, "In this matter of what may be called railway car politeness, the women have quite as much to learn as the men." [96]

One may question whether this was a true crisis for American gentility. To read etiquette books and social critics too literally is to accept a world in which, at any given moment, people are becoming ruder. Yet the debate about ladies' place in public moved beyond the parlor and into the expanding consumer culture. In 1897, the superintendent of the Boston, Revere Beach & Lynn Railroad ordered, "Conductors and motormen in addressing women passengers shall substitute the word 'Madame' for 'Lady.'" The order came in response to workers' confusion when addressing female passengers. "Women patrons of the road were sometimes addressed as 'Missis,' sometimes as 'Miss,' not infrequently as 'Lady,' and occasionally as 'Madame,' and it was often the case that the person addressed as 'Mrs.' should have been addressed as 'Miss,' if strict propriety was observed, and vice versa." In frustration, many trainmen had resorted to 'Lady,' but this appellation proved "distasteful to women who are ladies and inappropriate to other women." Even "Madame" failed to please everyone; the *Railway Age* recommended that the American Society of Railroad Superintendents find "a comprehensive and appropriate word of public address for women of all ages and conditions." [97] Despite the silliness of such deliberations, it is worth taking the terms of this broader debate seriously. Public life in the cars remained no place for a lady in part because the very nature of her identity was opposed to the social life of the cars. She could not thrive in an environment of unfixed identities, and the demands of travel made her too much of a burden to both herself and others.

Unable to identify ladies, the railroad companies turned their attention to the complaints of male travelers. At midcentury, public life had been perceived as unruly and filled with inconveniences and petty insults. By the final decades of the century, the semipublic world created by the railroads inspired expectations of comfort and fueled a shift in gender roles by encouraging passengers to claim their money's worth. Although they failed to provide an explicit definition of "gentlemen's rights," changes in railway policy suggest a growing recognition that men should not be compelled to surrender seats and that women were not entitled to more than that for which they had paid. An observer of railway car life defended "the modest unassuming man who is content to take his own share of what comfort may be provided for travellers and to get the fair reasonable worth of his money and no more." This reasonable male figure stood in stark contrast to "the snappish woman entrenched among her bundles and bags and bridling and fumbling over the necessity of compressing herself within the space she has paid for, entirely unconscious that the severest trial falls upon the person who has to sit beside her." [98] The rights of purchase conferred by the expanding consumer culture complicated the rules of gender deference, provided men with new rights, and transformed men into the civilizing agents of public life.

After the 1870s, railroad companies increasingly provided amenities for male travelers, refined spaces for men who could afford to separate themselves from the undifferentiated mass. No longer presumed to travel only as the long-suffering and dutiful protectors of ladies, gentlemen travelers enjoyed genteel spaces designed to guarantee their physical and social comfort. As railroad companies expected women to delight in the "cute" dressing tables and "cosy" seats of the domesticated train, they believed respectable male travelers would appreciate luxurious smoking and library cars set aside for their use. The *Railway Age* reported that "the Chicago, Burlington & Quincy has won the affections of a considerable class of travelers by putting on its mainline several elegant 'palace smoking cars,'" that provided men an alternative to the "horrible emigrant cars which still afford the only resort for smokers on a good many roads." [99] Here men could claim their respectability as gentlemen free from the demands of ladies.

The commercialization of public life in the cars left gender segregation in place by creating more luxurious accommodations set aside for men. [100] In 1886, the *Railway Age* noted the new demands of male travelers, as well as the improved amenities, when it wrote that "a man's boudoir will do, but it must be as dainty in its fittings as a ladies.'" [101] According to the Pennsylvania Railroad, the new and improved "Smoking Car is the paradise of men." Here, men relaxed and socialized among the "luxurious rattan chairs, divans, tables, and writing desks." [102] The company's "Mexico Special" included "a gentleman's car" equipped with a barber shop, a bath-

Gentleman traveler at home aboard (1891). Courtesy of the Warshaw Collection of Business Americana—Railroads, Archives Center, National Museum of American History, Behring Center, Smithsonian Institution.

room with hot and cold water, and a smoking saloon "furnished with library chairs, a lounge, a sofa, and two writing desks." The car so closely resembled "one's club [that it] cannot fail to receive the [e]ndorsement of masculine appreciation."[103] The Baltimore & Ohio boasted smoking rooms "finished in Circasian walnut, exquisitely inlaid; the chairs upholstered in olive-green leather; the ceilings of red and gold, the general design being Italian renaissance."[104] And the Chicago, Milwaukee & St. Paul Railway announced that the buffet library car was "literally a man's club on wheels"—a place where male travelers could find cigars, mineral water, and liquors as well as "a meal equal to any served in the best hotels or in one's own home."[105] The comfort of women was perceived in terms of domesticity; men's comfort was associated with business. Railroad companies therefore stocked their cars with the most recent newspapers, periodicals, and books as well as with writing paper. Some trains even posted stock quotations and provided secretaries or stenographers.[106]

Women continued to receive luxurious amenities, but rather than reflecting values of gender deference these new comforts revealed a changing perception of the lady. No longer the uplifting agents of men, ladies could not be trusted to themselves. The persistence of gender segregation and the elaboration of ladies' accommodations did not necessarily reflect increased respect for the lady or her rights. In 1868, the author of "Womanhood and American Chivalry" noted that the proliferation of feminine luxuries no longer implied chivalry: "While there may be a disposition to surround woman with as much comfort, and even luxury, as could have been accorded to her at the most over-liberal period, there is a marked tendency to pull her down from the pedestal on which she is enthroned."[107] In 1885, the *Indianapolis Journal* printed an article questioning Pullman's decision to create separate ladies' apartments within their sleeping cars. If ladies were "left to themselves in one apartment, with no men to watch the proceedings, there might be some ugly words and possible hair pulling."[108] Similarly, when the *Chicago Tribune* announced the all-female drawing-room cars on some western railway lines, it underscored that the cars' design accommodated the foibles of their intended inhabitants. The new "Adamless Eden on Wheels" provided tea in elegant urns, hairpins, and an abundance of mirrors and powder puffs. This paradise, however, was not above moral reproach: an accompanying cartoon depicted female passengers vainly gazing into mirrors, greedily fighting over novels in the car's library, and smoking in the all-female smoking compartment.[109]

Initially intended to create a small and distinct semipublic domain for women travelers, by the early decades of the twentieth century sex-segregated spaces and amenities reflected the reluctance of white men to inconvenience themselves in the name of chivalry. No longer willing to pay a personal price to make women comfortable by giving up seats or fetching meals, male travelers embraced a world of gendered amenities that made *them* more comfortable. The connotations of "the lady" and the nature of gender segregation aboard the trains had shifted. Previously seen by the railroads and the courts as too good or too pure for the rough-and-tumble world of public transport, ladies were now decried as too demanding or too selfish. In 1880, the *Railway Age* suggested a separate car "so that the poor tired male beings going home at night might be secure against being turned out of their seats by a drove of women." [110] By the 1890s, the railroads no longer separated male and female passengers only to protect women; they provided distinct spaces so that ladies and gentlemen might enjoy different services and amenities. This new type of gender separation offered men protection from the seemingly endless demands of women—an escape from the codes of deference and chivalry that had defined Victorian gender relations. The result was a rearrangement of those relations that continued to place women on the margins of public life.

As with the domestic amenities considered in the previous chapter, black travelers were excluded from the revised system of gender segregation. Even black ladies and gentlemen who could afford a first-class ticket or reserve a Pullman berth were often turned away. Indeed, their exclusion was justified in the name of comfort. It was argued that only by separating races could the railroads ensure the safety and comfort of both white and black passengers, as was their obligation under the law of common carriers. And so, segregation was validated as part of the reimagining of public spaces as sites in which people should feel at ease.

Black women nonetheless learned to speak the new language of consumer comfort and tried to use it to their advantage. The November 15, 1895, issue of the *Railway Age and Northwestern Railroader* reported on a black woman who sued the Louisville & Nashville Railroad because a white passenger traveling in the Jim Crow car had insulted her. The Kentucky court of appeals found that under the separate coach law, the railroad was liable for the white man's bad conduct.[111] The woman was entitled to travel in an all-black car—this was what her ticket bought her. Anna Julia Cooper likewise asserted her right to the comfort she could afford. She explained, "When I . . . apply for first-class accommodations on a railway train, I do so . . . because I want comfort—not because I want association with those who frequent these places." All she and other African Americans wanted was to live in "whatever of comfort, luxury, or emoluments [their] talent or [their] money can in an impartial market secure." [112] Cooper understood that comfort in public was no longer the result of morality or deference but was something that one bought.

Gentlemen for Hire

CONDUCTORS, PORTERS, AND
COURTESY AS SERVICE

Railroad conductor Charles B. George recounted in his autobiography the day in 1864 when W. S. Johnston beckoned him into
Chicago's Wells Street Depot. "At one end of the room stood a table
covered with packages, and about it were gathered a number of
friends." The packages contained a "beautiful silver service of nine
pieces," and the "friends," including Mr. Johnston, were passengers
who rode frequently with George. Two years later the conductor "was
given an exquisite set of pie forks, of English make, and valued at
seventy-five dollars." These gifts were only two of many he received
over the years from passengers grateful for his attentive service. By
1897 he had acquired "hosts of souvenirs . . . curiosities and odds and
ends enough to more than fill a cabinet."[1] So why then describe these
particular gifts in detail? Although it is impossible to say for sure, it
is likely that George valued these gifts for what they said about him.
Both the silver service and the pie forks suggest refined domesticity.
With these gifts, his passengers identified George as a gentleman.

As noted previously, many travelers used the vocabulary of courtesy and etiquette when describing the railroad staff most responsible for their comfort: white conductors and black porters. In letters,
diaries, and travel accounts, conductors and porters were frequently
described as "gentlemanly" or "civil" and the assistance they provided
as "courtesy."[2] Benjamin Franklin Taylor advised travelers, "As a rule,
it is the conductors who treat you with the most courtesy and kindness."[3] Julia Shubrick expressed gratitude to a "very civil" conductor.[4]
Lillian Leland made special mention of "the gentlemanly Pullman
conductor of the Denver & Rio Grande Railroad."[5] M. M. Shaw praised
"the good-looking and gentlemanly train conductor" as well as the

"A Short Stop at a Way Station. The Polite Conductor," Currier and Ives (1875). Courtesy of the Library of Congress, LC-USZ62-1378.

Pullman porter, "a genteel colored man in a neat uniform."[6] Jennie Kimball recounted the ease of travel when "the Porter, who is a gentleman of color, stands to relieve you of your bags, shawls, etc. etc."[7] During a journey from New Orleans to Los Angeles, Alice Dunbar-Nelson described the porter as "urbane and suave."[8] And Emily Faithfull proclaimed, "The conductors and porters in these drawing-room and sleeping-cars are some of the most polite men to be found in all of America."[9]

"Working-class gentlemen" played a pivotal role in the life and values of the American traveling public, acting as supporting characters in the late-nineteenth-century story of public domesticity. These workers seemed to guarantee that good manners—and the Victorian gender roles they defined—would not be sacrificed as travelers sought to get their money's worth. They preserved notions of gender deference and helped ease passengers' transition from Victorian restraint to modern consumerism. By being both gentlemen and workers, they freed male travelers to be both gentlemen and consumers while enabling women to pay for the privileges of ladyhood. They were, in effect, "professional gentlemen" or "gentlemen for hire," bringing the best qualities of the private sphere to public life.[10] They assisted women on and off trains; they carried luggage; they made travelers comfortable by making up their berths and by regulating the temperature in the cars. They rendered an unruly public space more homelike, transplanting the personal attention of private society to the rails and doing much of the work that male passengers had previously done, but without complaint. *Peck's Sun* noted this transfer of responsibilities, explaining that when a man entrusted his family to a good conductor, "you feel as secure as though your wife and children were under the escort of your brother."[11] And according to New York's *Daily Times*, "Our wives and children, when we may not accompany them in these homes upon the rail, are only away from our immediate vision . . . the anxious care of natural guardians being supplanted by the courteous vigilance of the agents of the company."[12]

It is no coincidence then that the final decades of the nineteenth century saw the proliferation of workers whose jobs were to make respectable travelers "at home" while abroad. They helped to protect women's domesticity in public while freeing male travelers of their obligations to female passengers. In the 1870s, for example, Fred Harvey, founder of the Harvey House restaurants, brought "civilized dining" to the railway depots of the American West. More important, his famed "Harvey Girls," with their neat uniforms and good morals, were celebrated for their feminine respectability and Victorian domesticity.[13] During the 1880s and 1890s, tour guides "personally conducted" travelers, freeing them "of the many petty cares and annoyances inseparable from ordinary travel." One tour agency promised that ladies "are enabled, not only to travel without special escort, but also without becoming dependent on other travelers." Instead "experienced conductors accompany every party, and the travelers are relieved of all personal care and responsibility."[14] In the 1880s, the Pennsylvania Railroad provided chaperones that had "especial charge of ladies." The first woman so employed explained, "I go through the train . . . and introduce myself to the ladies. I tell them . . . I am there to give them all the information and help in my power." It was her job to "devote herself to those who have no escorts."[15]

Railroad companies and American travelers hoped that the veneer of courtesy ("the gentlemanly worker") could both blur and define social divisions (male/female, black/white, worker/consumer) and create a public life of consumer comfort free of social strife. And, like Conductor George, many workers took pride in their gentility. Railroad man Joseph Taylor lauded "the polite and radiant conductor."[16] Herbert O. Holderness became a Pullman conductor because it was the only way he could "be a gentleman without means," and he appreciated the "paramount importance of civility and politeness" in his job.[17] African American porters likewise embraced the role of courtesy in their work, carefully drawing the distinction between politeness and servility. The former marked them as gentlemen, "the aristocracy of Negro labor."[18] The latter undermined their struggle for fair treatment from employers and passengers.[19] The *Pullman Porters' Review*, a Pullman Company publication, portrayed porters as courteous gentlemen, not servants: "By courtesy is not meant obeisance, bowing, etc. . . . [but] politeness which comes from the Latin verb, 'polite' to polish, to be finished, to be well bred, a smooth, refined, sober and polished gentility."[20]

Much has been written about workers' struggles to define this line between service and servility.[21] Customers struggled with this distinction too. For them, accepting conductors and porters' gentility proved hard work, as the divisions of class and race reinforced the view that trainmen were workers first and gentlemen second. (Conductor George's prized silver set might have indicated that his passengers included him among the genteel, but it more clearly rewarded him for a job well done.) Much as comfortable furniture and domestic touches failed to turn railroad cars into homes, good manners did not turn workers and customers into "friends." Instead, dependent upon conductors and porters to make them at home aboard, passengers confronted the limitations of public domesticity. No matter how courteous and refined workers were, neither they nor their passengers could ultimately ignore that the "courtesy" they provided was work—that it was a service required from employers and paid for by passengers. Even as the domestication of the railroad produced new types of jobs, the social and economic conditions of the workplace challenged the cultural assumptions that called them into being.

During the closing decades of the nineteenth century, railroad companies encouraged their workers to cast themselves in the role of gentlemen. Surely this effort reflected the values of many railroad company executives and managers as well as those of workers. It also reflected an understanding of passengers' desires: courtesy was good for business. Courteous and gentlemanly workers made respectable travel possible and cultivated passenger loyalty. The Erie Road advertised the politeness of its staff. The Pennsylvania Railroad asked its passenger conductors to "remember that the popularity of the Route depends greatly upon the manner in which Passengers are treated by Conductors and Train Men."[22] The *Bee Line Gazette* made the link between courteousness and profit even more explicit: "Politeness pays in every walk and calling in life, but in none more than in that of railway conductor. . . . [He] is a living advertisement of his line."[23] After thirty-six years of railroad service, John Droege came to a similar conclusion: "The passenger conductor . . . can do more to popularize or unpopularize the road for which he works than any one man."[24] Joseph Taylor elaborated on this role, explaining that "a gentlemen sends his wife and family East regularly twice a year by the same route, and by the train of which a certain conductor is in charge the greatest part of the distance, simply because, years ago, that official gained the confidence of the family by trifling acts of courtesy and consideration."[25]

Few companies considered employees' acts of courtesy "trifling." According to Howard Elliott, chairman of the board and president of the New York, New Haven & Hartford Railroad, "a railroad that has a reputation for good service has an asset of incalculable value."[26] Conventional wisdom held that polite and thoughtful service could make up for a delayed train or a missed connection. ("If the train is thirty minutes late . . . you arrive at your destination an enthusiastic admirer of the road which has such courteous men in its employ.") By contrast indifferent service could neutralize the effects of punctual travel or elegant accommodations. ("A cross and crabbed conductor does more to drive away passenger traffic . . . than belated trains.")[27] No wonder the *Railway Age* declared in 1884, "That courtesy is productive capital in railway management is indisputable. . . . Patient and enduring courtesy on the part of officers and employees may be classed with steel rails and first rate equipment as paying investment for a railway."[28] By century's end, many railroad companies made considerable investments in hiring, training, and policing gentlemanly workers.

In the 1830s, officials and trade journals advised that prospective conductors be "'sober,' 'prompt,' and 'honest' and 'exhibit gentlemanly behavior towards passengers.'" According to historian Walter Licht, the first generation of American railroad conductors "adorned in top coats and fine silk hats, ever tending to the comfort of their

The gentlemanly trainman (trade card, no date). The text in the upper left corner reads: "Conceive him if you can, An Erie R.R. young man. With a suit of blue clothes, brass buttons in rows, a very polite young man." Courtesy of the Warshaw Collection of Business Americana—Railroads, Archives Center, National Museum of American History, Behring Center, Smithsonian Institution.

passengers, and wary of insubordination in the ranks, . . . appeared the epitome of taste and responsibility."[29] Conductor George fondly recalled, "The distinguishing characteristic of the old-time conductor was his fine silk hat. Slouch and stiff hats were good enough for the ordinary citizen," but the conductor required better.[30]

As the industry matured, however, companies decided that some workers required help becoming gentlemen. The railroading lifestyle—long stretches away from home, the temptations of saloons, the lure of urban entertainments—could corrupt even the most upstanding men. In order to protect their workers, companies invested in a version of public domesticity similar to the one they sold to their respectable passengers. In the 1880s and 1890s many cooperated with branches of the Railroad Division of the Young Men's Christian Association to fund dormitories and reading rooms that offered railroad men moral and domestic accommodations while out on the road. The intent was "to provide convenient, attractive and homelike quarters for the use of men during their spare time and to surround them with good influences, and those educational advantages which are more appreciated by railroad men than by any other class."[31] Other companies went a step further, building their own homes and libraries. The Pennsylvania Railroad, for example, provided quarters for conductors in its Philadelphia Broad Street Station "so that the men who use them can stay all night as comfortably as they could at their own homes."[32]

Many of these "homes" resembled the luxurious railroad cars of the period, their designs suggesting that railroads viewed their employees as gentlemen. According to one observer, the "luxuriousness" of the New York Central's facility was evidence that Cornelius Vanderbilt, the road's owner, "loves his neighbor as himself, even if that neighbor be a plain brakeman earning but low wages."[33] The Pennsylvania Railroad conductors' home included a library decorated with a Brussels carpet, chairs, sofas, and chess tables as well as a reading room well stocked with newspapers, magazines, atlases, and encyclopedias. In addition, the quarters housed a Steinway piano and a violin so that conductors ("assisted by their lady friends") could hold an informal concert or entertainment. According to the *Railway Age*, the décor and amenities were "intended to cater to tastes of a higher order, as though the company considered its employees intelligent, cultivated gentlemen, and intended to treat them as such."[34]

The Southern Pacific Railway seemed to hold trainmen in similar regard; its clubhouses offered "hot and cold baths, a library of fiction and reference books, correspondence tables on which may be found neat club stationery, a billiard and pool hall, a gaming and recreation room, barber shop, cigar counter, a restaurant which is open twenty-four hours day, and a large number of bedrooms." To gain access, a railway man needed only pledge that he was the employee of a railroad company and agree "to conduct myself as a gentleman while enjoying any of the privileges of the club."[35]

But if such facilities were built to serve gentlemen while away from home, they also were intended to instruct railroad men in the ways of refinement, keep them from immoral influences, and train better workers. The general manager of the Santa Fe Railroad claimed that investing in employee reading rooms led to better service on the line. The rooms "have a tendency to make men more temperate, which insures safety as well as economy. . . . The investment has been a very profitable one for the company."[36] According to the road's superintendent of reading rooms, "By surrounding [workers] with books, magazines, lectures, and illustrated science, they do have the same opportunities for self-development as the high-officials. . . . An employee so treated will become proud of his reputation as an intelligent and refined citizen."[37] The management of the Seaboard Air Line hoped that its combination library, reading room, and air brake instruction room would "materially promote its interests by assisting in securing the greatest intelligence on the part of its own employees." The trappings of refined domesticity ("numerous portraits, engravings, photographs, etc., nicely framed and giving a very satisfactory air of completeness and comfort") reflected a bit of wishful thinking on the part of railroad companies.[38] They wanted their employees to be gentlemen, and they invested in the amenities to make them so.[39]

While employee homes and clubs focused on leisure and genteel amenities to improve the morals of trainmen, company rule books detailed the work expected of these gentlemen for hire. They marked the transformation of courtesy from a personal attribute of gentlemen (a sensibility to be instilled though refined domesticity) into the job of trainmen (a list of tasks to be mastered). By the second half of the century, rule books had grown longer as they detailed not only technical tasks but also the polite conduct required of workers.[40] The Pullman Palace Car Company ordered its conductors and porters "to promote the comfort of passengers" while maintaining "a courteous and obliging manner."[41] The Philadelphia, Wilmington & Baltimore Rail Road Company instructed conductors to be "polite and obliging" and warned that "profane and indecent language will not be tolerated."[42] The Pennsylvania Railroad required its conductors "to be courteous to all," and the company rule book specified, "They must be respectful and considerate in their intercourse with Passengers, giving them politely any information desired, and use every endeavor to contribute to their pleasure and comfort." Brakemen, who on passenger trains often helped travelers board and alight, were told to "give polite attention to [passengers'] wishes."[43]

Such instruction became more important over the latter half of the century. By the 1870s, many passenger conductors were men who had moved up through the ranks of the railroad hierarchy and developed their professional skills in the freight service. Unlike the first generation of passenger conductors, they were often ill prepared for passenger service. As one observer noted, the passenger department viewed passengers as patrons to be courted; the transportation division saw them as parcels to be moved.[44] Although a passenger conductor had mastered the technical and administrative aspects of his job, too often he retained "the somewhat rough habits of the freight train." In fact, "in his long apprenticeship on a freight train he has very likely been learning how *not* to fulfill the additional requirements of a passenger conductor."[45] The 1884 edition of the Pennsylvania Railroad's *Rules for the Government of the Transportation Department* specifically noted that most passenger conductors began their careers as brakemen on freight trains and therefore had not learned to treat passengers courteously. In order to redress this gap in training, companies required workers to be "perfectly conversant with the Rules and Regulations" and to carry the leather-bound rule books with them while on the job.[46]

According to one railroad observer, the codification and enforcement of rules did "much to improve the morals of [railroad] employees in general" and placed them "upon a thorough respectable level upon which they, being gentlemen by nature, find it no way difficult to sail."[47] But did railroads and their passengers view trainmen as "gentlemen by nature"? The imposition of rules suggests that employers and passengers considered workers gentlemen by design. The codification of politeness makes sense only in the context of rudeness, and stories of impolite trainmen circulated alongside those praising courteous and gentlemanly workers. In 1885 the *Buffalo Courier* happily reported that the New York Central & Hudson River Railroad was preparing a rule book for its conductors and porters. "Both employees will be required to consider themselves the servants of the traveling public and cater to their smallest wants."[48] Two years later, the *New York Times* encouraged the "traveling public" to protest the poor state of "railroad manners." The *Times* warned that rudeness was inevitable "unless a wholesome fear of discipline prevents [trainmen], and this discipline can be enforced only in cases of rudeness that are brought to the notice of authorities."[49] According to another contemporary account, the Rutland & Burlington Railroad posted a sign in its cars alerting conductors, brakemen, and baggagemen (and, of course, passengers) that "any departure from civility of conduct and that courtesy due to patrons of the road, will render them unfit for its services, and they will be dismissed accordingly."[50]

In addition to investing in workers' "homes" and rule books, many railroads hired detective agencies to check up on employees. Detectives' findings often confirmed that conductors and porters were honest gentlemen. A report from the Pinkerton agency described a brakeman as "gentlemanly looking," while a spotter for the Pullman Palace Car Company recalled, "I found the Pullman conductor, generally speaking, a polite dignified and intelligent man, who endeavored to perform his duties for the best interests of the company. The porters were no less attentive to passengers."[51] Detectives, however, also reported conductors who insulted women and embezzled fares. According to Allan Pinkerton, founder of the National Detective Agency, "No kind of operation carried on by the Detective, requires more system and care, than that of testing the honesty of Railroad Passenger Conductors."[52] The stakes of such investigations were high; men's jobs and reputations were on the line. (One retired railway "spotter," as they were called, expressed regret that many of his colleagues were themselves corrupt.)[53] Surveillance was meant to keep conductors and porters vigilant. As Pinkerton explained to the companies that hired him, the threat of spotters served to keep many trainmen honest, "thus exhibiting the practical advantages of the tests applied upon [the] Railroad."[54]

Another detective summarized his job: "[I] enter the car the same as an ordinary passenger and . . . carefully note the number of passengers who rode during the journey. Where they boarded and where they left it. The degree of attention that was given to each passenger by the conductor and porter, the conditions of the berths."[55] A surveillance report submitted by the Pinkerton Agency to the Philadelphia & Reading Railroad noted that a conductor stood on the platform smoking a cigar, a brakeman had been offered and refused a drink, and another conductor "evidently passed a woman free from Schwenksville to the junction. He sat and talked with her a short time."[56] Spotters also recorded whether conductors canceled tickets, collected fares, and turned in all the money they collected. Detective agencies even employed women as spotters to measure the scruples of trainmen. George Farley explained, "Whenever I have a difficult piece of work — such as a leary and suspicious conductor to test — I invariably give the case to a lady, or ask my operative to take his wife with him."[57] Clarence Ray, another railway spotter, suggested, "The right kind of woman could be used to advantage as a spotter making traveling alone safer for other women."[58]

In the end, railroads and their passengers told conflicting stories about gentlemen for hire. At times, they described men of refinement and discriminating taste. At others, they portrayed men who needed rules and surveillance to keep them in line. Workers themselves provided their own narratives reconciling these different interpretations. Their stories emphasized the connection between money and gentility. Accepting courtesy as part of their jobs, workers saw that a gentleman was defined not only by his conduct but by his consumption. If railroads expected their workers to be gentlemen, they should pay wages that would support a gentlemanly lifestyle. An anecdote circulated among railroad men told of a railway president who asked a prospective conductor whether he had a diamond ring, a fast horse, a house and lot, or money in the bank. When the man said no, the president replied, "Then you can't have a place on my road. You're sure to want all these things, and I don't want you to make them out of us."[59] Likewise, a Pullman conductor complained, "The Pullman Company, with its small pay, the expensive surroundings the employees are forced to face, and the rules under which they are forced to work has caused more men to become dishonest than any other one thing in this country."[60] Another conductor suggested that his employers do away with spotters and "expend the money now used in secret service to better thy servant's condition and place him above temptation."[61]

If passengers, railroads, and workers viewed courtesy as part of a trainman's job, it was but one task among many. A Pullman conductor explained that in the course of his job he might be called upon "to quote a timetable, Xenophon's *Anabasis*, or Horace's *Odes*; find a lady's diamond ring after she has dropped it through the sink hole of the wash basin, reduce a dislocation of the jaw, or quiet a drunken man on the verge of delirious tremens." In short, his passengers expected him to be "all things to all men."[62] A less colorful accounting of a conductor's duties might include checking the supplies and cleanliness of the cars, collecting and turning in fares, counting tickets and passengers, seating passengers, answering travelers' questions, handling disorderly passengers, enforcing company rules, regulating the car's temperature and ventilation, calling out station stops, helping passengers alight at the right stations, and assisting them with parcels. In addition, "he should see that no time is lost at stations, have a thorough understanding of the time card, and all the rules and regulations affecting the duties of employes, an eye to the condition of the track, trestles, bridges, culverts, and embankments; he should frequently examine the breaks, couplings, and bell-ropes of his cars."[63] Finally, he needed to stay alert to any delay or irregularity that might endanger the smooth operation of the rail system and be prepared in case of accident.

The nature of rail travel—the speed, the scale of operation, the rigid organization—often made the cars inhospitable to passengers' notions of courteousness, and the competing responsibilities of conductors compromised their ability to treat passengers politely. In 1871, after considering "the constant unceasing petty annoyances" routinely encountered on the job, a convention of passenger conductors asked, "Would it be singular if we became harsh in our manners and brusque in our speech?"[64] One observer noted, "Every day and perhaps a number of times a day, [a conductor] must collect fares of fifty or a hundred persons in less time than he ought to have for ten."[65] Imagine if just one of those passengers objected to the fare, needed clarification of the timetable, or had only a vague notion of his route. In such situations, a good conductor moved the passenger along or fell behind schedule, kept track of his accounts or risked charges of embezzlement, and remained attentive to all his passengers or faced the consequences of complaint and company investigation. John Droege, showing sympathy for the trainmen's predicament, explained, "Lack of courtesy is not always intentional. Many passengers are unable to distinguish between courteous, quick treatment and that which is abrupt and discourteous."[66]

By necessity, company policies gradually transformed "courtesy" into standardized and impersonal work; courtesy became "service." The distinction was subtle, but it was noted by both passengers and trainmen. The first blurred the line between worker and passenger through personal contact and individual acts of kindness. The second, by contrast, was meant to keep that division clear.[67] Although Victorian etiquette was defined by rules, many passengers espoused the belief that courtesy was more pleasing because it was offered freely and spontaneously. (This was, after all, the point of gentlemen passengers' complaint that women claimed gender deference as a right.) Rule books, however, left little room for individual acts of kindness, instructing workers to "avoid unnecessary conversation" and "all familiarity" with passengers—precisely the type of personal gestures men like Conductor George took pride in.[68] Attempting to reconcile the appeal of courtesy with the demand for service, the Pullman Palace Car Company advised its conductors, porters, and waiters to use judgment when interacting with the traveling public and "not, by adhering too strictly to the letter of a rule, disobey the spirit of it."[69]

Such advice reflected passengers' persistent desire for courteous trainmen who took personal care of them. Even as they demanded the regimentation and predictability of service, they continued to imagine a public realm peopled by thoughtful friends rather than dutiful employees. In 1896 the *Pittsburgh Post* lamented that the Baltimore & Ohio Railroad banned its conductors and brakemen from assisting ladies aboard. Apparently "a handsome and well-meaning conductor" had helped a young lady and soiled her dress with grease. She complained, and "beautiful young ladies must hereafter struggle up the steep declivity without the proffered assistance of the brakemen or conductors." Julia Shubrick fondly recalled the conductor who offered her his arm and escorted her half a mile through a snowstorm.[70] Other travelers spoke of conductors who loaned them money during an emergency or of porters who recalled the names of passengers even after several months. By emphasizing such kindnesses, passengers denied the commercial nature of the service they received while incorporating these acts into their expectations as consumers.

Few tasks revealed the tension between passengers' expectation of courtesy and workers' obligation of service like the enforcement of company policies regarding "disorderly" passengers. Although advertised to passengers as workers eager to please them, trainmen were often required by railroad companies to exercise authority over customers. Any lapse on the part of a passenger was ultimately the responsibility of the conductor, as rule books regulated the behavior not only of employees but of passengers as well. In 1864, for example, the Indianapolis & Madison Rail Road declared that "in the event of any Passenger being drunk or disorderly, to the annoyance of others, [the conductor] must use all gentle means to stop the nuisance." The Pennsylvania Railroad instructed its conductors to "maintain good order among the passengers, and not permit rudeness or profanity."[71] The company's sense of "good order" included ensuring passengers kept their feet and luggage off the seat cushions, securing passengers' possessions during travel, and preventing gambling in the cars. Many passengers applauded these efforts as an attempt to protect polite and respectable travelers from the rudeness of others. No doubt they accepted such policies as part and parcel of the public domesticity they desired. But for every grateful passenger there was another one resentful of moving her traveling case or having his friendly card game called into question.

In order to reconcile passengers' expectations and workers' responsibilities, railroads instructed conductors and porters to enforce policies without offending—using gentlemanly coercion to persuade passengers to treat one another courteously. The Philadelphia & Reading Railroad advised its brakemen to enforce the rules of the road "in a quiet and gentlemanly manner." The Pennsylvania Railroad instructed conductors to "make Passengers as comfortable as circumstances will permit, and bear in mind that no provocation will justify rudeness or incivility toward them." This often required considerable ingenuity. On one road, conductors tactfully told men entering into a game of cards, "Gentlemen, if you know each other, well and good; if not I want to caution you, because we are having many complaints regarding the results of card games."[72] Such a warning avoided direct accusation of wrongdoing. Other situations were more delicate. For example, when a woman accused a fellow passenger of stealing her watch, the conductor was in a tight spot. He must accuse one passenger of theft or the other of lying; after searching the alleged thief to no avail, it was no easy task to suggest politely that the watch was perhaps "misplaced" in the front of the woman's dress.[73]

Company rule books dictated that disorderly passengers be treated politely, but trainmen did not always feel that they could comply. A gathering of Philadelphia conductors lamented, "How many of us daily submit to taunts and jibes from men who are our inferiors?" They knew too well that not all passengers were gentlemen, and under certain circumstances "the conductor cannot give himself up completely to learning gentility, for he still has need for his old severity."[74] When a passenger refused to pay, or insulted ladies, or was simply spoiling for a fight, a conductor had no choice but to remove him. Most railroads explicitly instructed, "If [disorderly] conduct is persisted in to the annoyance of other passengers it becomes the duty of the Conductor to eject the offending party."[75] This was no parlor game; it was rough work. Joseph Taylor explained that, when politeness failed to win over a stubborn passenger or silence a boisterous one, "a proper conductor, mindful of his Company's possible liabilities for damages in such a crisis, gently but firmly introduces his left hand in the region of the offender's thorax, and with the right grasps the baggy excrescence about his base (he is always male), gives him an animated movement along the aisle of the car, and softly dumps him—somewhere outside."[76]

But even rude passengers claimed the right to polite service. A railroad company, as Taylor mentioned, was legally responsible if its workers failed to remove a known nuisance from the cars; it had an obligation to protect its well-behaved passengers from insult and injury. This obligation was, however, balanced by the need for restraint.[77] Overzealousness exposed the railroad and its workers to legal liability. One admirer of railroad men advised that when removing a drunk passenger, "Care must be taken . . . not to punish him or use the least bit of unnecessary severity, for he will, when sobered off, quite likely be induced by a sharp lawyer to sue the railroad company for damages by assault."[78] Moreover, he would likely win. When John Peck sued the New York Central & Hudson River Railroad after being ejected from a ladies' car in 1871, the New York State Court of Appeals ruled that the railroad had the right to set aside a car for ladies and that Peck had no claim to enter the ladies' car. Nonetheless, the court also decided that the trainman had overstepped his duty while removing Peck. According to the court he "could lawfully use so much force as was needful to effect the result sought for. . . . For an excess of force beyond that degree, he would be liable," as would his employer.[79] Or as the *New York Times* reported, "His authority was strictly limited to using such gentle and considerate force as would remove the intruder, without giving him any useless mortification, suffering, or injury."[80] And so, faced with a disorderly passenger, a conductor made a complex calculation. Such was the nature of the working-class gentleman's service.

On the American railroad, courtesy was a good usually reserved for whites, and African American women seldom described white conductors as "civil" or "genteel." Their experiences highlight that the "service" railroad men provided was both more and less than courtesy. Some, such as Anna Julia Cooper, saw "these same 'gentlemanly and efficient' conductors . . . deliberately fold their arms and turn round when the Black Woman's turn came to alight."[81] Others, such as Alice Dunbar-Nelson, mocked the solicitousness of the "fresh white youth [who] wanted to move me out [of the Jim Crow car], to the hysterical delight of the colored passengers, who knew me."[82] More common was the experience of Frances Ellen Watkins Harper, who recalled "the conductor [who] put up his hand and [stopped] the car rather than let me ride."[83] Like Mary Church Terrell, African American women remembered the stern conductor who refused their entry to the first-class ladies' car, explaining that the Jim Crow car "was first-class enough for you."[84] Many, such as Pauline E. Hopkins, described "the brutality of the conductor who ordered her out of the comfortable day-coach into the dirt and discomfort of the 'Jim Crow' car."[85] Or, like Ida B. Wells, they told stories of being "pretty roughly handled" by conductors and baggage men determined to eject them from the first-class accommodations for which they had paid.[86]

Most African American women did not regard their poor treatment as "rudeness." Instead they spoke of justice. They understood that what was for sale on the railroads were not acts of courtesy bestowed by individual workers but something broader—inclusion in a new public order shaped by commercial relationships. Anna Julia Cooper focused on this larger context by identifying workers' politeness for what it was: "Courtesy 'for revenue only' is not politeness, but diplomacy." Like the railroad companies, she understood that courteous workers were good for business and that trainmen alone did not determine the treatment black travelers received. They had jobs to do and rule books to follow. "A railroad conductor is not asked to dictate measures, nor to make or pass laws. His bread and butter are conditioned on his managing his part of the machinery as he is told to do." Cooper "could not take it as a want of courtesy on the conductor's part" when he informed her of company policies. Dismissing him as rude—even if he growled, "Here gurl, . . . you better git out 'n dis kyar 'f yer don't, I'll put yer out"—missed the larger point.[87] Such "rudeness" was evidence that she was not included in the "traveling public," that she stood outside the realm of public domesticity.

The treatment of African American travelers makes evident that railroad workers were empowered by their employers, by the courts, and, to some degree, by white public opinion to control passengers under particular circumstances—that the rights of purchase were not absolute. In this respect, the treatment of black women reveals more than that nineteenth-century American institutions were racist; it lays bare the strain of coercion within the domesticated public life emerging at this time. On the one hand, the railroads fostered a sense that consumer choices could make "respectable" people comfortable in public. On the other hand, they set limits on passengers to fulfill a particular vision of a well-ordered public life, determining where they could sit and how they could act. Although black travelers experienced the consequences of this contradiction most acutely, they were not the only ones to do so. Significantly, many white travelers spoke of this same tension when they encountered black railroad workers, especially the "gentlemanly" Pullman porter. In both cases, white racism heightened tensions about the authority of workers over paying customers and shattered the façade of courtesy.

Since the industry's beginnings in the early nineteenth century, African Americans worked for the American railroads. Their access to jobs, however, was always limited by discrimination. In the South, African Americans worked as firemen, as brakemen, and on section and maintenance-of-way gangs. In some regions of the country they worked at freight handling, track laying, and road maintenance. Railroad companies and white unions, however, excluded black workers from high-skilled, well-paid jobs. They were barred from work as conductors or engineers. Instead, African American railroad workers were most visible in the service sector—as waiters, redcaps, and porters.[88] Beginning in the 1870s, George Pullman hired newly emancipated African Americans as porters in his palace cars, and the position quickly became identified as a "black man's job."[89] By employing only black men as porters, Pullman not only tapped a cheap labor force but also played upon whites' notion of blacks as natural servants. In an often quoted passage, Pullman associate Joseph Husband boasted, "Trained as a race by years of personal service in various capacities, and by nature adapted faithfully to perform their duties under circumstances which necessitate unfailing good nature, solicitude, and faithfulness, the Pullman porters occupy a unique place in the great fields of employment."[90]

Like the white conductors with whom they worked, African American porters served as working-class gentlemen—men whose courtesy and hard work smoothed the way for travelers. As previously noted, white passengers viewed them in this light, describing them as "genteel" or as "gentlemen of color."[91] Respectable black travelers also appreciated the porter's gentlemanly presence, both on the trains and off. As members of the black middle class, porters were admired for their neat uniforms and professional bearing. (In the words of a popular song: "We don't carry razors, or wear striped blazers, Or with the lower folks associate, Aristocratic, and not erratic, We're always at your service, never late.")[92] Service work was often a stepping-stone on the path of political, professional, or entrepreneurial ambition. Many black men worked on the trains during the summer to put themselves through college, and porters often held prominent positions in their communities. Moreover, with the institution of Jim Crow, the mobility of porters and their contact with whites added to their special standing. African American parents entrusted children traveling alone to the watchful eyes of the porter in the hope that he could provide protection from the insults and dangers of rail travel, another example of working-class gentlemen taking on the role of surrogate family member or protector in a complex and threatening public.[93]

As was the case with the conductor, the porter's many responsibilities made courteousness very hard work indeed. Before becoming a conductor himself, Herbert Holderness noted that each Pullman conductor "was attended by a colored gentleman (also in uniform), who appeared to be doing all the work."[94] This was an apt descrip-

Pullman porter as gentleman. From "Railway Passenger Travel," Scribner's Magazine, *September 1888. Courtesy of the New York University Libraries.*

tion of the porter's job. He was on constant call to satisfy the requests of passengers—carrying bags, opening and closing windows, lighting lamps, making up and closing berths. Giving "any assistance in [his] power," the porter also saw to the personal needs of his passengers, as he was called upon to polish shoes and brush down clothes. In addition, he was responsible for keeping his car clean. An 1888 rule book instructed, "The Porter should be almost constantly on his feet and working up the car with a cloth or duster." [95] Other duties included cleaning washstands, basins, urinals, and spittoons as well as keeping track of bed linen, blankets, combs, and pillows. Securing Pullman inventory no doubt added to tensions between porters and passengers. Should any items go missing, the company held the porter financially responsible. On trains with library cars, porters were responsible for distributing and returning books. Again, the porter was accountable for any losses.

While Pullman expected its porters to give gentlemanly attention to passengers and enforce its policies, the company did not provide them with the same trappings of gentility bestowed upon white railroad men. The company supported genteel black leisure by funding Chicago's Wabash Avenue YMCA, and in the 1920s it provided music lessons and organized porters into bands and choruses.[96] But on the job, porters repeatedly confronted insults to their standing as public gentlemen, as company policies excluded African Americans from the consumption that defined respectable public life. Although it did not directly instruct its porters to enforce Jim Crow, the Pullman Company followed state statutes, and when traveling through states with separate coach laws porters had little choice but to obey the orders of white conductors or face dismissal.[97] Even in states without segregation laws, company policies limited porters' mobility, dictating where they were permitted to polish shoes (on a camp stool "next to the gentlemen's washstand") and sleep for the few hours they were off duty (in the smoking room or in "an upper end berth" designated by the conductor, but "in no instance . . . a berth in a section over a lady passenger"). Company rules even required porters to use particular blankets and to provide their own combs and hairbrushes, forbidding them from using "those furnished for passengers' use." [98]

In spite of company attempts to mark his separate and inferior status, the porter, by the very nature of his job, exerted considerable power over his passengers. In his reminiscences, Holderness described the porter as "the *deus ex machina*, whose word is law and by whose frown or favor the passenger is either very comfortable or supremely unhappy." [99] His "deft work," for example, transformed railroad seats into sleeping berths. [100] E. W. Sanborn lovingly described a porter making up his berth—"letting down the adjoining berth, taking out the shiny partition and sliding it into place, pushing the lower seats together, exhuming the sheets and pillows from the crypts, letting down the 'upper,' reaching for the mattress and blankets." Despite his respect for the porter's skill, Sanborn, like many white passengers, resented the porter's control; by making up berths the porter also set the bedtime of his passengers. [101] "For air, food, warmth and sleep we are at the mercy of the porter." Even brushing passengers' clothes served as a "rite symbolic of his control over our persons." Sanborn concluded that the porter was the "monarch" of the Pullman car. [102] An 1880 article in the *New York Times* similarly identified the porter as "the real despot of the sleeping car," accusing him of collecting passengers' shoes "not necessarily with a view to blackening them, but as a guarantee that they will not venture to get out bed without permission." [103]

Many of the complaints about "despotism" focused on the issue of tipping—a practice associated with porters more than any other group of trainmen. Again and again travelers spoke of tipping as evidence of porters' abuse of power. Sanborn complained that porters attended to him "with an intensity meant to impress upon him that [they] are not adequately paid by their responsible employers." [104] One traveler compared a request for a tip to political graft. Likening the power of porters to the corrupt politics of urban machines, he implored, "Let us resist the sleeping coach porter, with his unjustifiable demand for twenty-five cents; so shall we get in the habit of facing down the Tweeds, and the Sweeneys, and the Halls." [105] Caroline Dall suggested that porters were agents of women's disenfranchisement, noting that they paid more attention to male travelers familiar with the practices of tipping. [106] No doubt such complaints served as a code for racist sentiments: a belief that black men should not exercise any type of power over white passengers. Conductors, after all, were not singled out as "monarchs" and "despots" even though their authority was more pronounced than that of porters.

But again, focusing exclusively on racism reveals only part of the story. It is difficult to see how the practice of tipping empowered porters, let alone turned them into "kings." Reliance on tips kept porters' livelihoods uncertain. Pullman used the promise of tips to keep porters' wages low, while racism limited opportunities for other respectable employment. Some porters, echoing Sanborn, likened their service to a confidence game and believed that hustling for tips was beneath them.[107] Even white railroad men noted that the tipping system exposed porters to insult and added to the burdens of an already demanding job. Pullman conductor Charles Walbourn pleaded with passengers, "When the porter comes to you in the morning with his broom, don't be too hard on him. Remember as you give him his quarter that it is not so much his imposition on you for his tip, as that is the way he is forced to make his living."[108] Confronted with the injustice of the porters' situation, Holderness suggested that they be authorized to collect a 25-cent fee for all services rendered. He concluded, "Politeness, good humor, readiness to see what a gentleman or lady may want and, if possible accommodate them. . . . All these good qualities are surely worth a quarter of any passenger's money, especially when it is considered that the porter's living depends upon the tipping system."[109]

Holderness's simple plan reveals precisely why passengers may have bristled at tipping black gentlemen for hire; not because the customary 25 cents was more than most travelers could afford, and not simply because the porter was a black man, but because his open hand made explicit what so many travelers tried to ignore: workers' courtesy was a commodity. Rail travelers had exchanged the demands of fellow passengers for the restrictions set by the railroads and the attentions of their workers—both white and black. Railroad companies promised passengers workers who could impose order on an unruly public; travelers paid for the privilege of being at home aboard. Often the nature of this transaction was romanticized. Railroads sold their particular vision of comfort using terms like "courtesy," and white passengers responded in similar terms recognizing workers as "gentlemanly," "civil," "genteel." But as Anna Julia Cooper pointed out, "Courtesy 'for revenue only' is not politeness." Porters' expectations of and need for regular tips underscored that "courtesy" had become "service," and made extravagant personal gifts like Conductor George's silver service relics of the past. Imagining workers as courteous friends in a public of shared values, white passengers instead encountered men who knew their politeness was a job.

Nerves of Steel

NEW WOMEN FIT FOR

PUBLIC LIFE

Elmore Elliott Peake's story "The Night Run of the 'Overland'" appeared in *McClure's Magazine* in June 1900.[1] In the opening scene, Ben and Sylvia Fox sit at home listening for the sounds of the Overland train on its usual run. Despite the familiarity of this domestic scene, Peake asserted that the Foxes were no "ordinary couple." Sylvia is nursing Ben through an illness. Ben is a railroad engineer, a man of rugged strength, gentle birth, and thoughtful temperament—all of which "shone through even the pallor of sickness." In short, Ben is an accomplished man of the rails. Sylvia is "striking [with] her loose gown, girdled at the waist with a tasseled cord, only half conceal[ing] the sturdy, sweeping lines of the form beneath. Her blue eyes . . . fixed solicitously upon her husband's face, were dark with what seemed an habitual earnestness of purpose, and her sweet mouth drooped seriously." As the Overland approaches, the Foxes hear the alarming sound of grinding brakes. Moments later, there is a knock at the door. C. W. Howard, the railroad company's general superintendent, pushes his way through the door and announces that the Overland's engineer has "had a stroke of apoplexy fifteen miles back." He asks Ben to drive the engine from Valley Junction to Stockton. Ben, too ill to drive the engine, suggests that Sylvia go in his place. After all, "she knows the engine as well as I, and every inch of the road." "Sylvia," he says, "you must go. It is your duty." Without asking to whom she owes this duty, Sylvia quickly changes into a short walking skirt, dons one of Ben's caps, and kisses her husband good-bye.[2]

Minutes later, Sylvia stands before the locomotive, "the great black hulk of iron and steel." As she contemplates the power of the engine, the darkness of the night, and the fragility of the human life within the cars, the superintendent praises her as "a brave little woman." He then tells her that an important railroad executive he is eager to impress is aboard the train. "Don't lose your nerve—but make time whatever else you do." The commercial well-being of the railroad company depends upon Sylvia's ability not only to drive the engine but to bring the train in on time. Despite the daunting challenge, Sylvia "bore herself with the firm, subdued mien of one who knows the gravity of her task, yet has faith in herself for its performance." Understanding that "her train was but one wheel—nay, but one cog on one wheel—in the vast and complicated machine of transportation," Sylvia goes to work.[3]

Peake quickly transported both Sylvia and the reader from a timeless image of home life (a wife caring for her husband) to the nexus of late-nineteenth-century modernity (the engine cab of a locomotive), where the demands of technology and commerce met. He both recapitulated and exaggerated the journey of female travelers as they stepped beyond the domestic sphere and set out on the railways. Peake even hinted at the increased proximity of these two worlds in his story's subtitle, "A Story of Domestic Life Among Railroad People." Sylvia is a woman equally suited for both settings—she neither imagines the engine as some larger, louder domestic appliance, nor does she play the lady and presume upon the courtesies of the railroad men. Instead, once in the engine cab, "Sylvia worked with the fireman with a fine intelligence which only the initiated could understand." She displays the bravery, loyalty, and knowledge usually associated with men on the line. Yet Peake never suggested that she was a "railroad man." However brave or knowledgeable, Sylvia remains a woman; her skill fills the fireman not with camaraderie but with "chivalric pride." Even Sylvia marvels that "a puny human hand—a woman's hand, moreover, contrived for the soft offices of love—could stay that grand momentum" of the powerful engine.[4]

In Peake's story, the juxtaposition of woman and railroad revealed the potential power of each: technology was more powerful, yet more responsive, when a feminine hand held the throttle; woman was more fragile, yet more in control, as she stood in the engine cab and proved herself capable of managing perhaps the most challenging technology of modern life. Peake did not simply portray these unexpected configurations of gender and technology but manipulated them to heighten the suspense of his story. In a hushed conversation, the general superintendent tells the visiting railroad executive, "I've got the best railroad story to give to the papers that has been brought out in years, and if I don't get several thousand dollars' worth of free advertising out of it, my name isn't C. W. Howard. . . . 'Overland' at this moment is in the hands of a girl." Through Howard, Peake hinted that his own story was designed to have popular appeal—the idea of a woman driving an engine simply must. Howard's (and Peake's) assumption is soon proven correct. As the Overland pulls into Stockton, a throng gathers to cheer the female engineer. "When Sylvia appeared in the gangway, her glorious sun-kissed hair glistening with melted snow, and her pale face streaked with soot, the generous crowd burst into yells of applause." Sylvia is celebrated for both her skill and her femininity; more precisely, she is celebrated because the former fails to diminish the latter.[5]

Peake's story followed the broad outlines of other popular railway stories in which fearless engineers save the day; however, it also transcended and transformed that narrative formula. By 1900, "railroad literature" was a common feature in popular magazines. One student of railroad fiction has identified the period between 1890 and 1910 as the "golden age" of the genre. During these two decades, stories of manly action, adventure, and achievement upon the rails appeared regularly in *McClure's*, *Scribner's*, the *Saturday Evening Post*, and *Youth's Companion*.[6] Authors like Frank H. Spearman, Cy Warman, Francis Lynde, and Frank L. Packard described in careful detail the achievements of brave and honest railroad men. Highlighting the courage, loyalty, and smarts of ordinary men, these stories captured the romance of life on the rails and created an image of railroad men as American heroes—men who routinely met extraordinary challenges. Peake bent the rules by placing a woman in a setting so strongly identified with male heroics.

Sylvia's triumph is particularly striking when contrasted with the fate of the railroad men in the story. Peake repeatedly suggested that manliness was somehow compromised or endangered by the railroad: Ben is home ill with some unnamed disease; the Overland's first engineer suffers a stroke; Superintendent Howard hesitates to "tell the boys [about Sylvia] for the sake of their nerves." But when Sylvia's nerves are tested, they do not fail her. She brings the train into Stockton twenty seconds ahead of schedule. Only after reaching her destination does she yield to the strain. Stepping down from the engine cab she sees the railroad executive Superintendent Howard wanted to impress: he is Mr. Staniford, president of the Mississippi Valley, Omaha, & Western Railway and Sylvia's estranged father. When he pushes through the crowd to stand before his daughter, her "over-strained nerves gave way under the double excitement and laying her head wearily upon his shoulder, and with her hands upon his neck, she began to cry in a choked pitiful little way." She is undone by womanly emotion, not nervous strain.[7]

Through Sylvia, Peake showed that a woman could both meet the challenges of modern life and retain the ideals of femininity and family responsibility. Driving the engine does not compromise her standing as a true Victorian woman; neither the thrill of the engine nor the importance of her accomplishment alter her role as a duti-ful daughter. Reunited with her father, Sylvia seeks out the comfort only he can offer. In the story's final line, she sobs, "Oh, papa, call me your dear little red-head once more!" Starting out on her journey as a dutiful wife, she concludes it as an adoring daughter. Her role in the engine cab is additive, not transformative. Sylvia is a domestic woman at home in public, even a public that was not rendered homelike. She is a lady who inspires chivalry in men but neither demands nor ex-pects it. She meets and even enjoys the physical challenges of modern life but is not broken by them; she becomes neither hysterical nor manly when confronted with the powerful engine.

The woman Peake imagined was a new cultural type, one forged by the demands of American life over the last quarter of the nine-teenth century. The Victorian lady considered previously proved her-self ill-suited to public life—too dependent, too demanding, too silly and rude—but Sylvia moved easily into public life, suggesting another context for considering how the social and cultural changes posed by the railroad reshaped Victorian gender identities and confounded the ideal of separate spheres. Capable yet feminine, strong yet demure, she embodied the possibility of a public life that maintained gen-der difference without burdening men with the protection of women. Reconciling the demands of the railroad with familiar qualities of Victorian womanhood, Peake showed his readers a "New Woman." He rewrote the joke about the fine woman and the locomotive that opened Chapter 2, but the pairing now inspired admiration rather than laughter.

Historians of women have long scrutinized this "New Woman" of the late nineteenth century, and many have celebrated her as an important challenge to the constraints of Victorianism and the separate spheres ideal. She revealed herself from 1890 to 1920 in a variety of guises; she was the eager college student, the no-nonsense settlement house worker, the middle-class clubwoman, the young working girl of the department store or factory, the stylish Gibson Girl.[8] Many men praised her strength of both mind and body, but others deemed the New Woman threatening.[9] The New Woman was, from the time of her emergence, an embattled figure because she threatened the status quo. For example, nineteenth-century doctors and educators sought to keep the New Woman in her place and proclaimed that she would ruin her health with too much "brainwork." She would be unsexed or, worse still, rendered mannish. According to experts, the New Woman's intellectual pursuits overstimulated her brain, robbed her ovaries of energy, and caused sterility or cancer.[10] Thus the New Woman not only challenged manhood but endangered womanhood, the white race, and, by implication, the American nation.

Peake's story, however, suggests an alternate way of conceptualizing the New Woman. Sylvia represents a popular vision of strong and capable womanhood. Beginning in the 1890s, popular fiction, railroad company advertisements, tour brochures, and newspaper accounts increasingly presented similar images of the New Woman. Some scholars may dismiss these commercial and popular images as simply the appropriation of more potent and political forms of New Womanhood, but in so doing they risk overlooking important markers of cultural change.[11] Recent scholarship on masculinity has interpreted the late-nineteenth-century preoccupation with healthy and heroic men as an effort to reformulate notions of manhood to meet the demands of modern life. In a variety of popular "texts," from boxing matches and football games to historical fiction, scholars have found images of powerful manhood, nationhood, and white racial dominance linked to narratives of American territorial and commercial expansion.[12] If, as this scholarship suggests, new meanings of manhood were created to meet the demands of modern life, it stands to reason that new images of womanhood were needed as well.

Yet few women's historians who have studied the New Woman have considered her in concert with popular images of manliness. She is instead interpreted as aspiring to a life associated with a fading Victorian notion of masculinity marked by self-control, social and political involvement, and a cultivated intellect. Other images of healthy and strong New Women have been embraced as feminist figures isolated from concerns for nation or race.[13] But a New Woman, one fit for life on the rails, emerged alongside and in conversation with popular notions of strong manliness, and it is impossible to understand her without also exploring these visions of masculinity. Understanding how and why images of competent women like Sylvia circulated broadly and had such popular appeal offers an opportunity to investigate not only the nature of changing gender ideals but also the realignment of public and private. The acceptance of such New Women represents the end point of this study's composite travel narrative from public domesticity, through an expanding and segmented commercial society, to the public adventures the railroad offered women in the opening decades of the twentieth century—a journey that can also be understood as a movement from Victorian to modern, from a culture of separate spheres to the public-private hybrid of American consumer culture.

～～ As the story of Sylvia Fox suggests, the juxtaposition of women and the railroad had taken on new meaning by the beginning of the twentieth century. Now more than a punch line, this unlikely pairing remained popular as it revealed the considerable advances of both humanity and technology. The popular appeal of such displays was not lost on railroad executives. Like Peake's fictional Superintendent Howard, they understood that news of white women doing a man's job brought their lines publicity. In August 1901, the *Railway Age* published an unconfirmed story about two women in the employ of the Southern Pacific Railroad. One was reported to be a trainmaster in New Mexico; the other a mechanic and designer of a new type of engine. The *Railway Age*, seeking to prove the veracity of these "newspaper romances," asked "whether the two heroines (the trainmistress and the locomotive designer) have actual existence or are imaginary beings." It even suggested "that these romantic characters might not be unconnected with the devices of railway advertising."[14]

S. F. B. Morse, traffic manager of the Atlantic system of the Southern Pacific Company, responded that "the Southern Pacific's passenger department is known to tell the truth—frequently. It surely will not make use of imaginary characters to attract attention to its deservedly popular route. . . . We have never tried to impose upon the unsophisticated public by representing fiction to be fact; consequently so far as we are concerned your insinuation does not go." A second letter confirmed that a Mrs. Pease was serving as dispatcher in Gila Bend, New Mexico. A letter published two weeks later, however, revealed that the story of the "lady mechanic" was very likely untrue. H. J. Small of the Southern Pacific Company was "wholly unable to locate the lady who invented the new type of locomotive."[15] This enthusiastic exchange underscores the vitality of these images and the chord they struck with the public.

Despite Morse's protestations, railroad companies did use "imaginary characters" to promote their lines. Beginning in the 1890s railroad brochures increasingly featured fictional images of women railroad passengers outdoors enjoying vigorous, albeit respectable, activities. Although these illustrations did not show women taming the engines nor doing men's work, they did reveal a new emphasis on female vitality and stood in contrast to images of women as domestic travelers. For example, railroads promoted vacation spots along their routes with pictures of women playing sports, posing on beaches, or walking the seashore with binoculars. Phoebe Snow, the best known of the "imaginary characters" embodying this ideal, was the fictional spokesperson for the Delaware, Lackawanna & Western Railroad from 1900 to 1917. Always clad in white linen and speaking in rhyming jingles, she promoted the ease of travel upon the line and praised the Lackawanna's clean, anthracite-burning engines. Over time, she also advertised her own skill in negotiating the public life and challenges of railroad travel.

Initially presented in a series of streetcar advertisements, Phoebe Snow proved so popular that she soon found her way into magazine and newspaper ads and onto billboards. Originally conceived as a symbol of the Victorian feminine ideal of domesticity, she evolved into a robust and capable traveler; later advertisements depicted her enjoying golf, tennis, and bicycling. She became so well known that a popular vaudeville joke told of a little boy who, when asked to name the two most famous women in the world, answered "my Mamma's Mamma and Phoebe Snow." Her name was used to sell women's clothing and handbags, and it appeared on a line of tennis, boating, and horseback-riding attire. Blurring the line between real and imaginary characters, admiring girls sent her fan mail.[16] Such confusion and broad-based popularity show that the images of New Women on the rails were more than marketing ploys to keep women traveling and suggest that they had broader resonance. Phoebe Snow's appeal suggests that she spoke to issues beyond the virtues of anthracite.

Images of fit and capable white women were often created by and appealed to men. Phoebe Snow, the creation of ad man Earnest Elmo Calkins, received marriage proposals from would-be suitors.[17] And although Sylvia Fox's feat was unusual within railroad literature, capable women often figured as romantic interests for male protagonists. In this genre, written almost exclusively by and for men, women proved themselves worthy of love by skillfully meeting the challenges of railroad life. In Francis Lynde's *A Romance in Transit* (1897), Fred Brockway, a passenger agent, falls in love with Gertrude, the daughter of a railroad president, but refuses to admit his feelings because he is intimidated by her family's wealth. One evening, Gertrude confides in Fred, "I have often thought I should like to ride on an engine," and asks to ride that night. Fred is impressed by her pluck: "Brockway caught his breath. 'Do you—would you trust me to take you on the engine to-night?'" In the cab, Gertrude proves herself a worthy partner. She even tries her hand at driving the engine "cling[ing] to the throttle as if she were afraid it was alive and would escape, but her eyes sparkl[ing] and the flush of excitement mount[ing] swiftly to cheek and brow."[18] All concerns about Gertrude's wealth and Fred's relative poverty disappear when confronted with the sight of her in the engine cab. The power of the machine reveals that Gertrude and Fred share the same strength of spirit.

In Frank Spearman's *The Daughter of a Magnate* (1903), the romantic bond between Gertrude Brock, the title character, and Ab Glover, a railroad engineer, is solidified by time spent together in the engine cab. They meet on a tour of the treacherous lines through the Sierra Mountains. Gertrude accompanies her father in his private car; Ab serves as their guide. During a break in their journey, Gertrude and Ab walk through a rail yard. As they approach a train, Gertrude expresses a desire to climb into the cab and start the engine. Within moments, "the heiress to many millions grasped the throttle, unlatched it and pulled at the lever vigorously with both hands." Although Gertrude screams when the engine hisses and begins to move, Ab admires her as she laughs at her "blackened gloves" and "begrimed skirt." The experience changes them. According to Spearman, "they had crossed the railroad yard strangers; they recrossed it quite other." Once again, class difference is erased by a shared moment of daring. By boarding the engine, Gertrude "made herself a heroine to every yardman in sight," to Ab, and presumably to Spearman's male readers as well.[19] A review of Spearman's story in the *Railway Age* praised the characters as "true to life," noting "the daughter of the magnate does not forget to be a daughter of Eve while fulfilling the other role."[20] Earlier women's fiction portrayed the parlor car as a public stage on which women might display their domestic skills to would-be suitors; Peake, Lynde, and Spearman used the engine cab as a setting to display the womanly accomplishments they admired. In the engine cab, women tried on manly roles and displayed a willingness to embrace the power and excitement of modern life.

Fiction writers and their readers were not the only ones to express admiration for women willing and able to face the challenges of life in the age of rail travel. Male journalists and editors presented and interpreted the experiences of women travelers according to their own values and concerns. In 1890, for example, an unnamed editor introduced Lillian Leland's published travel letters by praising her considerable abilities and outlining her impressive qualities. He called attention to Leland's "nervous energy and power of endurance seldom found in a woman" and noted that even with her "retiring and reserved manner" she was "capable of facing the greatest possible danger without flinching, or the most aggravating difficulty without annoyance." He compared her favorably to other famous women travelers, most notably Ida Pfeiffer and Isabella Bird, well-known European travelers often praised for their manly perseverance in the face of difficult journeys.[21] W. H. Davenport Adams, author of *Celebrated Women Travellers of the Nineteenth Century* (1883), praised Pfeiffer by noting that "if a spirit like hers, so daring, so persevering, so tenacious, had been given to a man, history would have counted a Magellan or a Captain Hook the more." And Miss Bird "carried in her bosom a man's heart, and was never wanting in courage or resolution."[22] Like Leland, both Pfeiffer and Bird were praised for their feminine reserve and their uncommon heroic (read "masculine") qualities.

The similarity of these descriptions is telling. Even though they traveled under different circumstances (Pfeiffer set out on her voyage in 1841 when she was a forty-five-year-old widow; Bird, age twenty-three, undertook her travels in 1854 at her doctor's urging), Leland, Pfeiffer, and Bird came to stand for a vision of womanly drive and ability. In the hands of male interpreters, these three different lives represented women's ability to meet the challenges associated with navigating, literally and figuratively, the world beyond women's usual sphere. They came to represent, as it were, a new railroad type: the extraordinary woman of manly abilities. Removed from their contexts and presented to an eager readership, real-life women like Leland and Bird came to resemble the daring, albeit fictional, Gertrudes of the engine cab. Like the railroad types presented earlier, these daring women were readily recognizable to those in the know; yet the liveliness of their specific experiences and personalities was flattened as they were rendered generic.[23]

The issues of male authorship and admiration, the blurring between real and imaginary characters, and the nature of women's capacity to travel through modern public life all converged to great effect in Nellie Bly's 1889 circumnavigation of the globe. On 14 November 1889, the *New York World* reporter set out from New Jersey, hoping to outpace Jules Verne's fictional character Phileas Fogg by traveling around the world in fewer than eighty days. Unlike Verne's protagonist, who traveled by a wide variety of transports, including elephant and ice-boat, Bly traveled by cruise ship and railroad car. She visited London, Paris, Singapore, Hong Kong, and Yokohama.[24] Unable to print many of Bly's dispatches due to delays, the *World* fueled interest in her journey by encouraging readers to enter a contest and guess the precise day, hour, minute, and second of her return. Readers were invited to "guess early and often," and on 5 December 1889, the newspaper announced receipt of nearly 300,000 guesses. The *World* also sustained interest in Bly's journey by printing excerpts of letters and news stories wishing the plucky traveler well. These came from across the country and abroad.[25] Bly caused such a sensation that *Cosmopolitan* sent one of its reporters, Elizabeth Bisland, around the world in an effort to steal some headlines, and *Life* lampooned Bly by sending a fictitious reporter named "Sadie McGinty" off on her own daring enterprise — "around New York in 80 years!" The latter claimed that the feat would stand as "evidence of a great journal's enterprise and a plucky woman's nerve." Thus, Nellie Bly, with her real and fictional imitators, created a community of readers rapt by the notion of a woman traveler's effort to negotiate a complex and threatening world.[26]

It is tempting to end this study with a description of the crowds cheering Nellie Bly as she sped across the United States aboard a special train; to mention that during her flying trip across the country she, of course, took a turn in the engine cab and placed her hand upon the throttle;[27] perhaps to note that the *World*'s circulation increased considerably during her journey and that upon her return Bly's image was used to sell real estate, cakes, cigars, elastic stockings, and Dr. Morse's Indian Root Pills "for Biliousness, Headache, and Constipation." For a dollar, one might purchase "Round the World with Nellie Bly," a popular board game recreating the famed journey, complete with "plenty of excitement on land and sea." Such fanfare, after all, suggests the end of women's journey away from the confining values of separate spheres. By the time she completed her trip around the world in 72 days, 6 hours, and 11 minutes, handily outdoing Phileas Fogg, Bly was a national celebrity. Even P. T. Barnum drew inspiration from the journalist's example: "From the great amount of public attention she is attracting. . . . I begin to look in her direction for new popular features in my show."[28] Barnum's emulation confirms that the lone woman traveler was no longer a problem in American culture. Crowds cheered her; concerned spectators hung on her every movement; and railroad companies, entertainers, and hucksters got rich exploiting her image.

Barnum's desire to cash in on Nellie Bly raises an intriguing question: What was the appeal of her travels? How did images of daring women like Sylvia Fox, Lillian Leland, Phoebe Snow, and Nellie Bly find a place in turn-of-the-century popular culture? Most secondary studies of Bly's career depict the appeal of her journey as that of a straightforward adventure narrative. Such studies celebrate Bly as a lone woman who, speaking no language other than English, met the challenges of circumnavigation with only one small suitcase and no special arrangements for her conveyance. Bly's journey is portrayed, in the same language used by the *World*, as "the spectacle of a young fearless woman racing from country to country, alone and unprotected."[29] She emerges as a daring woman—a New Woman willing to cross boundaries, real and metaphorical, for her career. But this interpretation fails to ring true when placed beside scholarship on the New Woman. Why would the world embrace so controversial a figure? These women were more than simply figures of female emancipation, daring, and adventure. Upon closer scrutiny, the images of capable women circulating within late-nineteenth- and

BETTER GAMES FOR CHILDREN

No. 4122—NELLIE BLY

In the year 1889, the New York World sent one of its reporters, Mrs. Nellie Seaman, known as Nellie Bly, on a record making trip around the world. The trip was made in 72 days, 6 hours, 11 minutes—remarkable time with the transportation facilities available in those days.* The Nellie Bly Game board shows the route traveled by Nelly Bly.

The long ocean voyages, the stirring adventures which she experienced, and the many places of prominence which Nellie Bly actually visited, are portrayed on the game board. The moves are governed by spinning a dial, and two, three or four may play. Beautiful folding game board size 15½ x 16.

*The present record for a trip around the world is held by John Henry Mears who in 1913 made the journey in 35 days, 21 hours, 36 minutes.

Size, 8¾ x 16½.   Price, $1.00

BETTER GAMES FOR CHILDREN

No. 4131—PHOEBE SNOW

In this game dainty Phoebe Snow needs help to get from New York to San Francisco in the quickest possible time. She has to change cars many times, is delayed by wrecks and other obstacles, but finally reaches her destination and the player who succeeds in landing her there, wins the game. It's great fun to travel with Phoebe Snow and every boy and girl will like this game. Phoebe Snow is a dial game, played on a beautifully lithographed folding board.

Size, 8¾ x 16½.   Price, $1.00

Advertisement for Nellie Bly and Phoebe Snow board games, Bradley's Games (c. 1916). The description at top refers to Bly as "Mrs. Nellie Seaman" and notes that John Henry Mears set the record for circumnavigation in 1913, making the journey in 35 days, 21 hours, 36 minutes. The other describes Phoebe Snow as "dainty" and invites players to help her on her cross-country trip. Author's collection.

"Nellie Bly on the Fly" (trade card, c. 1890). According to this advertisement for Dr. Morse's Indian Root Pills, "Men don't monopolize success." Author's collection.

early-twentieth-century popular culture prove more complex, even contradictory, than they first appear.

Although fit for public life, these popular New Women remained tied to the private identities associated with Victorian womanhood. The two fictional Gertrudes, after their time in the engine cab, return to the domestic life of the private car. The daring experiences and excitement of the engine cab merely tested their worthiness as future brides. In both Spearman's and Lynde's stories, the engine cab remains a site of manly action, and the female protagonists ultimately leave the engine to become wives. Likewise, although Bly's journey was replete with exciting adventures and personal challenges, the reporter's successes abroad were often depicted in the press in terms of conventional feminine roles. At times, the coverage even depicted Bly's journey as a quest for a husband. According to one report, "the real question [raised by her tour] is whether a charming Miss Bly will ever succeed in going round the world at all—as Miss Bly." [30] And a well-wisher remarked at the announcement of Bly's journey: "Miss Bly has proved herself a remarkable young woman, and I hope she will get a good husband." [31] By depicting her as a would-be bride, the press could assert that Bly, who exhibited more than masculine strength, was never anything less than a lady. The *Wilmington Star* assured readers that although Bly was ahead of schedule on her journey, "it does not necessarily follow from this that she is a 'fast' young lady. On the contrary, she is a good, well-behaved girl, who crosses her t's and dots her i's." [32]

Even the letters printed in the newspaper upheld traditional gender expectations. This tendency was reflected in the *World*'s observation that Bly "is bidden God-speed by manly men and prayers for her safe return are offered by sympathetic and warm-hearted women." [33] Presumably, Bly appealed to both types of readers. A letter from "Five Girls in Mount Vernon" expressed admiration for Bly and pleaded, "Will you tell us about Nellie Bly personally? We have read so much about her that we are very anxious to know." The letter continued: "Everything she writes is so good and her descriptions of the places she has visited are so perfect and we admire her so much for her ability that we want to know all about her. She is about how old? Handsome, ordinary or plain? (She is so smart, she could not be homely.) Tell us all about her. She is a wonder in our minds, and we are waiting to read her description of her trip around the world. The fact is Mr. Editor, we five girls think we must know more about Nellie Bly." The editor responded with a brief description: "The young lady in question is about twenty-three years of age; height, 5 feet and 3 inches; a pronounced brunette, with gray eyes; fairly good-looking." As for Bly "personally," the editor responded, "She is quiet, reserved, her manners are genteel, though she is full of determination, and, girls, she does not chew gum." Thus, even as Nellie Bly held out the possibility of a more expansive public life for women, the men who shaped her public persona presented her achievements in a more traditional light.[34]

On 5 January 1890, while Nellie Bly was still making her way around the globe, the *World* printed a story by the journalist Nell Nelson detailing her own "midnight ride on the Washington Express." The editor introduced it as an account of "a plucky young woman's remarkable experiences." Nelson described her ride in the engine cab—the speed, heat, noise, and jarring motion. But with the help of the brave fireman she was able, in time, to settle her nerves. She told readers, "This hero at the furnace was my tower of strength and his comfort made a man of me as it were." Soon Nelson "swallowed cinders at a gulp, took a side-saddle seat on the narrow bunk, set my teeth together and . . . had my heart in pendulum swing, if accelerated a trifle." Now, Nelson could note the details of her journey. She taught her readers how to read railroad signals, described the watering of the engine, and recounted the frenzy accompanying an encounter with a wrecked freight train. In the end, Nelson announced that she was "glad I made the engine trip, but . . . I would not live again the horror." Like the characters of railroad fiction, Nelson saw her time in the engine cab as both brief and novel. The only hint of transgression was her confession that she was "costumed for the occasion in leather leggings, Turkish trousers, hat and ulster, sacrificing my skirts for better security against accidents."[35] Yet the main illustration for the story shows Nelson clad in a dress and awkwardly standing on the engine cab's platform, eliminating any hint of female impropriety.[36]

Why circulate accounts of daring women only to reaffirm traditional notions of womanhood? Why embrace images of female heroism only to assert that such moments are fleeting? It is possible to interpret Sylvia Fox or Nell Nelson as attempts to appropriate and commercialize the social and political ideals of New Womanhood; to dismiss them as watered-down versions of women who more truly threatened the status quo. But there is another, richer interpretation: that the popular versions of New Women who earned the admiration of women and captured the hearts of men were part of a different, but related, cultural conversation. Simultaneous with the emergence of these daring and adventuresome women, the American public embraced new ideals of strong and heroic manliness. Scholars like T. J. Jackson Lears, Amy Kaplan, and Gail Bederman have incorporated these images of manly vigor into analyses of antimodernism, territorial expansion, racial politics, and the defining of American civilization itself.[37] They portray a broad anxiety about men's vulnerability to the enervating forces of modern life and catalog numerous attempts to repudiate this fear. These studies of manliness suggest that Phoebe Snow, Nellie Bly, and the other real and imagined women of the rails addressed more than a debate about women's roles and abilities. In short, the popular images of New Womanhood on the rails may have been one strand in a web of concerns surrounding technological progress, racial health, and the fate of American civilization—the very issues that shaped so many other railroad narratives.

In the last quarter of the nineteenth century, the railroad was not only a means of territorial and commercial expansion but a site of manly conquest. Fiction writers, journalists, railroad workers, and companies circulated images of heroic railroad men as a shorthand for man's ability to come to terms with both the power of technology and the complexity and uncertainty of large-scale business enterprise. No figure captured these two challenges more aptly than the railroad engineer. In 1888, *Scribner's Magazine* drew special attention to the engineer, "the popular 'hero of the rail,'" who must "ride in the most dangerous part of the train, take charge of a steam boiler that may explode and blow him to atoms, and of machinery that may break and kill him, and try to keep up vigilance which only a being more than human could successfully maintain."[38] The engineer seemed the quintessential figure of modern American life; powerful and fearless, yet subject to the forces of business and technology. In the engine cab, he worked to control a machine more powerful than himself and, all the while, needed to conform to the schedule and policies of the railroad company. If somewhere down the line a trackman, signalman, or switchman failed in his duties, or if bad weather damaged the tracks, he would, through no fault of his own, endanger himself, his passengers, and the larger network of rail travel.

In sum, the engineer embodied both the systems of order associated with modern business and the untamable and unpredictable forces such systems sought to control. Because railroad workers repeatedly met this challenge of modernity, the praise heaped upon them suggested that they were somehow set apart from the rest of humanity—members of what one railroad observer described in 1874 as "a new and distinct profession in the practice of which peculiar qualifications are indispensable," or, more simply, as a "new social class of 'Railroad Men.'"[39] Countless articles and memoirs enumerated both the remarkable demands upon and the corresponding qualities of such men. Imagine, for example, riding an engine a mile a minute on a starless night or through a driving rain.[40] The ability to endure such strain marked the engineer as a unique example of American manly vigor and confirmed the strength of his nerves. In the words of one turn-of-the-century observer: "Railroad men are generally healthy and strong. They do not need football games to keep them in good physical condition. . . . Being obliged to possess such bodies, it is evident that rich blood course through their brains and their minds be bright and active."[41]

As was often the case, Victorians turned such qualities into inherent biological traits, and the term they used to capture the particular qualities that set railroad men apart was "nerve." Nineteenth-century medical science believed that humans possessed a limited amount of "nervous force" with which to meet the stresses of life; inadequate nerve resulted in disease. The railroad engineer possessed an abundance of nervous force. Joseph Taylor, railroad man and author, explained that the engineer's "nervous system is perpetually on the strain, and if he allows his attention to be withdrawn for a moment from his duty—either by a thought of his family of other personal affairs (the claims of his stomach, for instance)—that very moment the whole of the precious human freight behind him may be cast into wreck and death."[42] The conductor Charles B. George noted that "engineers must not only look out for themselves, but for the hundreds who are back of them in the passenger coaches."[43] At the end of the nineteenth century, then, the railroads, despite their domesticated car interiors and their lady passengers, remained an important site for constructing a vision of manly vigor.

The engineer was frequently portrayed as the most heroic of all railroad men precisely because he carried the burden of safeguarding the domesticated scenes taking place in the cars. In 1893, Edwin Price implored his fellow locomotive engineers to "think of your important trust. Although the Millionaires of the World do not come to you and introduce themselves or in any manner seem to recognize you, yet they do honor you by placing themselves and Family in your care as you are running at the rate of fifty to sixty miles per hour." Again, the engine cab and its demands overshadowed class divisions. "In the darkness, as they sleep almost as comfortable as in their own golden chamber in their costly palace, . . . the Engineer takes them in safety." [44] Popular songs like "My Papa's The Engineer" and "My Dad's The Engineer" echoed Price's sentiments. In both songs, a young girl soothes a carload of frightened passengers: "'Daddy's on the engine, Don't be afraid, Daddy knows what he's doing,' Said the little maid." [45] The engineer, facing down dangers that passengers could ill afford to contemplate, stood as the train's surrogate and often unseen patriarch, leading his family across the continent.

The figure of the railroad engineer spoke to a variety of cultural issues and addressed concerns about modern life—concerns about speed and technology, interdependence, and large business enterprise; yet the very conditions that fueled the reformulation of late-nineteenth-century manliness and called the manly engineer into being likewise threatened that cultural ideal. Throughout the second half of the nineteenth century, stories of heroic railroad men circulated beside popular, medical, and legal accounts of men undone— unnerved, as it were—by life on the rails. As the engine cab offered the greatest stage for manly heroics, it revealed the frailty of men when confronted with technology and business's growing demands. In short, the railroad man could also embody the weaknesses and vulnerabilities his popular image sought to redress. Moreover, in so doing, the railroad worker served as a surrogate for all Americans threatened by the demands of modern life.

One humorous account told of an engineer who took the strains of his work to bed: "The other night, now, my wife started up in bed and screamed as if she was being murdered. 'What are you doing?' she cried; and bless your life! Sir, there was I, pulling her slender arm with all my might, while my foot was steadied against—something else, trying to 'reverse.'" [46] Other stories were less amusing. In May 1880, the *Railway Age* reported the death of engineer William Phillips at the age of thirty-nine. He had run a train from Jersey City to Pittsburgh, 443 miles nonstop, and in less than the scheduled time. Phillips never recovered from the nervous strain of that trip.[47] In railroad publications, advertisements for nerve tonics and health remedies confirmed that a life spent on the rails often took its toll. A typical testimonial announced: "If any class of people suffer from kidney disease it is railroad engineers, occasioned by the continual jar of the engine. I have suffered many years with kidney and liver disease, Rheumatism, and great exhaustion and nervousness."[48] Ironically, then, railroad men were a distinct class not only because of their considerable nerve but also because of their ill health.

The coexistence of strength and weakness in the railroad man challenged Victorian notions of manliness and revealed that a figure could be both manly and vulnerable. Beginning in the 1850s, medical professionals turned their attention to sorting out why healthy men paid so dearly when exposed to the demands of the railroad. The answer was that the railroad was so powerful that it created its own ailments. A study conducted in England during the 1860s and reprinted in the United States found that "in order to stand the wear and tear of constant travelling, a man must not only be of strong constitution, but he must begin young. . . . After thirty or thirty-five, men are no longer able to acquire this necessary tolerance."[49] Nervous diseases like "railway spine" and "railway brain," brought on by trauma or psychic shock, rendered virile men weak, crippling them with symptoms similar to those of hysteria, nervous exhaustion, epilepsy, even dementia.[50] More troubling was the study's implied message that the same illnesses that threatened railroad workers could easily afflict members of the traveling public.

In 1867, the British physician John Eric Erichsen was among the first to diagnose railway injuries and argue for their unique standing among modern ailments. According to Erichsen, "in no ordinary accident can the shock be so great as in those that occur on railways." The doctor attributed the exceptional nature of railroad-related shock to "the rapidity of the movement, the momentum of the person injured, the suddenness of the arrest, the helplessness of the sufferers, and the natural perturbation of mind that must disturb even the bravest [men]."[51] Rather than finding fault with men's nerves, Erichsen noted the railroad's relentless and overwhelming ability to debilitate even healthy men. Many doctors and laymen were troubled by once healthy men rendered weak, nervous, even overly emotional—qualities often associated with Victorian ideals of feminine frailty.[52]

The array of symptoms associated with railroad injuries threatened not only men's health but the very division between manliness and femininity. Dr. Erichsen explained, however, that such fears were based upon imprecise diagnoses. Although many railroad-related ailments often looked like hysteria ("a disease of women rather than men"), they were distinct diseases marked by great trauma to the nervous system. Erichsen concluded that any man would be rightly upset to see his strength, health, and livelihood endangered by nervous disease: "That such an unhappy sufferer should occasionally be unnerved and give way to mental emotion is natural enough. It certainly appears to me that the term 'hysteria,' elastic as it is, can scarcely, with any regard to truth or justice, be strained so far as to embrace those feelings that naturally spring from the contemplation of so gloomy a prospect as this." According to the doctor, the underlying cause of railway injury was physical, not emotional. And so, any emotional upset a man experienced after a railroad accident was not hysteria but the normal response of a healthy man rendered ill. By so interpreting these ailments, Erichsen drew a line between the very real physical suffering of men and the emotional weakness of women.[53]

If exposure to the uncertainties and dangers of rail travel could strain a railroad man's nerves, imagine the impact upon a woman.[54] Although women did not drive engines (fictional accounts and daring journalists notwithstanding), they were subject to the strains of rail travel as passengers. Women—vulnerable as they were to emotional upsets—worried about the speed of the trains, the sturdiness of bridge trestles, and the possibility of derailment or collision. Even in the comfortable passenger cars they experienced the jarring motion and considerable noise of the tracks. Could a woman meet the mental and physical demands of railroad life? Did she possess adequate nervous force? In 1872, Dr. Ely Van De Warker answered these questions in the *Georgia Medical Companion*. He extrapolated from studies of European railway employees: "With all this evidence of the gravity of the functional and structural lesion on the more sturdy and robust physique of man, we have no trouble in concluding that woman—taking into consideration the less amount of exposure attending her life—must suffer in increased proportion." The suffering of men provided "corroborative evidence" for the much greater suffering of women. Van De Warker concluded that because "woman cannot, from the nature of her organization, make a successful habitual railroad traveller," physicians should dissuade women—especially pregnant, nervous, and aged women—from traveling by rail.[55]

Like Erichsen, Dr. Van De Warker reinforced the boundary between male and female gender roles. He presented case studies of women railroad passengers rendered ill during travel; significantly, nearly all the cases emphasized the negative impact of rail travel upon women's reproductive organs. Common problems arising from women's train travel included premature labor, miscarriage, ovarian irritation, and menstrual irregularity. Such ailments were "the result, probably of combined mechanical causes, and of nervous shock." Van De Warker asserted that most of the women he had studied were previously healthy and "that the peculiar method of transit is cause" of their illness. Apparently the strain diverted woman's limited nerve force from the taxing and more important demands of her reproductive organs. He concluded that any woman who routinely traveled by railroad did so "at the expense of her future usefulness."[56] Not only did women prove themselves "poor travellers, the world over," but rail travel could turn them into poor women.[57] The woman railroad traveler, like the transgressive New Woman, threatened not only her own health but that of future generations by wasting her limited nervous force on inappropriate activities.

Concerns about the railroad's impact upon an individual's productive and reproductive capacities—indeed, manliness and femininity—spoke to larger anxieties about the health of the modernizing American nation.[58] Throughout the 1870s and 1880s, American periodicals compared "the Health and Physical Habits of English and American Women," investigated "The Health of American Women," and asked "Are Americans Less Healthy than Europeans?"[59] Ironically, by the 1890s, popular images of the female railroad travelers offered a very reassuring answer. Much as the "new social class of railroad men" answered growing concerns about the vulnerability of manliness, images of healthy and daring women passengers stood in opposition to the sickly and exhausted female traveler. These New Women of the rails proved that American women could be both strong and womanly—fit for both the engine cab and family life. The balance between vigor and femininity was crucial, as many Victorians perceived sexual difference as a vital part of any advanced civilization.[60] Only in primitive cultures was the line between men and women's roles blurred. To forfeit womanliness in the drive for national vigor would undermine America's standing in the hierarchy of civilized nations.[61]

At first glance, the transition from the "haggard and weary" women travelers described by Van De Warker to the healthy and vital female passengers of later railroad advertisements, fiction, and journalism is jarring. That a culture could move from the former to the latter in so short a time—that the two very different images could even coexist—is puzzling. Yet late Victorian culture reveals tremendous capacity for living with and attempting to reconcile such contradictions: on the one hand, nineteenth-century physicians agreed that modern life taxed the human nervous system and caused disease. On the other hand, they believed that the advances of modern life had the potential to foster good health. George Beard, author of *American Nervousness: Its Causes and Consequences*, perhaps the best-known exponent of this contradiction, interpreted nervous disease in the United States as evidence of the nation's status as a "modern civilization." To Beard, pervasive nervousness was a cause for nationalistic pride: "All this is modern, and originally American: and no age, no country, and no form of civilization, not Greece, nor Rome, not Spain, nor the Netherlands in the days of their glory, possessed such maladies." Disease was a symbol of progress, and in time, Beard argued, progress would cure disease. "The evil of American nervousness, like all other evils, tends within certain limits to correct itself." The same nationalism that led Beard to see nervousness as evidence of American civilization's advance encouraged him to believe in that civilization's curative powers. As civilization and technology advanced they would undo the damage they had wrought on the nation's nerves. Beard concluded that "American inventions are now assisting both American men and American women to diminish their nervousness; palace cars and elevators and sewing machines are types of recent improvements that help to diminish the friction of modern life."[62]

As might be expected, the railroads embraced and promoted this image of themselves as the cure for modernity's stresses and strains; through technological and cultural innovations such as the parlor car the railroads were able to position themselves as saviors rather than destroyers of individual and national health. For example, the addition of domestic amenities not only eased women's entry into public but soothed the nerves of male and female travelers by mimicking the secure environment of the home and suggesting the permanence of a heavily constructed dwelling. The lush upholstery, thick carpets, and heavy drapery that gave the parlor car its domestic and luxurious appearance also insulated passengers from the physical and nervous shocks of travel.[63] Polite and attentive employees similarly protected travelers from the exhausting demands of public life. All of these developments made it possible to cast the railroad as a site of rejuvenation, not fatigue, and permitted the railroads to emphasize the restorative and healing experience of travel. The railroad had accelerated American life, intensified the demands of business, and created new types of dangers and disease, but it could also carry weary travelers to the healing powers of the natural landscape and vigorous physical activity without aggravating the conditions such vacations were intended to redress.

In February 1880, the *Railway Age* explained that "nervous ailments . . . all impel their unfortunate bearers to seek in the recreation of travel and the strange scenes the rest and health of which their pursuits or surroundings have robbed them." [64] Nine years later, the Union Pacific noted that "the question 'Where shall we go for health and pleasure?' assumes greater importance each succeeding year." The Union Pacific's passenger department published a volume to "assist those who are in doubt in settling this important point, as well as to show them what a wonderful country lies between the Missouri River and the Pacific Coast." [65] In 1890, the Great Northern Railway made its case for the healing powers of train travel in a pamphlet entitled *Vacation Gospel*. In the introductory passages, Rev. Dr. Bridgman preached the benefits of vacation: "The man whose mind is long and often on the rack of anxious thought needs the change and relaxation which delightful journeyings and pleasant saunterings alone can give." The sermon was followed by a map detailing the railway's lines and connections.[66] By advertising the restful nature of rail travel and the restorative value of vacation, the railroads resolved the contradictory nature of the progress they embodied and established themselves as the promoters of national health.

It is in this context that a vision of strong and capable female railroad passengers can best be understood: as civilization both caused and cured disease, and the railroad both taxed and rejuvenated the nerves, women could be both ill suited for and rendered fit by the experience of rail travel. And so, healthy and active women such as Phoebe Snow emerged as advertising shorthand for the virtues of a railway vacation. Indeed "vacation" is an ideal metaphor for women's time in the engine cab: a railway adventure allowed women a temporary release of vigor and offered momentary excitement to bring a healthy flush to their cheeks. But in the end, women adventurers, both fictional and real, returned to home and hearth, restored and with a new appreciation for the manly strength that endured such trials on a regular basis. Despite the celebration of accomplished women, public daring and competence remained male qualities. As Nell Nelson noted in her account of her ride in the engine cab, the fireman "made a man out of me." Nellie Bly was praised broadly for "her grit [that] has been more than masculine." [67] To be brave and calm in the face of a roaring engine was a manly feat, even for a woman.

Note that a woman's daring depended upon the greater bravery and chivalry of men. Neither fictional Gertrude strode into the engine cab unattended. And Lillian Leland's "unchaperoned" journey was possible, in the words of her editor, because she was "everywhere the recipient of kind, respectful and courteous treatment" from male travelers.[68] Likewise, courteous men mitigated the dangers of Bly's circumnavigation. What, inquired one source, could possibly go wrong "when she 'a charming American of nineteen-years-old'. . . throws herself upon the hitherto undoubted courtesy and chivalry of the Atlantic and Pacific liners?" [69] Elizabeth Bisland informed readers that throughout her "entire journey I never met with other than the most exquisite and unfailing courtesy and consideration. . . . It seems to me this speaks very highly of the civilization . . . when a woman's strongest protection is that she is unprotected." [70] Phoebe Snow similarly reflected upon the good manners of the train staff on the Delaware, Lackawanna & Western Railroad. According to one of her famous rhyming advertisements, "Miss Snow you see / Was sure to be / The object of / Much courtesy / For day and night / They're all polite / upon the Road of Anthracite." [71] By completing a whirlwind journey, then, the female traveler revealed not just her own strength or nerve but the accomplishments of the men who made such experiences possible, and, by extension, she paid tribute to the modern civilization that supported such achievements.

This "American Girl," celebrated in fiction and analyzed in countless articles, became for many the most important female type in the final decade of the nineteenth century.[72] That American women could face up to the strains of technology and commerce, of high speeds and countless details, and all the while remain womanly, reflected well not only on them but on American civilization—on the freedom, courtesy, and manly protection American men provided. (Perhaps this larger symbolic role explains the repeated confusion surrounding the real or imagined nature of these women travelers: fact or fiction, they served equally well as metaphors for national strength.) By celebrating women in the engine cab, the symbolic center of modern life, Americans embraced images of womanly competence without sacrificing traditional gender roles. At her best, the American Girl was beautiful, fearless, athletic, confident, and innocent of vice. In many respects she resembled her contemporary, the New Woman. But unlike the New Woman, whose accomplishments reflected the capabilities of her sex alone, the American Girl embodied the achievements of her nation and asserted that American civilization would continue its forward march with neither men nor women unsexed by the demands of modern life.

In 1880 the *Nation* noted the American Girl's arrival, and during the 1890s other periodicals investigated her origins and studied her reception in Europe.[73] In 1884 the *New York World* explained that this uniquely American creation was the result of "the ennobling ideas of domestic life that prevail in the United States, . . . the primal disposition to deal justly with women that had its origins with our Saxon culture, . . . [and] the liberality of our political institutions."[74] Thus, five years before giving the world Nellie Bly, the newspaper extolled the daring woman whose abilities paid honor to her nation. Much of the coverage of Bly's journey portrayed her achievements in this light. The paper noted, "The pluck and nerve in undertaking such a trip will be heartily applauded by every admirer of the American girl."[75] Similarly, a telegram from one of Bly's admirers celebrated the relationship between Bly and her nation: "It is pardonable in us Americans to say that your indomitable will and pluck are but characteristics of model young America."[76] The *Memphis Sunday Times* described her tour as "one of the most thoroughly modern and American exhibitions."[77] And in the final days of Bly's journey, the *World* awaited her homecoming "as a tribute to American pluck, American womanhood and American perseverance."[78]

The differences between American Girls and New Women reveal the unsteady ground upon which women acted in public. Did the daring women described in this chapter serve as evidence of women's newly recognized abilities and growing public presence? Sylvia Fox, Phoebe Snow, Nellie Bly, and Nell Nelson were public actors, yet the public world they inhabited was different from that imagined earlier in the century. The accomplished woman traveler or daring rider of the engine was a figure more complicated than a protofeminist New Woman. Although she was a new creation, the achievements she embodied were not those of all women. She was instead rooted in a more varied array of values—those often associated with the changing ideals of late-nineteenth-century manliness. Placing these brave and capable white women in this context reveals the shifting boundary between private and public. As new images of vigorous and strong men circulated in the culture, they were joined by representations of women worthy of them. And like their male counterparts, these female ideals spoke to concerns about national health and American civilization as well as social difference and racial dominance. In popular narratives, white men and women, often regardless of class, joined together in a struggle to match the power of technology and meet the demands of modern commercial culture.

Although engine cab romances often crossed class lines in the celebration of nerve and American womanhood, they left growing assumptions about racial difference and separation unchallenged. American Girls were subsumed within other debates that marginalized them as public actors or held up their achievements to serve racist or nationalistic ends. Nellie Bly and Phoebe Snow were exciting and accomplished female actors, but the public they inhabited was rather limited. In real and fictional accounts, strong and healthy woman travelers represented a strong and healthy nation that was imagined as white. The creator of Phoebe Snow explained that the original advertising campaign was an explicit celebration of whiteness. It "told how the Girl in White met a Man in White upon the Road of Anthracite, and was finally married by a Bishop who happened to be traveling on the same train, who was also clothed in white."[79] As African American travelers were routinely excluded from the domesticated public, they were absent from stories of the American Girl and her triumphs—the latter accounts confirming that the risks once posed by social diversity had been erased by racial segregation. Coal soot, not the presence of African Americans, threatened Phoebe Snow's "whiteness."

Yet gender difference helped sustain the belief that railroad cars and other semipublic commercial spaces were still "public" in the midcentury sense of the word: first by continuing to highlight that white women were somehow at risk; then by emphasizing that women were often unruly and rude public actors, selfish and unable to navigate commercial life effectively; and finally by emphasizing the exceptional nature of those women able to meet the demands of public life successfully. Even as the public life of rail travel became more domesticated, it remained a manly domain in contrast to the private sphere—regendered rather than ungendered by women's presence. Understanding this transformation and the place of women as actors and symbols within it explains how women entered into public but did not move about as men did.

EPILOGUE

Since beginning this work, I have been struck by the number of people who still tell railroad stories. Many of their tales echo those told at the end of nineteenth century—taking the train to visit a distant relative, wondering at the vastness of the American West, encountering a world of strangers and unfamiliar types, traveling in surroundings seldom encountered at home. People who do not have personal stories to share often ask whether I have seen a particular film in which the train figures prominently as a site of anonymity (*The Lady Vanishes*), criminal intrigue (*Strangers on a Train*), surrogate family (*Some Like It Hot*), romance (*The Harvey Girls*), or consumer frenzy (*The Music Man*). (For the record, yes, I have.) Friends and family send newspaper clippings hinting at the continuing relevance of my study. Articles about the reintroduction of "women only" cars on East Japan Railways, the "subway trance" that prevents New Yorkers from getting to know one another, and even the "transcontinental railroad as the Internet of 1869" all point to the railroad's staying power as an important public space and cultural symbol.[1]

The appearance of continuity, however, can be deceiving. The modern impulse to tell railroad stories is infused with nostalgia. The railroad is no longer the essential link in the nation's personal transportation network, having been surpassed in importance by automobiles and airplanes. Most Americans who now ride the train do so as part of a daily commute, with long-distance train travel the choice mainly of railroad aficionados and nervous fliers. Those travelers who opt for "the romance of the rails" often board with imaginings of what used to be. They celebrate the trains for their ability to bring strangers together, to reveal the Main Streets of small towns and the back lots of cities. Railroad journeys no longer stand for progress, but for what progress has erased for many passengers—exposure to social diversity and the seamier aspects of American life.[2] The train is seldom praised for its ability to simulate the experiences of home, but for its evocation of a public life reminiscent of the mid-nineteenth-century ideal. Describing a train trip from New York to Chicago for the *Wall Street Journal*, Terry Teachout writes, "If you want a sweet taste of what America was like in a slower, quieter age, book a bedroom on the Lake Shore Limited. You can always sleep at home." [3]

Ironically, in the minds of many Americans today, the railroad stands for a version of public life that it helped domesticate over a hundred years ago. Yet public domesticity still shapes travelers' expectations, and assumptions about gender inform this ideal. Mothers load children into minivan "homes" fully loaded with reading lights, cup holders, reclining seats, and even DVD players—a modern family room on wheels. Airlines entice businessmen to fly first-class with promises of eager attendants, seats that turn into beds, and the homey touch of fresh-baked cookies. [4] Even aboard the railroad, men and women seek some of the comforts of home: although the sparsely decorated "roomettes" on Amtrak's trains are a far cry from the domestic splendor of a Pullman sleeper, the company's Acela train offers passengers a "quiet car" where they can escape the intrusion of cell phones, laptop computers, CD and digital music players, as well as the conversation of other passengers. The modern conveniences of home and office have entered public life to so great a degree that they have become public nuisances in their own right.

Indeed, laments about rapidly declining manners also reveal the current state of public domesticity. [5] New terms like "road rage" and "air rage" have entered the American lexicon to describe the menacing behavior of the rudest travelers. Drivers note with irritation that road etiquette varies from one part of the country to another: "While it may be easy to discern . . . rude behavior in an airport or on a plane," the *New York Times* warns motorists that "speed limits along with a lot of unwritten traffic laws, vary not by state but by driver." [6] Air travel is no Utopia of the well-mannered; passengers complain about a new array of social types: "seatback kickers," "oblivious cell phone talkers," and "overhead bin stuffers." One passenger, observing a "reckless seat recliner," pondered "the duties and respectful rights of passengers" to one another. [7] Others complain about "supercilious flying waitresses or hostile counter clerks . . . [and] the hostage-kidnapper relationship that begins once that airplane door is closed." [8] One flight attendant, in turn, recalled a more genteel age of air travel when "men would not think of boarding a flight unless they were wearing a coat and tie." Another noted that passengers have no respect for the skills she brings to their care: "They don't know I have been trained to defibrillate, do C.P.R., apply first aid, even deliver a baby."[9]

These contemporary travel narratives, so similar to their nineteenth-century antecedents, reveal our expectations for public life. In the words of one modern-day traveler, "We want what we were promised—ease and speed and gentility, exoticism and elegance."[10] Twenty-first-century travel stories about bad manners, annoying social types, legal rights, the despotic power of service workers, and consumers' unrealistic expectations confirm that the boundary between the public and private realms continues to be drawn, crossed, and redrawn in the small spaces of travel. They tell us that we cannot be fully "at home" in public—that despite the blurring of the line between private and public life, no amenities, no set of rules can prevent us from bumping up against one another. In the end, the ongoing romance of railroad stories, with their nostalgic (albeit, historically inaccurate) celebration of a lively and messy public life, suggest that many Americans long for precisely this type of social contact. I, for one, take some comfort in this.

NOTES

Abbreviations

The following abbreviations are used throughout the notes.

AC   Archives Center, National Museum of American History, Smithsonian Institution, Washington, D.C.

BL   Beinecke Rare Book and Manuscript Library, Yale University, New Haven, Conn.

HML   Hagley Museum and Library, Wilmington, Del.

NL   Newberry Library, Chicago, Ill.

NMAH National Museum of American History, Smithsonian Institution, Washington, D.C.

Introduction

1. On women and the ideological importance of their presumed exclusion from market relations see Stanley, "Home Life," 74-96.

Throughout this study I have tried to use the language of "respectability" in addition to that of class. Although the separate spheres ideal and other Victorian values were most closely associated with the new urban middle class, they circulated beyond this group. On this point, see Howe, *Victorian America*, 10. According to Howe, "Working-class people were brought within the ambience of Victorian culture. A culture can reach out beyond the social group with which it originates and become a vital element in the consciousness of others. . . . American Victorianism, then, had a life beyond the middle class, just as it had a life beyond British-Americans and Protestants."

2. By public culture, I mean not simply how people conduct themselves beyond the domestic sphere, but the ways in which they imagine and order the world crowded with anonymous social actors of different sexes, classes, and races. Public culture is, by definition, contested, existing in the play of different groups and their competing values and expectations. It is a multi-sided conversation about power and access, influence and opportunity. On public culture see Bender, "Metropolitan Life." For another notion of public culture see Elsa Barkley Brown, "Polyrhythm and Improvization." She writes, "History is everybody talking at once, multiple rhythms being

played simultaneously. . . . In fact, at any given moment millions of people are talking all at once" (85).

3. I refer here to the work of economic historians like Rostow and Fogel.

4. Studies considering the railroad's place in American cultural life often fail to question the gendered assumptions that inform the history of the railroad. See Stilgoe, *Metropolitan Corridor*, ix. On "the enduring force of the identification between technology and manliness," see Wajcman, *Feminism Confronts Technology*, 137.

5. "The Pacific Railroad," 175. The article concludes with a strong indictment of women who seek to move beyond their true sphere and claim suffrage: "It is worthwhile for the women who are clamoring for the suffrage to reflect whether the right to vote does not imply a capacity for the hard work of subduing the world, mental and physical, to which so far only men have been found competent" (175).

6. This study seeks throughout to consider narration as an important historical process and as a powerful agent of cultural change. On discourse and its ability to shape experience see Joan Scott, "The Evidence of Experience." She seeks a reading of the past that "would not assume a direct correspondence between words and things, nor confine itself to single meanings, nor aim for the resolution of contradictions. . . . Rather it would grant to 'the literary' an integral, even irreducible, status of its own." Such an approach would "open new possibilities for analyzing discursive productions of social and political reality as complex, contradictory processes" (793-94).

For a study that weaves together both the experience of rapid and sweeping historical changes and the narrative efforts that gave meaning to them, see Walkowitz, *City of Dreadful Delight*. Walkowitz's consideration of both experience and social construction has shaped my thinking about the railroad's significance in nineteenth-century America and how it sheds light on the transformation of Victorian gender roles.

7. Beebe, *Mr. Pullman's Elegant Palace Car*. See pages 27, 29, 31, 118, and 175 for a sample of images portraying women aboard.

8. Lynne Kirby makes a similar observation concerning the centrality of gender in considerations of the railroad. See her study, "The Railroad and the Cinema."

9. These values define "Victorianism" and "Victorian culture" as they are used throughout this study. On the value of studying Victorianism as a unit of American cultural history see Howe, *Victorian America*, 3-28.

10. Railroad historians have long claimed their subject's centrality to

any understanding of the past. See Albro Martin, *Railroads Triumphant*, 399. He claims, "Indeed, almost everything that has been written about the rise of material civilization in America during the past century and a half has been, in one way or another, about railroads."

11. Foucault, "Of Other Spaces," 23-24. Foucault considers the railroad briefly as part of his larger discussion of "heterotopias," or "counter-sites, a kind of effectively enacted utopia in which the real sites, all the other real sites that can be found within the culture, are simultaneously represented, contested, and inverted. Places of this kind are outside of all places, even though it may be possible to indicate their location in reality" (24).

12. On the cultural ambiguity of the railroad see Marx, *The Machine in the Garden*, 191-92. According to Marx, the railroad was "an instrument of power, speed, noise, fire, iron, smoke—at once a testament to the will of man rising over natural obstacles, and yet confined to a predetermined path. It suggest[ed] a new sort of fate." For a nineteenth-century observer "to see a powerful, efficient machine in the landscape [was] to know the superiority of the present to the past." But Marx also understood that the railroad was more than a transparent representation of the Victorian drive for progress or technology's triumph over the landscape. The railroad raised difficult questions about the ambiguity of change.

13. Many scholars have explained the emergence of new identities by pointing to the transformative power of experience. Most famously, E. P. Thompson's *The Making of the English Working Class* locates working-class identity in a series of shared experiences. But some scholars now reject experience itself as a stable category and instead argue that it too is socially constructed. For this argument see Joan Scott, "The Evidence of Experience." I believe the railroads bridge these differing evaluations of experience: because the nineteenth-century railroad was repeatedly depicted as a transformative space, the discussions surrounding it offer insight into how personal and historical change were themselves negotiated or socially constructed.

14. Certeau, *The Practice of Everyday Life*, 112.

15. Berman, *All That Is Solid Melts into Air*, 5.

On the railroad as an embodiment of modernity see Schivelbusch, *The Railway Journey*. In the foreword to that work, Alan Trachtenberg notes that "in their railway journeys nineteenth-century people encountered the new conditions of their lives; they encountered themselves as moderns, as dwellers within new structures of regulation and need" (xv).

16. On railroads as an important site in the emergence of Jim Crow see

Woodward, *Strange Career of Jim Crow*; Grace Hale, *Making Whiteness*; Ayers, *Promise of the New South*; McMillen, *Dark Journey*. According to Ayers, "The railroads were even more 'modern' than the cities themselves" (145). On segregation as a product of modernization see Cell, *Highest Stage of White Supremacy*.

17. Quoted in Grace Hale, *Making Whiteness*, 50.

The name "Jim Crow" applied to railroad cars for African Americans originated not in the South but in Massachusetts in 1841. See Ruchames, "Jim Crow Railroads in Massachusetts," 62.

18. See William Taylor, "The Evolution of Public Space," 290. He claims that at the end of the nineteenth century new commercial spaces "expanded the perception of what was public to include their own arenas, which were, strictly speaking, privately owned and administered, but which served and addressed the public in dramatic ways. Those who promoted the building of such monumental new institutions and services were referred to as 'public-spirited,' and they modestly held themselves to be responsive to public opinion."

Mary Ryan's work also suggests the flexible meaning of "the public," noting that during the nineteenth century women followed a code of "public conduct," took up "public space," were subjects of "public policy," and participated in "public discourse." Thus a city street, a department store, the state, and its authority are all categorized as public. Ryan, *Women in Public*, 3.

19. For a sophisticated and thorough historiography of women's historians' use of separate spheres see Kerber, "Separate Spheres."

20. On multiple "publics" see Fraser, "Rethinking the Public Sphere." According to Fraser, "The view that women were excluded from the public sphere turns out to be ideological; it rests on a class- and gender-biased notion of publicity, one which accepts at face value the bourgeois public's claim to be *the* public. . . . On the contrary, virtually contemporaneous with the bourgeois public there arose a host of competing counterpublics, including nationalist publics, popular peasant publics, elite women's publics, and working-class publics" (116).

For examples of studies considering separate female publics see Stansell, *City of Women*; Abelson, *When Ladies Go A-Thieving*; Benson, *Counter Cultures*; Leach, "Transformations in a Culture of Consumption"; and Brandimarte, "'To Make the World More Homelike.'"

21. See, for example, Baker, "The Domestication of Politics." Also Ryan, *Women in Public*; and Faust, *Mothers of Invention*.

22. Kwolek-Folland, *Engendering Business* is one example of this last approach.

23. See "No More Separate Spheres!"

24. The works on the domestication of public life chronicle numerous efforts between the 1830s and the 1920s to make women feel "at home" (and therefore respectable) in public settings. Gender-segregated spaces for ladies emerging at this time included separate ladies' entrances in theaters, special park lawns reserved for ladies and children, and even a ladies' pond for skating in New York City's Central Park. As respectable women gained access to more numerous and varied spaces beyond the home (hotels, stores, colleges, various workplaces, and even entire cities), domesticated public facilities proliferated to serve them.

25. William Leach has argued that the rise of commercial public spaces in the latter half of the nineteenth century marked the emergence of "a public life in cultural tension in which the lives of women and men inter- fused and competed for influence." Leach, "Transformations in a Culture of Consumption," 336.

26. I want to make it clear that both passengers and railroad pro- fessionals engaged in this process of cultural construction. The domes- tic train cannot be understood simply as an attempt at social control by railroad officials nor as a straightforward reflection of consumers' de- mands. The domesticated train is instead best understood as a reflection of both shared and competing values—the outcome of contested responses to broad social and technological changes. The cars never resembled homes exactly, nor did the life of the cars mirror precisely domestic life, but rail- road car companies encouraged the idea that the resemblance was strong, and passengers acted as though they believed them.

27. For considerations of these domesticated commercial sites see Brucken, "In the Public Eye"; Abelson, *When Ladies Go A-Thieving*; Leach, "Transformations in a Culture of Consumption"; Grier, *Culture and Com- fort*; Levine *Highbrow/Lowbrow*; Rosenzweig and Blackmar, *The Park and the People*; Ryan, *Women in Public*.

Chapter One

1. Charles Adams, *The Railroads*, 3-6.

On Adams's career, especially his tenure on the Massachusetts Board of Railroad Commissioners, see McCraw, *Prophets of Regulation*, 1-56. Adams spent a considerable portion of his life contemplating the administration of railroads. In addition to his ten years of service on the Massachusetts

Board, he spent three years with the Eastern Trunk Line Association and served as president of the Union Pacific Railroad from 1884 to 1890.

2. This debate is captured quite nicely in Ward, *Railroads and the Character of America*.

3. Charles Adams, *The Railroads*, 3-6.

4. For the most important and inclusive secondary account of the inventions and refinements that characterized the American railroad car see John White, *The American Railroad Passenger Car*.

5. At times, these various innovations were in use simultaneously on different lines or in different regions of the country, amplifying the sense of endless variation and rendering any simplistic chronology of car design elusive.

6. For tables of track mileage see Hughes, *American Economic History*, 165 and 256.

7. Holbrook, *The Story of American Railroads*, 36. On the evolution of railway timetables, consult Lomazzi, *Railroad Timetables*. On the railroads and the institution of standard time see O'Malley, *Keeping Watch*, 55-98.

8. Whitman, "To a Locomotive in Winter," in *Leaves of Grass*, 581-82.

9. See Whitman's "Passage to India," in *Leaves of Grass*, 509-12. Here he depicts the railroad's power to reveal the North American continent in all its variations of topography and climate. The railroad, according to the poet, tied the Atlantic to the Pacific and thus fulfilled Columbus's dream of a passage to India.

On the increase in passenger traffic see Albro Martin, *Railroads Triumphant*, 123. Between 1890 and 1920, passenger traffic grew faster than freight traffic. By 1910 passenger volume reached 972 million, and total passenger-miles stood at 3.2 million. According to the *Nation*, the 1890 Census Bulletin reported that the number of railroad passengers carried on New England lines nearly doubled between 1880 and 1889. During the same period, the number of passengers on the Chicago & Northwestern Railway increased 190 percent. Most of this increase was attributed to an increase in suburban travel. See "A Decade of Railway Travel," 374. Although passenger travel did not grow at the same impressive rates west of Chicago, the railroads nonetheless created unprecedented opportunities for travel in this region. In the absence of suburban commuting, western passenger travel was dominated by the tourist industry. On railroad companies' attempts to lure tourists to the West see McLuhan, *Dream Tracks*. For more on the evolution of the railroad and the rise of tourism see Aron, *Working at Play*; Sears, *Sacred Places*; and Cocks, *Doing the Town*.

10. Chandler, *Visible Hand*, 79-121.

11. Rail gauge was standardized in 1886. See Woodward, *Origins of the New South*, 123-24, on the day the southern railroads converted to standard gauge.

Railroads adopted standard time on 18 November 1883, when they divided the country into four time zones. Although "railroad time" dictated travel, standard time did not receive federal sanction until Congress passed the Standard Time Act in March 1918. See O'Malley, *Keeping Watch*, 55-98.

12. Richard Sennett has identified anonymity and social confusion as central to his definition of the city. According to Sennett, the simplest definition of a city is "a human settlement in which strangers are likely to meet . . . [and] in which such problems of enactment are most likely to rise as a matter of routine." Sennett, *The Fall of Public Man*, 39.

Other works exploring the relationship between urban life and anonymity include Halttunen, *Confidence Men and Painted Women*; Kasson, *Rudeness and Civility*; Brand, *The Spectator and the City*; and Wolff, "The Invisible Flaneuse."

13. According to Edward Ayers in his study of the postbellum South, "the railroad cars and waiting rooms were marked by the same anonymity that was coming to characterize the towns and cities . . . , the same diversity within confined spaces, the same display of class by clothing and demeanor, the same crowding of men and women, the same crowding of different races." Ayers, *Promise of the New South*, 145.

Many scholars have focused on the railroad as an urban institution. See, for example, Condit, *The Railroad and the City*. According to Condit, "The constantly expanding station not only shaped the urban fabric and the pattern of land use but became a special kind of urbanistic institution, a microcity mirroring the urban life around it. The train became a mobile equivalent, a special kind of microcity moving over the ground" (x). For a different approach see Richards and MacKenzie, *The Railway Station*, on the railroad station as a cultural and social "city gate." On the railroads as a cultural agent carrying urban values and experiences, "invading the land, transforming the sensory texture of rural life," see Marx, *The Machine in the Garden*, 32. For an interpretation that ties the railroad to the urban built environment and cultural life see Stilgoe, *Metropolitan Corridor*.

14. In important ways the steamboat captured the same urban qualities of railroad travel—a point that is aptly made in Herman Melville's *The Confidence Man*. Much as Melville's steamboat carried social uncertainty

and identity confusion up and down the Mississippi River, the railroad transported them across the country. But the steamboats never cohered as a transportation network to the same degree that the railroads did; nor do they afford the same consideration of business rationalization.

15. "A Queer Mixture," 375.

16. Chapple, "Types of Railroad Travellers," 550.

17. Outis, *Lake Superior*, 17.

18. Pritchett, "Politics of a Pullman Car," 195.

19. Cited in Nye, *American Technological Sublime*, 71.

20. The period between 1890 and 1910 has been referred to as the "Golden Age of railroad literature." Donovan, *The Railroad in Literature*, 5.

21. Chicago, Rock Island & Pacific Railway, General Ticket and Passenger Department, *Santa Claus' Christmas Train*, (Chicago: Porter & Babcock, 1880) in Warshaw Collection, "Railroads," box 80, AC.

22. On the transformation of Christmas see Nissenbaum, *The Battle for Christmas*. On the celebration of Christmas in consumer emporia at the turn of the century see also Abelson, *When Ladies Go A-Thieving*, 42-43; and Leach, *Land of Desire*, 88-90.

23. Howells, *Their Wedding Journey*, 90-91.
Niagara Falls' popularity as a honeymoon destination dates back to the late 1830s. For more on Niagara as a honeymoon spot and tourist destination see Sears, *Sacred Places*, 12. He identifies "the golden age of the Niagara honeymoon" as beginning after the Civil War and continuing into the 1930s.

24. Chapple, "Types of Railroad Travellers," 545.

25. "American Railway Traveling," 200. The article contends that the differences between American and European travel were so great that the foreign traveler "has to learn what travelling means in America" (196).

26. Schivelbusch, *The Railway Journey*, 89-112.

27. See, for example, "English and American Railroads Compared"; "English and American Railways"; "English and American Railroads"; "Railroad Travel in England and America."

28. The celebration of American scenery was a favorite theme of many railroad companies. The emphasis of scenery visible through the train window transformed the train journey (especially a long-distance journey) into a unique form of entertainment rather than a tedious ordeal. Such depictions can be found in most guidebooks of the period.

29. On the movement of goods between hinterland and city see Cronon, *Nature's Metropolis*, 97.

30. This term is from Wiebe, *The Search for Order*, 44. See also Howe, *Victorian America*, 11. Howe writes, "Society became ever more absorbed into the network of railways, print, and telegraphy which brought cosmopolitan Victorian culture to the countryside, permeating it with the values of modernization."

31. Lynde, *A Romance in Transit*, 43. Lynde expresses some ambivalence about this civilizing process. The novel's hero, Fred Brockway, refers to it as "railway diathesis" and mourns the exchange of originality for sophistication that follows the path of the railroad's tracks. Nonetheless, Brockway is a railway man and embodies the excitement and power that drew many men to the rails in both fiction and life.

32. Bain, *Tobacco in Song and Story*, 103.

33. Dreiser, *Sister Carrie*, 1.

34. Donan, *The Heart of the Continent*, 3.

35. For a railroad narrative that self-consciously celebrated the meeting of East and West see the *Transcontinental*. The newspaper was published from 23 May to 4 July 1870 on the Pullman Hotel Express as it traveled between Boston and San Francisco and chronicled incidents of the transcontinental excursion of the Boston Board of Trade. The first issue of the newspaper announced that the party carried aboard "a bottle of sea water [from the Massachusetts Bay] . . . to be taken to San Francisco and there emptied into the Pacific Ocean." In case the symbolism of this act eluded the *Transcontinental*'s readers, the article explained that "this train will be the first through entire train which has ever crossed from Atlantic to Pacific direct, every car going through with only through passengers, [and] the incident is not without historic interest."

36. Cunniff, "The Comforts of Railroad Travel," 3580.

37. The narrative of American civilization and progress encapsulated by the nineteenth-century railroad reflects contemporary assumptions by white Americans about the unity of their interests and their racial superiority to native peoples. For a sophisticated discussion of the varied meanings and usages of "civilization" see Bederman, *Manliness and Civilization*, 25–31.

38. Nye, *American Technological Sublime*, 32.

39. According to art historian Susan Danly, after the Civil War, "Travelers could now experience the sublime landscape they had previously known only in art. . . . To capitalize on that notion, the railroads advertised the train window as the frame of nature." See Danly and Marx, *The Railroad in American Art*, 31. See also Marx, *The Machine in the Garden*, 237–39.

40. Babcock, *Our American Resorts*, vii. Many guidebooks from this period point to the necessity of escape from everyday responsibilities and demands. This was especially true for "invalids," who comprised a special category of nineteenth-century tourists. See, for example, Union Pacific Railway Passenger Department, *Description of the Western Resorts*. See also Sanborn, "In the Pullman Car," 468-70. Sanborn describes the strain that a railroad journey put on one's nerves ("The noise and shock on the sleeper are constant.") and praises the wonder of the landscape made accessible by rail travel ("As for him who would see summer and winter, cosmos and chaos, side by side, in one quarter-section, let him come from California in June by the Central Pacific."). Such juxtaposition and contradiction were common in writings about American rail travel. For example, in 1890 the Great Northern Railway Line published a sermon by Rev. Dr. Bridgeman under the title "Vacation Gospel." The pamphlet preached, "One cannot afford to burn the candle of life at both ends and stick a red hot poker in the middle." Vacation, and presumably rail travel, offered a necessary break from the demands of modern anxieties. Warshaw Collection, "Railroads," box 88, AC.

41. Dr. George Beard, the most famous proponent of the viewpoint, argued that Americans were nervous because of the advanced nature of their civilization and technology. Beard, *American Nervousness*, vi-viii.

42. Aron, *Working at Play*, 45; and John White, *The American Railroad Passenger Car*, 204. A contemporary observer noted that "there was comparatively little travel before the War, not only because there were few railroads, but because the nation had not yet been put into motion. Army life left a generation of restless men at home, and the Centennial Fair in Philadelphia, in 1876, finally gave an impetus to going about which has never since died out." See Iddings, "The Art of Travel," 351.

43. Andrews, *A Few Tales of the Rail*, 10-11.

44. Chapple, "Types of Railroad Travellers," 543-44. See also *The Railway Anecdote Book*, 47.

45. Such scenes were common in both social commentary and fiction. See Johnson, *Autobiography of an Ex-Coloured Man*, 157. The protagonist recalls:

> During the trip from Nashville to Atlanta I went into the smoking-compartment of the car to smoke a cigar. . . . From the general conversation I learned that a fat Jewish-looking man was a cigar-manufacturer, and was experimenting in growing Havana tobacco in Florida; that a slender bespectacled young man was from Ohio and a professor in some

State institution in Alabama; that a white-moustached, well-dressed man was an old Union soldier who had fought through the Civil War; and that a tall, raw-boned, red-faced man, who seemed bent on leaving nobody in ignorance of the fact that he was from Texas, was a cotton planter (157).

46. Iddings, "The Art of Travel," 352.

47. Burdette, "Rules for Travelers," 584.

48. "American Railway Traveling," 205.

49. References to card players appear in popular stories and advice manuals as well as in official rule books for railroad employees. Passengers were repeatedly warned, "Beware of playing cards with strangers who wish to start a friendly game of euchre which is subsequently changed to draw-poker or some other seductive and costly amusement." Knox, *How to Travel*, 22. See also *The Middle States*, 1. Examples of railroad companies' concerns about gamblers aboard can be found in Droege, *Passenger Terminals and Trains*, 189.

For secondary analyses of the gambler's significance as a social type in nineteenth-century American culture see Halttunen, *Confidence Men and Painted Women*, 16-20; and Fabian, *Card Sharps*.

50. Gardiner, *A Drummer's Parlor Stories*, 45-47.

51. *The Railway Anecdote Book*, 229.

52. The promise or danger of a kiss while passing through a dark tunnel was a common motif in jokes, anecdotes, and songs. See, for example, Stephe Smith, *Romance and Humor of the Rail*, 104, 106-7. The story also finds its way into Rogers, *Wrongs and Rights of a Traveller*, 45. A reference to a film version of this story involving an African American woman and a white man appears in Nasaw, *Going Out*, 167.

The kiss in the tunnel was soon instituted in amusement park attractions, especially "the tunnel of love." On such popular amusements see Kasson, *Amusing the Million*, 73-76. Also Peiss, *Cheap Amusements*, 133.

53. *The Railway Anecdote Book*, 229-31.

54. "The Charming Young Widow I Met in the Train," DeVincent Collection, "Railroad," box 24, folder A, AC.

On trusting the wrong person see also "Nomadic Flirtation"; and Allan Pinkerton, *Thirty Years a Detective*, 153-58.

55. Lofgren, *The Plessy Case*, 117. For a contemporary account of the railroad's dual nature as a public and private institution that addresses the law of common carriers see "Railroads and the People," 259, 264-65. The article quotes Chief Justice Waite of the Supreme Court ruling in the

Granger cases in March 1877 and calls for the "creation of an intelligent public opinion" to place limits "upon the growth and power of corporate life."

56. During the 1870s and 1880s, the Granger movement mobilized this sentiment among midwestern farmers and demanded state legislation to regulate the railroads—to temper the drive for private profits with a concern for the public interest. In 1887, Congress tentatively sanctioned this view by passing the Interstate Commerce Act, calling for regulation of railroad rates and forbidding discriminatory practices.

See Middleton, *Railways and Public Opinion*, for an overview (albeit biased toward the railroad interests) of changing attitudes toward the railroad.

57. Droege, *Passenger Terminals and Trains*, 188–89 on the importance of the private policing carried out by railroad companies.

58. Knox, *How to Travel*, 234. According to Knox, "A good illustration is that of a railway in Mississippi where some rowdies beat a passenger severely, and the latter sued the company for negligence. It was shown that the conductor simply asked the rowdies not to get him into trouble, and then left the car; the court held that the company was liable for his failure to use due diligence in protecting the passenger, and gave the latter $6,000 damages, but if the conductor had stopped the train, and called the brakemen and passengers to assist him, the damages would not have been allowed, even if the conductor had failed in his effort at protection."

59. Indianapolis and Madison Rail Road, *Instructions for Running Trains on the Indianapolis and Madison Rail Road*, 21. See also Licht, *Working for the Railroad*, 80–84.

60. A variety of cultural scholars have long identified the significance of self-control or "self-mastery" to American Victorianism and have noted that during the latter half of the century changing social and economic conditions challenged this ideal. Many economic and railroad historians specifically credit the railroad with initiating the socioeconomic changes that challenged Victorian notions of self-mastery and point to the development of a rapid all-weather transportation system as the necessary precondition for modern mass production and distribution of goods. It is important to recognize that rail passengers were not simply overwhelmed by these developments, but used their cultural values to confront change and produce a complex renegotiation of Victorianism.

On Victorian self-control see Bederman, *Manliness and Civilization*, 12–13. On the tension between self-control and the emergence of consumer culture see Abelson, *When Ladies Go A-Thieving*, 31–32. On the railroads and self-mastery see Schivelbusch, *The Railway Journey*, 73; and Sarah Gordon, "A Society of Travelers." Gordon notes that "passengers paid much of the price for the growth of corporate authority" (266).

61. These expressions of rail company control did often add to a passenger's experience of the cars as socially unfamiliar and challenging. On the challenges passengers faced when negotiating the complex of corporate rules see Sarah Gordon, "A Society of Travelers." Indeed, there was a sense that railway travelers needed to master a huge body of rules and details in order to travel successfully. These rules are the object of ridicule in Burdette, "Rules for Travelers."

62. Thomas, *Anecdotes and Incidents of Travel*, 48–49.

63. The language of "ownership" appears in Caldwell, "Traveling Reduced to a Science," 79–80. The mechanisms for ownership grew more elaborate in the 1870s and beyond with the proliferation of specialty cars equipped with berths, sections, and staterooms. For a useful overview of personally conducted tours see Cocks, *Doing the Town*, 113–18.

64. Cunniff, "The Comforts of Railroad Travel," 3580.

65. George, *Forty Years on the Rail*, 168.

66. The Pullman Palace Car Company especially embraced standard service. See, for example, Husband, *The Story of the Pullman Car*, 157–58. According to Husband: "Pullman service has revolutionized the method of travel. Night has been abolished, the sense of distance has been annihilated; fatigue has been reduced to a minimum. In the oldest districts of the east, along the valleys of western rivers, on the wide-spread plains, among the remote peaks of the Rockies, in the deserts of the great southwest, the Pullman car, served by the same trained employees, furnishes the same comforts, and gives the same night's repose."

67. Sanborn, "In the Pullman Car," 467. Sanborn's analysis cannot be fully understood without considering that many service employees were African American men. In his study of Pullman porters, Jack Santino notes that the Pullman porters' struggled to achieve a balance between service and control and that their efforts were complicated by racist attitudes of white passengers. Santino, *Miles of Smiles*, 12.

68. Howells, *Their Wedding Journey*, 87.

69. Pritchett, "Politics of a Pullman Car," 195.

70. George, *Forty Years on the Rail*, 211. See also Benjamin Taylor, *The World on Wheels and Other Sketches*, 67.

71. Chapple, "Types of Railroad Travellers," 543.

72. See, for example, Benjamin Taylor, *The World on Wheels*, 51–59.

In an effort to educate the traveling public, popular travel accounts and fiction frequently opened with a quick catalog of familiar railway types. Such a scene appears in Howells, *Their Wedding Journey*, 11–15. For a similar catalog see Lynde, *A Romance in Transit*, 1–2. Among those listed are a sun-browned ranchman, a pair of schoolteachers, a Mormon elder, a Denver banker, and "the inevitably newly married ones." It is worthy of note that many of these types were associated with specific geographic regions.

73. Chicago, Rock Island and Pacific Railway, *Nellie in Dreamland*.

74. Chapple, "Types of Railroad Travellers," 549.

See Stephe Smith, *Romance and Humor of the Rail*, 290, for the account of an elderly woman who dies while traveling in the cars with her daughter and son-in-law. For stories that consider travel during mourning and traveling to a funeral see Smith, 200–210 and 292. Jack Santino makes a similar observation in his study of Pullman porters. He notes, "Many of life's most private, personal moments, moments of birth and death, occurred in the presence of the Pullman porter." See Santino, *Miles of Smiles*, 82.

The collapse of private and public in rail travel was also invoked to vilify labor militancy. In 1894, the *Railway Age and Northwestern Railroader* printed an article declaring the American Railway Union's support of the striking Pullman workers "an unprovoked war on the public." This war was especially vicious because it attacked travelers beset by personal sorrows — "women and children, invalids and those hurrying to the bedsides of the sick and the graves of the dead." See the *Railway Age and Northwestern Railroader*, 29 June 1894, 361.

75. Howells, *Their Wedding Journey*, 15–16.

76. "The Baby on the Train" (1895) and "In the Baggage Coach Ahead" (1896) in the DeVincent Collection, "Railroads," box 24, folder C; and box 25, folder G, AC.

For other railroad stories focusing on grief during travel see George, *Forty Years on the Rail*, 236–39.

77. Stephe Smith, *Romance and Humor of the Rail*, 320–21. For another depiction of such intimacy see G. F. Thomas, *Anecdotes and Incidents of Travel*, 46.

78. *The Railway Anecdote Book*, 83. For others stories on the undermining of marital intimacy aboard see G. F. Thomas, *Anecdotes and Incidents of Travel*, 27–33, 48–49.

79. Benjamin Taylor, *The World on Wheels*, 51–53. Taylor described many

passengers with an inability to assume appropriate public conduct or posture. For example, Taylor decried "the man whose salivary glands are the most active part of him" and "the man who puts a pair of feet . . . upon the back of your seat" (53). As the "Hog" threatened property and the "Bouncers" strained propriety, the railway type designated "Might I?" endangered individual privacy. "Might I?," according to Taylor, intruded upon the well-guarded privacy of others. He assaulted fellow passengers with a barrage of questions: "Might I ask how far you are traveling? Might I inquire what business you follow? Might I inquire if you are married? Might I ask your name?" By taking full advantage of the intimacy of rail travel, "Might I?" attempted "to pull the cork from the bottle of your personal identity"—an act Taylor dubbed "the meanest kind of pilfering, though the law doesn't mention it" (55–56).

Chapter Two

1. *The Railway Anecdote Book*, 97.
A similar joke asked, "Why does an engineer always call his engine she?" Possible answers included "Because the more you throttle her the faster she goes." Or, "Because she runs the mail"; also, "Because there was so much bustle and bang about her" and, "Because she pulls the smoker." The final answer offered was "Because we couldn't get along without her." See *Railway Age*, 3 December 1885, 764.

2. According to the Costume Division at the Smithsonian Institution's National Museum of American History, women were not wearing long trains at the time this cartoon was published. The exaggerated lady's train may then be an attempt to emphasize women's dissimilarity with the train or to call greater attention to the pun. For the cartoon see *Harper's Bazar*, 12 December 1868, 944.

3. Indeed, railroad companies and passengers often displayed discomfort with the language of class and used appeals to respectability as a means of sorting passengers. The language of respectability, along with the democratic vocabulary of the American open coach, makes it difficult to trace the emergence of classed cars. Although first- and second-class cars are recorded throughout the nineteenth century, these cars were also designated as ladies' cars and smokers, respectively.

4. The repeated appearance of specific types of events in many different personal accounts and popular sources suggests that women travelers were having similar experiences in the cars or that they were developing conventions for depicting themselves in public. Either as lived experience or

cultural convention, taken together these individual stories offer insight into the possibilities and problems that arose when "respectable" women moved about in public. All reveal the complex negotiation of private and public values required of women in commercialized public spaces.

5. Many studies assert that women who traveled during the nineteenth century laid claim, in the very act of traveling, to uncharted social and cultural ground and bravely rejected the ideology of separate spheres. Such stories of heroic women throwing off the shackles of an oppressive domesticity uphold interpretations of nineteenth-century private and public spheres as rigidly distinct realms of personal action. In these accounts women appear as either protected yet suffocated when at home or endangered but free when on the move. Usually British or European and undertaking their journeys later in life, the women in these narratives traveled to "exotic" locales where they found adventure and romance. For this interpretation of women travelers see Frederick and McLeod, *Women and the Journey*; Robinson, *Unsuitable for Ladies* and *Wayward Women*; Birkett, *Spinsters Abroad*; Tinling, *Women into the Unknown*; and Hamalian, *Ladies on the Loose*.

6. Napheys, *The Physical Life of Women*, 88–89.

7. Hill, *Hill's Manual*, 167.

8. Stephe Smith, *Romance and Humor of the Rail*, 163–65. On the visibility of honeymooners among passengers see Chapple, "Types of Railroad Travellers," 545; and also Benjamin Taylor, *The World on Wheels*, 56–57. On newlyweds trying to evade detection see Gardiner, *A Drummer's Parlor Stories*, 27. For a fictional account of a wedding journey see Howells, *Their Wedding Journey*.

In an attempt to provide newlyweds with increased privacy, the Pullman Palace Car Company experimented with special honeymoon accommodations and stateroom suites for couples. Ultimately these specialized bridal accommodations called increased attention to couples seeking to avoid the public's notice and were discontinued. See Beebe, *Mr. Pullman's Elegant Palace Car*, 296.

9. An account of the Boston Board of Trade excursion can be found in the *Transcontinental*. Volume 1, numbers 1–12 were published daily on board the train as it traveled between Boston and San Francisco. The newspaper seems to have terminated with the journey.

10. John Thomas, *Fifty Years on the Rail*, 58–59. For a similar account of women traveling as part of a Pennsylvania Railroad Conductors Excur-

sion see M. M. Shaw, *Nine Thousand Miles*. For a very different example of a woman traveling with her husband see Miriam Florence Leslie, *California*.

11. Margaretta E. Du Pont Coleman to Margaretta E. Lammot Du Pont, 1 March 1885, Margaretta E. Du Pont Coleman Collection, HML.

For a less privileged take on the train as maintainer of family relationships see Moss "A Ride to Stroudsbourg."

12. Margaretta E. Du Pont Coleman to Margaretta E. Lammot Du Pont, 28 October 1880, Margaretta E. Du Pont Coleman Collection, HML.

Other travelers maintained their connection to their family while traveling by keeping journals that they would then share with loved ones at journey's end; see Socolofsky, "Private Journals of Florence Crawford," 15–61, 163–208.

For other accounts of women traveling to visit relatives see the diary of Gabrielle Josephine Crofton, HML. Also Pohanka, *A Summer on the Plains*; and Snell, "Roughing It on Her Kansas Claim."

13. Margaretta E. Du Pont Coleman to Bannen Coleman, 13 August 1890, Margaretta E. Du Pont Coleman Collection, HML.

14. Clendenin, Travel Diary, Western Americana Collection, BL. Women also traveled for brief pleasure excursions with female friends. See Ida B. Wells, *Memphis Diary of Ida B. Wells*, 76; and Russell, "Our Trip to Mount Hood."

For accounts of women who traveled to restore their health see Bird, *The Englishwoman in America* (London: John Murray, 1856) and *A Lady's Life*. Also Dall, *My First Holiday*, 3; and Leland, *Traveling Alone*, 1.

15. This example underscores that the domestic sphere was not simply a haven for women but the site of female labor. Brackett, "The Technique of Rest," 49–50.

16. Certainly some women traveled for reasons directly at odds with the ideology of separate spheres. Two notable examples of such female travelers are actresses and suffragists. These women were viewed by many contemporaries as transgressive, and their conduct frequently confirmed the importance of separate spheres for women rather than transformed the middle-class ideology. Such public women were seen as exceptions. For example in 1894, *The Ladies Home Journal* editor Edward Bok wrote: "We may admire the public singer on the concert platform; we are charmed by the actress on the stage; we are impressed by the woman who writes well or talks brilliantly. But after all, the woman who *holds* us, who not only commands but retains our respect, is the woman who is truest in her own

sphere, reigning over her kingdom of home and children with a grace and sweetness, compared to which a public life is the hollowest of mockeries." Quoted in Garvey, *The Adman in the Parlor*, 152.

17. Jones, "American Mothers and Daughters," 800. Jones pursued her interest in women and travel in her book *European Travel for Women*.

18. Joseph Taylor, *A Fast Life*, 116.

19. "Right Up and Down Woman," 173.

20. Jones, "American Mothers and Daughters," 800.

21. Rural people served a similar function in some stories. See Andrews, *A Few Tales of the Rail*, 10-11.

22. "Nomadic Flirtation."

23. Walbourn, *Confessions of a Pullman Conductor*, 7-27.

24. Dreiser, *Sister Carrie*, 5.

25. For positive self-depictions by traveling salesmen see Streeter, *Gems from an Old Drummers Grip*, 9-10. Depictions of salesmen as protectors of women can be found in Gardiner, *A Drummer's Parlor Stories*, 27-33; and Bain, *Tobacco in Song and Story*, 103-104.

26. Leland, *Traveling Alone*, 1.

27. Women were also expected to pack for their husbands, confirming that packing was seen as an extension of their domestic responsibilities. See Wayne, "My Valise and I," 77.

28. One guidebook suggested that women setting out on a long journey fill their baskets with "french bread, pound and sponge cake, crullers, sandwiches, hard-boiled eggs, roast chickens, deviled ham, bacon cut thin and crisped brown, and perfectly dry; canned fruits and meats; take salt, pepper, a tin cup, spoon, etc.; also comb, brush, towel, soap, sponge, soft paper, hand-mirror, and if you can stow away a very small basin, and a quart tin cup, all the better." See Hart, *The Traveler's Own Book*, 11. For other instructions on what to include in one's basket see also Henry Williams, *The Pacific Tourist*, 8.

29. Bird, *A Lady's Life*, 2.

30. Kimball, Diary of a Trip to California, 7-8, Western Americana Collection, BL.

For other sources recommending the use of lunch baskets see Florence Hartley, *The Ladies' Book of Etiquette*, 34, and Dall, *My First Holiday*, 20.

31. On the lunch basket and male dignity see Iddings, "The Art of Travel," 356. See also "The Disappearance of the Lunch Basket" on the declining need for carrying one's own food.

32. Florence Hartley, *The Ladies's Book of Etiquette*, 36.

A section or chapter on railroad travel was a common feature in late-nineteenth etiquette books. For examples of packing instructions and other advice about a lady's conduct during travel see also Eliza Leslie, *The Behavior Book*, 92-100; Ruth, *Decorum*, 136-45. See also Richard Wells, *Manners, Culture and Dress* (Wells's chapter on travel is almost identical to Ruth's).

On the value of a good veil see Cornelia Richards, *At Home and Abroad*, 21. According to Richards, when traveling on a train "a thick veil is indispensable, as you are liable to be much annoyed by dust, or smoke and cinders, also by the stares of rude or vulgar people with whom you are liable anywhere to come into close contact."

33. Benjamin Taylor, *The World on Wheels*, 155-56.

34. Quoted in Menken, *The Railroad Passenger Car*, 143.

35. Dall, *My First Holiday*, 19.

36. Clendenin, Travel Diary, 3, Western Americana Collection, BL. Clendenin confided that she and her companion "regret muchly the presence of several women, as they take up the dressing room so in the morning" (2). See also Adair, *My Diary*, 117.

The complaints expressed here were very common. See Louisa d'Andelot du Pont to Mary Belin du Pont, 1 May 1888, Longwood Manuscripts, HML.

37. Quoted in Menken, *The Railroad Passenger Car*, 187.

38. Ruth, *Decorum*, 145.

39. Ida B. Wells, *Memphis Diary of Ida B. Wells*, 86.

40. Florence Hartley, *The Ladies' Book of Etiquette and Manual of Politeness*, 38.

41. Eliza Leslie, *The Behavior Book*, 99-100.

42. Ruth, *Decorum*, 142.

43. Cooper, *A Voice from the South*, 89-90.

44. Dall, *My First Holiday*, 394.

45. Julia du Pont Shubrick to Gabrielle Shubrick Crofton, n.d., Longwood Manuscripts, HML.

46. Leland, *Traveling Alone*, 313.

47. Dall, *My First Holiday*, 3 and 20. See also Dickinson, *A Ragged Register*, 285-86.

48. Cooper, *A Voice from the South*, 90, 94-95.

49. "True and False Politeness" in Harper, *A Brighter Coming Day*, 400.

50. Margaretta E. Du Pont Coleman to Margaretta E. Lammot Du Pont, 1 March 1885, Margaretta E. Du Pont Coleman Collection, HML.

51. Dall, *My First Holiday*, 3.

52. Julia du Pont Shubrick to Gabrielle Shubrick Crofton, 9 March 18___, Longwood Manuscripts, HML.

53. For a rich and detailed discussion of the powers implied by the ability to observe and classify strangers on city streets see Walkowitz, *City of Dreadful Delight*, 15–39. Also consult Brand, *The Spectator and the City*; and Kasson, *Rudeness and Civility*, 80–81, 129–131.

On the place of gender in urban spectatorship see Nord, *Walking the Victorian Streets*; and Wolff, "The Invisible Flaneuse." According to Nord, "in the literature of the nineteenth-century city, the figure of the observer—the rambler, the stroller, the spectator, the flaneur—is a man" (1).

54. Kimball, Diary of a Trip to California, 11, Western Americana Collection, BL.

55. Armstrong, *On Habits and Manners*, 71–72.

56. Clendenin, Travel Diary, 3–4, Western Americana Collection, BL.

57. Margaretta E. Du Pont Coleman to Margaretta E. Lammot Du Pont, 1 March 1885, Margaretta E. Du Pont Coleman Collection, HML.

58. Louisa d'Andelot du Pont to Mary Belin du Pont, 19 January 1886, Longwood Manuscripts, HML.

59. Moss, "A Ride to Stroudsbourg," 44.

60. Leland, *Traveling Alone*, 304.

61. Dickinson, *A Ragged Register*, 83–5.

62. Ruth, *Decorum*, 143.

63. Louisa d'Andelot du Pont to Mary Belin du Pont, 6 May 1888 (postmark), Longwood Manuscripts, HML.

64. See Ruth, *Decorum*, 143, for the fine line defining appropriate "social intercourse while traveling."

65. Leland, *Traveling Alone*, 306. Dickinson, *A Ragged Register*, 129.

66. Dall, *My First Holiday*, 33.

67. Margaretta E. Du Pont Coleman to Margaretta E. Lammot Du Pont, 3 March 1885, Margaretta E. Du Pont Coleman Collection, HML.

For another account of socializing with "boys" met on the train see Clendenin, Travel Diary, 3 July 1894, Western Americana Collection, BL.

68. Letter dated 13 May 1867 reprinted in Still, *The Underground Railroad*, 768.

69. For Bird's observation of Chinese passengers as well as her negative impression of Digger Indians see *A Lady's Life*, 3–5.

70. Louisa d'Andelot du Pont to Mary Belin du Pont, 1 May 1888, Longwood Manuscripts, HML.

71. Steven E. Kagle and Lorenza Gramegna have argued that some women's diaries reflect a "borrowing from fictional works of plot elements, character behavior, and values that are so exaggerated, romanticized, and/or stylized that they would be questioned if presented in a realistic context." Some of the travel diaries and accounts in this study reflect a similar borrowing from travel guides with respect to the degree of detail recorded and the selection of particular details as worthy of note. Women seem to recall more than they could have possibly observed in so brief a time. Kagle and Gramegna, "Rewriting Her Life: Fictionalization and the Use of Fictional Modes in Early-American Women's Diaries," in Huff and Bunkers, *Inscribing the Daily*, 41.

72. Leland, *Traveling Alone*, 313. For another consideration of real versus storybook Indians see Faithfull, *Three Visits to America*, 201.

73. Martha Lawrence to Harrison and Cinthia Lawrence, 7 April 1876, Harrison Lawrence Family Correspondence, Western Americana Collection, BL.

74. Margaretta E. Du Pont Coleman to Margaretta E. Lammot Du Pont, 19 June 1888, Margaretta E. Du Pont Coleman Collection, HML.

75. Dunbar-Nelson, *Give Us Each Day*, 67 and 114.

76. Cindy Aron argues that the black middle class did not begin to participate in "vacation experiences" until the 1910s and 1920s, but notes that some African Americans traveled for pleasure as early as the 1890s. See Aron, *Working at Play*, 207, 222. Tera Hunter notes that working-class African Americans often took advantage of discount fares for shorter excursions to "carnivals, cakewalk contests, religious revivals, and state and regional fairs." See Hunter's *To 'Joy My Freedom*, 151.

77. Fannie Barrier Williams, "Vacation Values," 863.

78. For two examples of etiquette books written for African Americans see Armstrong, *On Habits and Manners*; and Charlotte Hawkins Brown, *"Mammy."* For the importance of etiquette to black women's self-image and safety among whites see Stephanie Shaw, *What a Woman Ought to Be*, 22.

79. *The Railway Anecdote Book*, 187. For reference to a film version of this story see Nasaw, *Going Out*, 167. Nasaw describes a 1903 Edwin Porter film, *What Happened in the Tunnel*. Nasaw summarizes the plot as follows: "A [white] 'masher' tries to kiss a pretty young girl as the train they are riding on enters a tunnel. When they reemerge into the light, the masher discovers to his horror that his lips are firmly planted on the black maid's face."

These anecdotes are clearly not only about black women's gentility but also about concerns over racial confusion and "sex across the color line." Rather than white men being lured into intimacy with black women, black women were subject to the insults, sexual and otherwise, of white men.

80. Terrell, *A Colored Woman*, 16.

81. Ida B. Wells, *Crusade for Justice*, 18–19.

82. Accounts of such treatment appear in autobiographies and fiction by many African American women. See Cooper, *A Voice from the South*, 91; Harper, *A Brighter Coming Day*, 218. For a fictional account see Hopkins, *Contending Forces*, 348.

83. Isabella (Lucy) Bird, *The Englishwoman in America* (London: John Murray, 1856) excerpted in Botkin and Harlow, *A Treasury of Railroad Folklore*, 81. Playing at being American or British is hardly comparable to the type of reimaging Wells undertook (see note 81), and it is not the intention here to conflate the two.

84. Clendenin, Travel Diary, 2, Western Americana Collection, BL.

85. Dickinson, *A Ragged Register*, 30.

86. Kimball, Diary of a Trip to California, 15, Western Americana Collection, BL.

87. Bird, *A Lady's Life*, 26.

88. Woodman, *Picturesque Alaska*, 16–17.

89. Ibid., 18, 33.

90. Dunbar-Nelson, *Give Us Each Day*, 230.

91. Clendenin, Travel Diary, 62–65, Western Americana Collection, BL. For firsthand accounts of the experience of riding on a car's platform see Bird, *A Lady's Life*, 26; and Leland, *Traveling Alone*, 350. On the thrill of passing through a tunnel while on the platform see Russell, "Our Trip to Mount Hood," 210. See also Dickinson's, *A Ragged Register*, 39, for an account of riding on the engine.

92. Susie Clark, *The Round Trip*, 6–7, 67, 191–93.

Chapter Three

1. Miriam Florence Leslie, *California; A Pleasure Trip*, 19. Frank Leslie's account of this same journey appears in *Frank Leslie's Illustrated Newspaper* throughout 1877 and 1878. In an article from 7 July 1877, Mr. Leslie echoes his wife's observations when he praises the inventiveness that made "the saloon of a passenger-coach . . . resemble a person's own parlor." Similarly, in an article from 25 August 1877 Leslie refers to a hotel car as "a luxurious home" and asserts, "Whatever one longs for in his own house is procurable in a hotel car."

2. Many historians have identified this nineteenth-century tendency to recast public spaces in domestic terms. In addition to works cited in the introduction see, for example, Kwolek-Folland, *Engendering Business*; and Aron, *Ladies and Gentlemen* on the domestication of the office.

3. Kimball, Diary of a Trip to California, 11, Western Americana Collection, BL.

4. Leland, *Traveling Alone*, 349.

5. Benjamin Taylor, *The World on Wheels*, 158.

6. Quoted in John White, *The American Railroad Passenger Car*, 209-10.

7. Susie Clark, *The Round Trip*, 5, 8.

8. Grier, *Culture and Comfort*, 20.

9. "Hardships on the Rails." To underscore the unevenness of the progress of railroad domestication, nearly a decade earlier in 1866 the *New York Times* ran a story on Pullman's sleeping car *Omaha* and claimed that it looked more like "an elegantly finished parlor than the interior of a railroad car." Cited in Sutton, *Travellers*, 57.

10. Miriam Florence Leslie, *California*, 19. On the shortcomings of the train as home see also "Woman and the Sleeping Car."

11. Clifford Clark, *The American Family Home*, 19.

12. Stevenson, *The Victorian Homefront*, 3.

13. Clifford Clark, *The American Family Home*, 104.

14. As with any cultural change, the transfer from one ideal of home to the next was uneven. In the words of architectural historian Gwendolyn Wright: "More than one model for the home and family have usually coexisted, although seldom in harmony." Gwendolyn Wright, *Building the Dream*, xvi.

15. On the changing nature of domesticity and for a discussion of the parlor's emergence as a site of consumption see Leavitt, *Catharine Beecher to Martha Stewart*, 8-39. See also Halttunen, "From Parlor to Living Room."

16. Hanford, *The Home Instructor*, 26.

17. The idea of home has long been an integral part of many travel experiences—the basis upon which the traveler draws comparisons and evaluates the journey. See Holloway, *The Hearthstone*, 32. According to Holloway, "Americans have to make new homes far distant from each other. But perhaps this necessity of frequent migration makes them cherish the idea of home the more."

On the importance of home in women's travel see Frederick and McLeod, *Women and the Journey*, xix.

18. *How to Make Home Happy*, v.

19. This was especially true of the parlor, where families met with not only friends and acquaintances but also carefully selected strangers. On the semipublic nature of the parlor see, among others, Halttunen, *Confidence Men and Painted Women*, 59, and Clifford Clark, *The American Family Home*, 42–43. The parlor, according to Clark, "helped fill the need for a more controlled social environment in which the rules governing social interaction could be formalized."

20. The home appears in this light in Garvey, *The Adman in the Parlor*, 83–87. The expansive role of the home and its importance as a site for learning how to meet the challenges of public experiences is also reflected in the contents of *How to Make Home Happy*. This household advice book included a section on travel, with special attention to train travel ("Always keep your head and arms inside the car window. . . . Do not ask the conductor foolish questions about the route" [217–18].) Even more striking, under the heading "Trying Emergencies" the author included a paragraph on railroad accidents in which he or she advised readers that "it is best never to jump from a train. . . . To mount the seat or reach the aisle is generally safer" (262).

21. One could write an entire book on the place of the railroad in Victorian childhood—especially boyhood. The train was a favorite motif in children's books and toys throughout the nineteenth century. For a history of model trains see Hollander, *All Aboard*, 17–19. On the popularity of model trains as a Christmas gift for boys see Stilgoe, *Metropolitan Corridor*, 4.

22. Lloyd, *Travels at Home*, 273.

23. Stevenson, *The Victorian Homefront*, 13.

24. The quotation appears on a stereograph in a series entitled "Picturesque Views of All Countries," Accession #71.53.953A, Photographic History Collection, NMAH.

25. Wilson, *Wilson's Lantern Journeys*, 196.

26. Lomazzi, *Railroad Timetables*, 87–98. Many of the railroad guides were written as travel narratives tracing the experiences of a small cast of characters and seem to be direct, albeit more commercial, descendants of works like Lloyd's cited above. See also Cunniff, "The Comforts of Railroad Travel," 3578. The Pullman Company's *The Story of Pullman* suggests that images of car interiors were included prominently in the circulated images of tourist sights. According to the Pullman Company, "illustrated magazine articles which appeared telling the story of a trip to California,

had as many pictures of Pullman interiors as they had of the big trees or Yosemite" (16).

For an example of a guidebook masquerading as a travel narrative see Wood, *An Unattended Journey*. Wood recounts the experiences of four girls as they travel to California. They meet at Denver and tell stories of their individual journeys to that city. As they travel across country they split into two sets of two and travel on separate lines and then meet again to tell about their experiences. Their accounts read like a standard guidebook listing sights of interest.

On the role of magazines and vicarious travel see Ohmann, *Selling Culture*, 231.

27. Northrop, *The Household Encyclopædia*, 233.

28. As Richard Bushman has argued, many middle-class homes that aspired to this ideal did not quite realize it by the 1830s or 1840s either. Not until the middle of the nineteenth century had "vernacular gentility ... become the possession of the American middle class." Houses and trains, therefore, both needed to evolve in order to conform to the cultural ideals of "home." Bushman, *The Refinement of America*, xiii.

29. This device is described in Sweet, *History of the Sleeping Car*, 12, Pullman Palace Car Company Collection, box 3A, AC.

30. Menken, *The Railroad Passenger Car*, 7.

For a discussion of railway spine see Schivelbusch, *The Railway Journey*, 134–49.

31. Ward, *Railroads and the Character of America*, 69–80.

32. "American Railway Traveling," 200.

33. Quoted in Charles Adams, *The Railroads*, 73–74.

34. Harding, *George M. Pullman*, 9.

35. The quotation is from L. Xavire Eyma, in *L'Illustration*, 22 July 1848 and is translated in Sweet, *History of the Sleeping Car*, 12, Pullman Palace Car Company Collection, box 3A, AC.

36. Pullman Company, *The Story of Pullman*, 12. See also Porter, "Railroad Passenger Travel," 308–10, on the vestibule trains.

Although the vestibule aided mobility and enabled the train to more closely approximate the conveniences of a home, the train was already considered in domestic terms before the vestibule's invention. For example, an 1879 guidebook for the Pittsburgh, Cincinnati and St. Louis Railway informed the would-be traveler that "secure in the possession of his berth, section, state-room or drawing-room, the favored passenger can sleep, sit, read, write, eat, converse, or comfortably stretch out and gaze out the wide plate-glass windows at the flying landscape." According to the author, a passenger could achieve this comfort for $2 above the cost of a first-class ticket. Caldwell, "Traveling Reduced to a Science," 79–80.

37. Shearer, *The Pacific Tourist*, 5–6.

38. George, *Forty Years on the Rail*, 243.

39. Caldwell, "Traveling Reduced to a Science," 82.

40. Quoted in Grant, *We Took the Train*, xvi–xviii.

41. Pennsylvania Railroad Co., *Tour to the Mardi Gras*, 5.

Some publications made comparisons between trains and other domesticated public spaces, especially hotels. One guidebook/advertisement brochure favorably compared the cars of the Denver and Rio Grande Railroad with their "plate glass mirrors, raw silk curtains, mahogany pannels [*sic*]" to "a *fin de siècle* apartment house." See Wood, *An Unattended Journey*, 68.

42. "The Pennsylvania Railroad."

43. Menken, *The Railroad Passenger Car*, 17.

44. Graves, *The Winter Resorts of Florida*, 11.

45. *Pennsylvania R.R. Around the World Via Washington and Transcontinental America*, Warshaw Collection, "Railroads," box 80, AC.

46. Jenkins, "Railway Stations," 315.

47. Both urban historians and railroad historians have presented the station in this light—as a "city gate" or even as some type of "microcity." See Droege, *Passenger Terminals and Trains*, 6; Condit, *The Railroad and the City*, x; Stilgoe, *Metropolitan Corridor*, 3; Richards and MacKenzie, *The Railway Station*, 7–9.

The urban nature of railway stations could also make them more public than the cars. After all, one did not need a ticket to enter a station.

48. *Benham's City Directory and Annual Advisor*, 1849–50, quoted in Meeks, *The Railroad Station*, 53.

49. "Railway-Stations," 67.

50. Howland, "Making Stations Attractive," 522. See also Gordon, "Gilded Stairs and Marble Halls."

51. Droege, *Passenger Terminals and Trains*, 23.

52. "Handicapped," 4. This conclusion may appear surprising to those familiar with the nineteenth-century American fascination with speed (steamboat races, fast mail trains, etc.). Nonetheless, speed was not enough to guarantee the United States' standing as an advanced nation.

53. The same article praises this particular train for having the "con-

veniences and elegancies of home" and compares it to a "richly appointed city mansion." See "A Royal Train," *Chicago Times*, 1887. Clipping, Pullman Collection, "Pullman Company Public Relations Department, History Files (1860–1968)," box 2, folder 78, NL.

54. Pamphlet, Warshaw Collection, "Railroads," box 67, folder labeled "Pullman/Sleeping Cars: General Works," AC.

55. Over time, new visions of progress would make themselves felt in the design of car interiors. In the final decade of the nineteenth century and the opening decades of the twentieth, the style of car interiors began to change, as older styles with their heavy draperies and thick carpets became associated with germs and other health threats. The late-nineteenth- and early-twentieth-century drive for hygiene pushed out the plush Pullman car and ushered in more stark, albeit, luxurious interiors.

56. Holloway, *The Hearthstone*, iv.

57. Etiquette books repeatedly advised readers to conduct themselves in public as they would at home. In other words, travelers should always be aware that their conduct was being observed and their reputations evaluated. For an example of this warning see *How to Make Home Happy*, 218. According to the author, "Discretion should be used in forming acquaintances while traveling. . . . Whether at home or abroad, the same rules of good behavior should prevail."

58. "Women and Children in America," 468.

59. Stanley Buder makes a similar argument in his study of Pullman when he writes, "The sleeping car became a visible symbol of the material promise of American industry and ingenuity." See Buder, *Pullman*, xi. On the home as a symbol and determinant of American civilization see Clifford Clark, *The American Family Home*, 4; and Grier, *Culture and Comfort*, 25.

60. Sanborn, "In the Pullman Car," 472.

61. Shearer, *The Pacific Tourist*, 6.

For a similar invocation of the contrast between the rugged landscape and the civilization within the cars see also the lyrics of George Brown's "The Tourists in a Pullman Car," DeVincent Collection, Railroads, box 24, folder B, AC.

62. Dickinson, *A Ragged Register*, 32.

63. *Transcontinental*, 27 May 1870, 2.

64. Susie Clark, *The Round Trip*, 144–45.

65. For an analysis of nineteenth-century family life and its relationship to middle-class morality see Ryan, *Cradle of the Middle Class*.

66. See Leyendecker, *Palace Car Prince*, for a more thorough biography of George Pullman.

67. For examples of this interpretation see Husband, *The Story of the Pullman Car*; and Beebe, *Mr. Pullman's Elegant Palace Car*. According to Beebe, "Before [Pullman's] first palace cars few enough Americans had any least conception of what constituted true luxury; three decades of first hand contact with the opulence available aboard the cars created a universal demand for rich living which had a profound effect on the American economy and national way of life that has not yet disappeared. For millions, their first contact with Turkey carpets, plate glass mirrors and velvet portieres was on palace cars. . . . Pullman left its impress on the entire national culture" (12).

68. Throughout his professional life Pullman acted on his belief that a well-designed home environment, whether the intended inhabitants were middle-class railroad passengers or industrial workers, would foster conduct conducive to public harmony. It is not my intention to downplay Pullman's love of profit, but only to suggest that the ways he sought to make his money reflect his beliefs about the importance of home as a social and cultural force. For this second interpretation of Pullman see Buder, *Pullman*, 60-61. See also Pullman's obituary in *Railway Age*, 22 October 1897, 865.

69. Pullman's quote appears in Doty, *The Town of Pullman*, 23.

Compare Pullman's statement with an excerpt from an article entitled "The Domestic Use of Design," in the *Furniture Gazette* from 12 April 1873: "There can be no doubt that altogether, independently of direct intellectual culture, either from books or society, the mind is moulded and coloured to a great extent by the persistent impressions produced upon it by the most familiar objects that daily meet the eye. . . . That a carefully regulated and intelligent change of the domestic scenery about a sick person is beneficial is obvious, and yet there are few who correctly apprehend to how great an extent the character, and especially the temper, may be affected by the nature of ordinary physical surroundings." Quoted in Grier, *Culture and Comfort*, 6.

70. Pullman Company, *The Story of Pullman*, 7.

71. In a variation of the quotation cited above Pullman is also quoted as having said, "Take the roughest man . . . and bring him into a room elegantly carpeted and furnished, and the effect upon his bearing is pronounced and immediate." Carter, *When Railroads Were New*, 173-74.

72. *Railway Age and Northwestern Railroader*, 26 January 1894, 47.

73. Women's ability to travel freely by train enabled the cars to be home-like and underscored the domesticity of American women and the superior character of American men who created a safe public setting for their women. According to Gail Bederman, for late-nineteenth-century Americans "gender . . . was an essential component of civilization. Indeed, one could identify advanced civilizations by the degree of their sexual differentiation. Savage (that is, nonwhite) men and women were believed to be almost identical, but men and women of the civilized races had evolved pronounced sexual differences. Civilized women were womanly—delicate, spiritual, dedicated to the home. And civilized men were the most manly ever evolved—firm of character; self-controlled; protectors of women and children." Bederman, *Manliness and Civilization*, 25.

74. "The Wife as a Traveler."

75. "Railway Advertising in Newspapers."

76. On the subject of women traveling with bouquets: the Michigan Central actually distributed bouquets of roses to its women passengers. In the year of the Columbian Exposition the line distributed 60,000 of them. See "A Vegetable Engine." During the Boston Board of Trade's transcontinental journey the female passengers gathered and arranged flowers during short stops along the route. See *Transcontinental*, 30 May 1870, 2.

77. This observation is based on a survey of *Godey's Lady's Book* from 1860 through the end of the magazine's run in the 1890s and the *Railway Age Gazette* from 1880 to 1920. I have also relied upon articles and stories found in *Poole's Index* of nineteenth-century periodicals.

78. Examples of stories in which the two lovers have met previously or know people in common include Riviere, "Experiences at the Sea Shore"; Rutledge, "A Railway Journey"; Victor, "In the Erie Tunnel"; and Couthoy, "A Railway Romance." The railroad companies also published romantic fiction in their advertising pamphlets. See, for example, *Cupid on the Rails*. Also Nixon, "A Chase for an Heiress."

79. Hull, "A Pullman Car Wooing."

80. "Floy's Journey"; Daly, *"For Love & Bears"*; and Spearman, *The Daughter of a Magnate*. For a review of Spearman's book see *Railway Age*, 1 January 1904, 18. On Spearman's place within the body of railroad fiction consult Donovan, *The Railroad in Literature*, 6.

For a similar interpretation of magazine fiction see Garvey, *The Adman in the Parlor*, 107-8.

81. "On the Way North," by Juliet Wilbor Tompkins, appeared in *Munsey's Magazine* in October 1895. It is reprinted in its entirety in Ohmann, *Selling Culture*, 297–305.

82. Thomson, "Romance on Wheels" pays special attention to proper conduct while aboard and interacting with strangers.

83. "Santa Claus on the Cars." It is not clear whether this story was printed as fiction or fact.

In 1880, the Chicago, Rock Island & Pacific Railway identified the railroad with the celebration of Christmas when it published a collection of children's Christmas stories presumably for distribution to young passengers. According to the first story, Santa no longer uses his sled but relies upon the railroad to distribute his gifts. See *Merry Christmas: Santa Claus' Christmas Train*, Warshaw Collection, "Railroad," box 80, AC.

84. Julia MacNair Wright, *On a Snow-Bound Train*. It is worth noting that in addition to *On a Snow-Bound Train*, Wright also wrote *The Complete Home: An Encyclopædia of Domestic Life and Affairs* (Philadelphia: Bradley, Garretson, 1879) in which she asserted the importance of the moral home: "Between the Home set up in Eden, and the Home before us in Eternity, stand the Homes of Earth in a long succession. It is therefore important that our Homes should be brought up to a standard in harmony with their origin and destiny. Here are 'Empire's primal Springs;' here are the Church and State in embryo; here all improvements and reforms must rise. For national and social disasters, for moral and financial evils, the cure begins in the Household" (3).

See also "The Snow Blockade" in Stephe Smith, *Romance and Humor of the Rail*, 231–50.

85. Stephe Smith, *Romance and Humor of the Rail*, 296. The other example is from "Not So Very Hoggish After All."

86. Holderness, *Reminiscences of a Pullman Conductor*, 49–50.

87. Howells, *The Sleeping-Car and Other Farces*, 46.

In a similar collapsing of the railroad car, the domestic, and the commercial, Cynthia Brandimarte's study of tea rooms describes a "homelike" restaurant in New York City that was designed to look like a sleeping car. According to Brandimarte, the Pullman Car Tea Shop "was created in a long and narrow commercial space lined with high back benches of Flemish oak and a six-foot-high wainscot topped with a narrow shelf. The operator, who had gotten the idea during train travel from Albany to New York, finished the walls and ceiling in a silver-gray paint and placed pots of scarlet geraniums atop the shelf. She hired black 'porters' and dressed them in

Pullman-like uniforms to serve the diners from tea wagons rolled up to each booth." Brandimarte, " 'To Make the World More Homelike,' " 10-11.

88. In Crane, *The Open Boat*, 80. "The Bride Comes to Yellow Sky" first appeared in *McClure's Magazine*, February 1898.

89. "Sleeping Car Progress."

90. Pullman Company, *The Story of Pullman*, 5-6.

By 1925 at least one decorating manual acknowledged Pullman's influence on home interiors but encouraged women to reject his particular aesthetic. Charles Almo Byers asked his readers,

> Now then, is there any hope for those of us who were cheated out of those cradle lessons in discrimination; whose childhood home associations were of the Early Pullman period of American home decoration; when the cozy corner held its sway and chenille curtains, crocheted tidies, beaded portieres, ubiquitous grill-work, plush upholstery and embroidered piano drapes formed dust catchers all over the house; when massive, ugly, battle-axe black walnut furniture was our heart's desire, and inflammatory color schemes in wall and floor coverings helped to make us a nation of color illiterates?

Despite this insulting depiction of Pullman's decorating taste the train car's influence on domestic design persisted in the efficient "Pullman kitchen." See Byers, *Modern Priscilla Home Furnishing Book*, 2.

91. "The Pennsylvania Railroad," 542, and Baltimore and Ohio Railroad, *Reasons Why*. According to Katherine Grier, a reading of popular periodicals suggests that "less prosperous rural women were interested in and knew about the furnishing practices of the urban middle classes by the 1870s." Railroad cars may have been one source of this knowledge. The commercial parlors of the nineteenth century "were an intermediary between the sources of tasteful furnishings and new consumers who were themselves deeply interested in having parlors and in furnishing them appropriately." See Grier, *Culture and Comfort*, 67, 20.

92. This issue of class on the rails is difficult to sort out because the enthusiasm for the train as an agent of democracy distorts contemporary accounts as well as the more celebratory secondary studies of the American railroad. The belief that the trains were democratic social spaces has been reinscribed without critique in many secondary accounts of nineteenth-century rail travel. See, for example, Alvarez, *Travel on Southern Antebellum Railroads*, 126. According to Alvarez, "The early railroad car was a conspicuous example of the American concept of an egalitarian society. Unlike his European counterpart, the American traveler was almost totally

lacking in the type of class consciousness which would have resulted in different cars for each social class. With the exception of Negroes, some immigrants, and those cars reserved for ladies, all passengers mingled together and shared equally the uncertainties of the road." Alvarez notes the exclusion of African Americans, immigrants, and women from this democratic space with no apparent irony.

93. George, *Forty Years on the Rail*, 222.

94. See "Railroad Travel in England and America," 418.

95. Iddings, "The Art of Travel," 353.

96. *Railway Age and Northwestern Railroader*, 8 February 1896, 67. The article noted a recent decline in class differentiation on British railways and warned that the opposite trend was taking hold in the United States. These changes, it said, were "the outward and visible sign of a deep-seated change which is going on in the spirits of the two peoples."

As early as 1870, some guidebooks were advising travelers of the different accommodations available in first-, second-, and even third-class cars. See Hart, *The Traveler's Own Book*, 11.

97. "Parlor-Car Manners."

See also *Railway Age*, 11 October 1889, 663. Apparently the desire for "more luxurious furnishings" and "comparative exclusiveness" inspired a proposal that "parlor street cars" be added to the elevated railways in New York City and to the cable roads of Chicago.

98. There is not a great deal of information on the history and physical design of emigrant cars. See John White, *The American Railroad Passenger Car*, especially Chapter 6. For primary observations of the condition of the passengers traveling in the emigrant cars see Miriam Florence Leslie, *California*, 284. For a positive depiction of the emigrant cars see Daly, *"For Love & Bears,"* 38.

99. Atchison, Topeka and Santa Fé Railroad, *In a Tourist Sleeper to California via Santa Fé Route* (December 1892), 4. The brochure also includes a brief history of the evolution from emigrant to tourist car. See also *The Pullman Exhibit at the Cotton States and International Exposition, 1895*, for more on tourist sleepers. Both documents in the Warshaw Collection, "Railroads" box 67, folder labeled "Pullman/Sleeping Cars: General Works," AC.

100. Emery, "Railroad Passenger Service," 67.

101. "The Family Car."

102. Cunniff, "The Comforts of Railroad Travel," 3577. Cunniff de-

scribes what he calls "these varied conveniences for different classes of people."

103. Terrell, *A Colored Woman*, 295. Terrell also recalled that the decision to travel Pullman exposed her to criticism from some members of the black community: "But, curiously enough, some colored people have been known to object to having representatives of their group travel in a Pullman car. I did not know this until I had an experience which proved conclusively that this is true" (305). Clearly, some viewed riding in a Pullman car (especially for the light-skinned Terrell) as a type of racial passing.

104. Albro Martin, *Railroads Triumphant*, 87.

105. *Railway Age*, 28 August 1903, 248.

106. "The 'Jim Crow Car.'"

107. *Railway Age*, 5 August 1887, 541.

108. Mathews, "Awakening of the Afro-American Woman," 151-53.

Chapter Four

1. Isabella (Lucy) Bird, *The Englishwoman in America*. (London: John Murray, 1856) excerpted in Botkin and Harlow, *A Treasury of Railroad Folklore*, 81.

Many British travelers commented upon the courtesies granted to American women in the cars. See, for example, Alex. Mackay, *The Western World; or Travels in the United States in 1846-47* (London, 1850), excerpted in Menken, *The Railroad Passenger Car*, 104-11. Mackay described a gentleman who passed an entire night holding a lady's carpet bag upon his lap rather than place it on the filthy floor, "as the ladies are used to such attentions in America."

2. See, for example, Ruth, *Decorum*, 16. According to Ruth: "In polite society great deference is paid to [a lady] and certain seemingly arbitrary requirements are made in her favor. Thus a gentleman is always expected to vacate his seat in favor of a lady who is unprovided with one."

3. "Courtesy in Travel."

4. Two other studies that consider the lady within the context of larger historical change are Aron, *Ladies and Gentlemen*; and Faust, *Mothers of Invention*.

5. For a thought-provoking take on the meaning and history of female privilege see Kerber, *No Constitutional Right*.

6. Frost, *Frost's Laws*, 102.

7. An alternative reading of this image could emphasize that the pro-

tected and genteel sphere of women exacted its toll in the public sphere of men. And, as this chapter demonstrates, for many men the price was simply too great.

8. Putnam, *The Lady*, xxxiii. Putnam's work examines the lady in ancient Greece, Rome, the Middle Ages, the Renaissance, and the antebellum South of the United States. She does not study the American lady after the Civil War; she does, however, acknowledge the lady's continued existence at the time of her writing.

9. Cooke, *Our Social Manual*, 359.

See Hemphill, "Manners for Americans" for a survey of conduct literature from 1740 to 1860. According to Hemphill, between 1820 and 1860 advice books encouraged men to spend time in the company of refined women in order to polish their own manners (473), and men, in turn, expected to offer women protection (476).

10. Cooke, *Our Social Manual*, 358. Ruth, *Decorum*, 16.

Similarly, in Cecil Hartley's chapter on "Politeness" he warns: "In the familiar intercourse of society, a well-bred man will be known by the delicacy and deference with which he behaves toward females." Cecil Hartley, *The Gentleman's Book of Etiquette*, 36.

11. After 1865, most etiquette books included sections on women's street etiquette and conduct during train travel. Nonetheless, some public places remained beyond the influence of ladies and off limits to respectable women. For example, many travelers presumed that a decent woman would not enter a smoking car. This assumption added to the insult of racial segregation for black ladies; Jim Crow cars were routinely smokers.

12. Houghton, *American Etiquette*, 15.

13. Florence Hartley, *The Ladies' Book of Etiquette*, 34.

14. Putnam, *The Lady*, xxvii.

See also Calvert, *The Gentleman*, 153. His definition of ladyhood ("it runs side by side with gentlemanhood") underscores the difficulty of fixing the qualities of the lady.

15. Frost, *Frost's Laws*, 99.

16. *Good Manners*, 269.

17. For an elaboration of this argument see Halttunen, *Confidence Men and Painted Women*, 92–123.

18. Allan Pinkerton, *Thirty Years a Detective*, 154. See also "A Female Deadbeat."

19. "How to Tell a Lady."

20. "Women and Children in America," 468.

21. Cecil Hartley, *The Gentleman's Book of Etiquette*, 69.

22. Cited in Blewett, *Men, Women, and Work*, 223. On working-class ladies see also Enstad, *Ladies of Labor*, 48-51; Peiss, *Cheap Amusements*, 62-67; Benson, *Counter Cultures*, 259.

23. *The Railway Anecdote Book*, 47.

Many etiquette books expressed this same belief. See, for example, Ruth, *Decorum*, 11, 15. He writes, "high birth and good breeding are the privileges of the few; but the habits and manners of a gentleman may be acquired by all." And, "The true gentleman is rare, but, fortunately there is no crime in counterfeiting his excellences. The best of it is that the counterfeit may, in course of time, develop into the real thing."

24. Frost, *Frost's Laws*, 99.

See also Harland, *House and Home*, 115-19. She informs readers that "philology and tradition clearly define a lady as one who has more to give than her neighbors, and whose province it is to dispense to the less fortunate. Viewed thus, the application is meaningful. To support it aright, there must be superiority to the commonality, largeness of heart, and liberality of hand." But she acknowledges, "American ladies—born and bred—do cook, nurse, and sweep rooms, usually in their own houses, occasionally in other people's, and for wages." Harland, nonetheless, pokes fun at working women who self-consciously seek out the title of lady—for example, referring to themselves as "wash-ladies," "salesladies," or even "foreladies." According to Harland, no man would claim to be a "foregentleman" or "salesgentlemen," and by scrambling to claim the title of lady, these women belittled the "dignity of true womanhood."

25. Putnam, *The Lady*, xxvii.

26. Terrell, *A Colored Woman*, 15-16. According to Stephanie Shaw, for African American women "'ladylike' behavior could not always save one from danger in a society in which many whites demonstrated little respect for black people in general, but without 'proper' behavior the dangers would certainly be intensified, the chances for abuse increased, and the opportunities for advancement diminished." Stephanie Shaw, *What a Woman Ought to Be*, 22.

27. Elsa Barkley Brown, "Polyrhythm and Improvization," 85.

28. McCabe, *National Encyclopædia*, 454.

The persistence of this gender deference is reflected in a 1903 rule book of the Philadelphia & Reading Railway Co. According to the publication, workers "must be respectful and courteous to all passengers, especially to women traveling alone, giving polite attention to their requests and all desired information as to routes, baggage or connections; but avoiding all familiarity and unnecessary conversation, either with passengers or other employees." See Philadelphia & Reading Railway Co., *Rules of the Operating Department*, 119.

29. Harvey & Co., *Popular California Excursions*.

30. Wood, *An Unattended Journey*, 5.

31. Pullman Palace Car Co., *Car Service Rules* (1893), 32, 45-46. Many of these special allowances, reflecting notions of women's frailty and dependence, identified ladies, and also children and invalids, as individuals requiring attention. See also Philadelphia & Reading Railway Co., *Rules of the Operating Department*, 8, on the treatment of "women, children and infirm persons."

32. Charles Sweet, *History of the Sleeping Car*, 4, Pullman Palace Car Company Collection, box 3A, AC. See also an advertisement from the *Baltimore Sun* cited in Menken, *The Railroad Passenger Car*, 14.

33. The full extent of these ladies' spaces is difficult to determine. A brief mention of the return of ladies' cars on the lines operated by the Brooklyn Rapid Transit Company in 1904 explained that this policy "would recall the old arrangement of a 'ladies' car' which used to be a feature on all regulated steam roads." The article, unfortunately, does not specify when or for how long this arrangement was common. See *Railway Age*, 12 February 1904, 239.

34. Menken, *The Railroad Passenger Car*, 14-15. See also *Bass v. Chicago & Northwestern Ry. Co.*, 36 Wis. 450; and *Peck v. New York Central & H. R.R. Co.*, 70 N.Y. 587.

On other gender-segregated spaces for ladies emerging at this time see Ryan, *Women in Public*, 76-82. Among the spaces noted by Ryan are separate ladies' entrances in theaters, special park lawns reserved for ladies and children, and even a ladies' pond for skating in Central Park.

35. Cited in Grant, *We Took the Train*, 22.

See also *Railway Age*, 19 May 1881, 274. According to an article on ladies' cars in India, "it cannot be objectionable for a male passenger to travel with his mother, wife, sister or daughter, when no other females require the compartment." For an example of a woman who challenged men's presence in ladies' spaces see "Right Up and Down Woman." 174.

36. Stephe Smith, *Romance and Humor of the Rail*, 292. Italics in the original.

37. Frost, *Frost's Laws*, 100.

38. Ruth, *Decorum*, 142.

39. "A Word for the Traveling Public," 2.

40. *Holly's Railroad Advocate*, 20 September 1856, quoted in Menken, *The Railroad Passenger Car*, 14-15. See also Stephe Smith, *Romance and Humor of the Rail*, 240.

41. The courts gave their approval to such policies. See Myron Bly, *Legal Hints for Travelers*, 31-32.

42. "American Railway Traveling," 197, 200.

43. Phelps, "Ladies' Car Humbug," 254.

44. In fact, in 1872 a superintendent of the Pinkerton Detective Agency matter-of-factly reported that he and another Pinkerton superintendent sat in the ladies' car during a recent inspection of the Pennsylvania & Reading Railroad. Indeed the superintendent "had some words with the conductor about getting into the ladies' car." The report suggests no wrongdoing concerning this issue and focuses on the conductor's failure to collect all fares. See Letter from Benj. Franklin, Supt., 19 August 1872, Reading Company Collection, HML.

45. Benjamin Taylor, *The World on Wheels*, 156-57.

46. Stephe Smith, *Romance and Humor of the Rail*, 293.

47. Licht, *Working for the Railroad*, 140.

48. James Macaulay, *Across the Ferry* (London, 1887), quoted in Menken, *The Railroad Passenger Car*, 154-55. Macaulay also noted that emigrant cars and the rising numbers of specialty cars did allow for class divisions.

49. Phelps, "Ladies' Car Humbug," 254.

50. This account is from *Peck v. New York Central & H. R.R. Co.*, 70 NY 587. The *New York Times* offered a slightly more colorful account of the Peck case on 1 February 1879. Under the heading "The Ladies' Car," the *Times* reported that the car was clearly labeled "Ladies' Car" when the plaintiff, erroneously referred to as "Pike," attempted to board it. After he was turned away by the brakeman, "Pike" bided his time and snuck into the car. When the brakeman later discovered that his instructions had been ignored he responded with anger and forcibly ejected "Pike" from the car.

51. "The Ladies' Car," 4.

52. *Peck v. New York Central & H. R.R. Co.*, 70 NY 587.

53. *Bass v. Chicago & Northwestern Ry. Co.*, 36 Wis. 460.

54. The paper was commenting on a similar case involving ladies traveling on horse cars. See "Ladies on the Horse Cars."

55. *Bass v. Chicago & Northwestern Ry. Co.*, 36 Wis. 460.

56. *Brown v. Memphis & Charleston Railroad Co.*, 5 Fed 499.

57. *Bass v. Chicago & Northwestern Ry. Co.*, 36 Wis. 460.

58. Increasingly, historians have examined the place of gender and class within the history of racial segregation and have recognized the special place of the black lady. See, for example, Gilmore, *Gender and Jim Crow*. On the exclusion of black women from the white ideal of "the lady" see Higginbotham, "African-American Women's History," 261–62. On the legal status of black ladies see Welke, *Recasting American Liberty*, 283–99.

59. Welke, *Recasting American Liberty*, 297–99. Also Welke, "When All the Women Were White," 283.

60. Cooper, *A Voice from the South*, 96.

Black men encountered a similar challenge. Could a black man with a first-class ticket claim entry to the first-class car when it was also designated the ladies' car? For an account of a black man expelled from the ladies' car see the *Cleveland Gazette*, 16 April 1887, 2. The incident took place on a Western and Atlanta train when the man entered the ladies' car at Chattanooga.

61. Ida B. Wells, *Memphis Diary of Ida B. Wells*, 76.

62. On the importance of class differences among blacks in the shaping of racial segregation see Minter, "The Codification of Jim Crow," 3–5, 8, 23, 41–43.

63. "The Model Woman: A Pen Picture of the Typical Southern Girl," *New York Freeman*, 18 February 1888, reprinted in Ida B. Wells, *Memphis Diary of Ida B. Wells*, 188.

64. Cooper, *A Voice from the South*, 93–94.

65. The dual audience for black respectability is best understood in terms of "race work" or "racial uplift." According to Evelyn Brooks Higginbotham, " 'Race work' or 'racial uplift' equated normality with conformity to white middle-class models of gender roles and sexuality. Given the extremely limited educational and income opportunities during the late nineteenth–early twentieth centuries, many black women linked mainstream domestic duties, codes of dress, sexual conduct, and public etiquette with both individual success and group progress. Black leaders argued that 'proper' and 'respectable' behavior proved blacks worthy of equal civil and political rights." These ideas are essential to any understanding of the black lady's significance. See "African American Women's History," 271.

66. Armstrong, *On Habits and Manners*, 70. According to Armstrong, education was the first step to becoming a lady. "It is not to those who are rich; it is not to those whom the accident of birth may have given special advantages; it is not even to those who are educated, or who claim the title

for themselves, that the name . . . 'lady' rightfully belongs. . . . Our first need is to make sure . . . that we know what is really meant by the words so frequently upon our lips" (5).

For another etiquette book addressed specifically to an African American audience see Woods, *The Negro In Etiquette*. Woods emphasizes the importance of treating black and white women with the same courtesy. See especially the chapters on "Street Etiquette" and "Why Colored Men Fail to Doff their Hats to White Ladies."

67. A little over fifty years later, Charlotte Hawkins Brown made no mention of racial segregation and its impact on African Americans' ability to travel respectably. See Charlotte Hawkins Brown, *"Mammy,"* 83–86.

68. Armstrong, *On Habits and Manners*, 79, 68.

69. This certainly is not the only example of women's belief that gender deference could overcome or exempt them from other social divisions or antagonisms. See Faust, *Mothers of Invention*, 198–99. Faust recounts that many white southern women of the elite classes put so much faith in the protections granted to ladies that they even expected advancing Union soldiers to respect them. According to Faust, "the privileges of gender did in fact provide considerable protection for Confederate females and served also as the foundation for their much vaunted belligerence. Most Yankee soldiers were reluctant to harm white southern women, particularly those who seemed to be ladies of the middle or upper class."

70. *The Chicago & Northwestern Railway Co. v. Williams*, 55 Ill. 185.

71. The November 1881 issue of the *Spice Mill*, a coffee and tea trade periodical, told of a similar case: "Jane Brown, a colored woman, bought a ticket entitling her to first-class passage from Corinth to Memphis, on the Memphis and Charleston Railroad. She took a seat in the ladies' car; the conductor ordered her to go forward into a smoking and emigrant car; she refused to go, and thereupon she was ejected with great violence. She brought suit for damages in the Federal Circuit Court, and a jury of white men awarded her $3,000." (342). The report of Brown's case can be found in *Brown v. Memphis & Charleston Railroad Co.*, 5 Fed 499. What is of interest here is that Brown's story found its way into the *Spice Mill* at all. A brief article on Brown's case also appeared under "Notes on Travel" in the *Railway Age*, 11 November 1880, 590.

The *Railway Age* also reported on *Gray v. Cincinnati Southern Railway Company*, U.S. Circuit Court, S.D. Ohio. According to the article the woman was excluded from the ladies' car although "she was lady-like in appearance and conduct, and was at the time carrying a sick child in her arms."

The court ruled she was entitled to damages. See "Legal Notes" in the *Railway Age*, 27 July 1882, 411.

72. This was the fate of Ida B. Wells's suit. See Welke, *Recasting American Liberty*, 306. Also, Welke, "When All the Women Were White," 293.

73. For a clear and concise table showing when the various southern states passed laws segregating the railroads see William Cohen, *At Freedom's Edge*, 217–18.

74. From the summary of *Day v. Owen*, 5 Mich. 520; and *West Chester & Philadelphia Railroad. v. Miles*, 55 Pa. 209 in Hutchinson, *Treatise on the Law of Carriers*, 1114.

75. Quotation is from Baldwin, *American Railroad Law*, 308. See *West Chester & Philadelphia Railroad. v. Miles*, 55 Pa. 209. See also Welke, "When All the Women Were White," 296.

76. *Day v. Owen*, 5 Mich. 520. Also cited in Seymour Thompson, *Law of Carriers of Passengers*, 309. This case refers to steamboats but was clearly relevant to rulings regarding travel by rail. See Welke, *Recasting American Liberty*, 327–29, on the legal relationship between gender and racial segregation.

77. See for example, *Heard v. Georgia R.R. Co.*, 3 I.C.C.R. 111, 508.

78. "Car for Colored People."

79. For examples of this interpretation see Gilmore, *Gender and Jim Crow*; and Stephanie Shaw, *What a Woman Ought to Be*.

80. Kraditor, *Ideas of the Woman Suffrage Movement*, 69–72.

81. Ironically, in the 1880s as African Americans challenged racial segregation, the courts began to question the wisdom of setting aside cars for ladies and considered the rights of men consigned to inferior accommodations. Even as gender segregation served as precedent for racial segregation, racial segregation threatened the privileges of gender for white women. See Welke, *Recasting American Liberty*, 331.

82. "American Railway Traveling," 205.

83. Rhodes, "Shall the American Girl Be Chaperoned?" 455. This type of complaint was not, of course, entirely new. Lucy Bird, in the passage at the beginning of this chapter, noted that ladies were frequently ungracious when claiming seats surrendered by male passengers. Similarly, in February 1857 *Appletons' Steam Guide* printed a brief article on "Railway Politeness" in which the author reported that he "kept statistics of female politeness for some months in the Sixth Avenue cars, and found that not more than one lady in twenty thanked me for giving up my seat to her" (43–44). See also "Women and Street Cars."

84. Mrs. Rhodes Campbell, "American Girl," 256.

85. "Courtesy in Travel."

86. "Women's Complaints about Car Seats."

87. "Womanhood and American Chivalry," 420.

88. Censor, *Don't*, 56.

89. Bugg, *The Correct Thing for Catholics*, 141.

90. Florence Hall, *Correct Thing in Good Society*, 181.

91. "Railway Manners."

92. "Courtesy in Travel." See also *New York Times*, 19 April 1881, 4; *Railway Age*, 23 July 1885, 473; and "Notes on Travel," *Railway Age*, 11 March 1886, 134.

93. Leland, *Traveling Alone*, 305.

94. Benjamin Taylor, *The World on Wheels*, 54–55.

95. *Railway Age*, 11 March 1886, 134.

96. *New York Times*, 19 April 1881, 4.

97. See the *Railway Age*, 6 August 1897, 635. As far as I know, the American Society of Railroad Superintendents suggested no alternative title.

According to at least one etiquette manual, "The indiscriminate use of *lady* and *gentleman* indicates want of culture." See Censor, *Don't*, 70–71.

98. "Railway Manners." For another example of women taking up more seats than they are entitled to, see the *New York Times*, 19 April 1881, 4.

See also Stephe Smith, *Romance and Humor of the Rail*, 240. In a story entitled "The Snow Blockade," a colonel observes, "There was some excuse for ladies' cars during the war, but now there is certainly none when all pay the same price for passage."

99. *Railway Age*, 29 July 1880, 402.

100. For an example of domestic language applied to the travel experience of men see *Railway Age*, 4 September 1903, 299. See also William Smith, *A Yorkshireman's Trip to the United States and Canada* (London, 1892), excerpted in Menken, *The Railroad Passenger Car*, 189. According to Smith, the "palace-cars" of the Pennsylvania Railroad's Chicago Limited "fully deserve the title, for they are indeed traveling palaces where one can obtain all the comforts of home."

101. "Do You Remember."

102. See pamphlet, *Pennsylvania R.R. Around the World via Washington and Transcontinental America* (1895) in Warshaw Collection, "Railroads," box 80, AC.

103. Pennsylvania Railroad Co., *Tour to the Mardi Gras*, 7.

104. *The Royal Limited* in Warshaw Collection, "Railroads," box 87, AC.

105. Quoted in Grant, *We Took the Train*, xvi.

106. On amenities for the lone male or business traveler see *Railway Age*, 29 July 1880, 402, on "palace smoking cars." See also "Do You Remember" on rising expectations of passengers; and "The Pennsylvania Railroad," 545, on the introduction of stenographers and typewriters aboard the Pennsylvania Limited.

107. "Womanhood and American Chivalry," 418.

108. Reprinted in the *Railway Age*, 8 January 1885, 26.

109. "Adamless Eden on Wheels."

Edward Filene also used the phrase "Adamless Eden" to describe his Boston department store, a space designed with female consumers' wishes in mind. See Benson, *Counter Cultures*, 76.

110. *Railway Age*, 15 July 1880, 371.

111. *Railway Age and Northwestern Railroader*, 15 November 1895, 562.

112. Cooper, *A Voice from the South*, 111-12.

Chapter Five

1. George, *Forty Years on the Rail*, 186-87. For a similar account of a conductor presented with a two-hundred-dollar silver tea service see Licht, *Working for the Railroad*, 140.

2. Conversely, failure to meet passengers' expectations was often dismissed as rudeness. For examples of references to railway workers as rude or discourteous see Dall, *My First Holiday*, 3, 20; and Dickinson, *A Ragged Register*, 285-86.

3. Benjamin Taylor, *The World on Wheels*, 67.

4. Julia du Pont Shubrick to Gabrielle Shubrick Crofton, 7 March [1852?], Longwood Manuscripts, HML.

5. Leland, *Traveling Alone*, 312.

6. M. M. Shaw, *Nine Thousand Miles*, 14, 18.

7. Kimball, Diary of a Trip to California, 10-11, Western Americana Collection, BL.

8. Dunbar-Nelson, *Give Us Each Day*, 356.

9. Faithfull, *Three Visits to America*, 47.

10. There were maids aboard the trains as well, but their numbers were limited and they tended to work on deluxe trains making limited runs. In 1926, the Pullman Company employed only two hundred maids, compared to over ten thousand porters. Finally, maids never took on the symbolic role associated with porters. See Chateavert, *Marching Together*, 22.

11. Reprinted as "Railway Conductors Defended."

12. *New York Daily Times*, 28 June 1869. Clipping, Pullman Collection, "Pullman Company Public Relations Department, History Files (1860–1968)," box 2, folder 99aa, NL.

13. On the Harvey Girls see Poling-Kempes, *The Harvey Girls*.

14. Raymond's Vacation Excursions, *Three Grand Trips to the Yellowstone National Park* (1888) in Warshaw Collection, "Tours," box 4, AC.

15. "A Chaperon on the Pennsylvania Road."

On Pennsylvania Railroad chaperones see also *Winter Pleasure Tours* (1890) and *Early Autumn Pleasure Trips* (1890) in Warshaw Collection, "Railroads," box 80, AC.

16. Joseph Taylor, *A Fast Life*, 34. See also "The Courteous Conductor."

17. Holderness, *Reminiscences of a Pullman Conductor*, 10, 15.

18. Arnesen, *Brotherhoods of Color*, 24.

19. In 1919, for example, the Brotherhood of Sleeping Car Porters Protective Union asserted that porters were "willing to work and at the same time be courteous." Quoted in ibid., 58.

20. "Teamwork on the Road," 372. The article concluded by condemning those porters who challenged the Pullman system (presumably by joining an independent porters' union). Such behavior endangered "teamwork." For an account of the various efforts to organize Pullman porters and the Pullman Company's responses see Bates, *Pullman Porters*.

21. See, for example, Arnesen, *Brotherhoods of Color*; Bates, *Pullman Porters*; Perata, *Those Pullman Blues*; and Santino, *Miles of Smiles*. All these studies focus on the twentieth century, especially the period after 1925. Nonetheless, the tensions they describe shed light on the experiences of late-nineteenth-century porters.

22. Pennsylvania Railroad Co., *Rules and Regulations* (1864), 45.

23. Reprinted as "The Courteous Conductor."

24. Droege, *Passenger Terminals and Trains*, 334.

25. Joseph Taylor, *A Fast Life*, 40.

26. Quoted in Droege, *Passenger Terminals and Trains*, 180.

27. "The Courteous Conductor." In 1915, *Railway Age Gazette* warned about the costs of discourtesy in similar language: "A surly conductor or a grouchy station employee may often needlessly drive business away by a simple act of discourtesy." See Roy Wright, "Making Friends for Your Railroad?" 130.

28. "Good Manners as a Factor."

29. Licht, *Working for the Railroad*, 44.

30. George, *Forty Years on the Rail*, 186–87.

31. "Y.M.C.A. Influence in Railroad Work," 10.

32. "A Conductor's Home."

33. B. B. Adams, "Every-Day Life of Railroad Men," 569.

34. "A Conductor's Home." Note that the vision of domesticity is incomplete without the inclusion of "lady friends." S. E. Busser, the superintendent of the Santa Fe Railroad's reading rooms, also commented on women's role in sustaining gentlemanly workers. Explaining the company's policy to hold dances at the reading rooms, he wrote, "Women don't run engines, but they do come pretty near to running the men that do. When the love of a pure, good woman handles the throttle of an engine, the passengers on the train can feel assured that they are as nearly safe as it is possible to be." Busser, "Santa Fe Reading Rooms," 131.

35. Athearn, "Saloons versus Railway Clubs," 210.

36. "Reading Rooms for Employes."

37. Busser, "Santa Fe Reading Rooms," 131.

38. "A Model Employes' Library."

39. Certainly railroad companies were not the only businesses turning toward welfare capitalism at this time; many companies sought to shape the morals and behavior of their employees—to bind labor and capital together through a system of shared values, and the values of refined domesticity were often deployed in this effort. One of the best-known examples is George Mortimer Pullman's company town just outside of Chicago. The town was constructed for the workers who built Pullman's famous cars. See Buder, *Pullman*, 60; and Pullman Company, *The Story of Pullman*, 19-23.

40. Licht, *Working for the Railroad*, 80.

41. According to the rule book such conduct was "imperatively required." See Pullman Palace Car Co., *Regulations for Employees*, 6.

42. *Regulations Governing Employés*, 40.

43. Pennsylvania Railroad Co., *Rules and Regulations* (1864), 45; and *Rules and Regulations* (1874), 51 and 53, both in the Pennsylvania Railroad Collection, HML.

44. Charles Paine, *The Art of Railroading*, 127-28.

45. B. B. Adams, "Every-Day Life of Railroad Men," 562-63.

46. Pennsylvania Company, *Rules for the Government of the Transportation Department* (1884), 128. See also Pennsylvania Railroad Co., *Rules and Regulations* (1864). Both in the Pennsylvania Railroad Collection, HML.

47. "Improvement in Character of Railway Men."

48. Reprinted as "Making Railway Journeys Pleasant."

49. "Railroad Manners." On passenger complaints see also Licht, *Working for the Railroad*, 102.

50. Stephe Smith, *Romance and Humor of the Rail*, 235.

51. Report dated 10 July 1872, Reading Company Collection, "Surveillance of Employees, Pinkerton Detective Agency," HML. Also Culver, *The Pullman Car Detective*, 138.

52. Allan Pinkerton, *Tests on Passenger Conductors* (1870), 4.

53. Ray, *The Railroad Spotter*, 53–54.

54. Allan Pinkerton, *Tests on Passenger Conductors* (1870), 4.

55. Culver, *The Pullman Car Detective*, 141–42.

56. Report dated 10 July 1872, Reading Company Collection, "Surveillance of Employees, Pinkerton Detective Agency," HML.

57. Culver, *The Pullman Car Detective*, 264.

58. Ray, *The Railroad Spotter*, 53.

59. George, *Forty Years on the Rail*, 172.

60. Walbourn, *Confessions of a Pullman Conductor*, 87.

61. Holderness, *Reminiscences of a Pullman Conductor*, 227.

62. Ibid., 197.

63. Joseph Taylor, *A Fast Life*, 48.

64. "Convention of Railway Passenger Conductors," 5.

65. B. B. Adams, "Every-Day Life of Railroad Men," 562.

66. Droege, *Passenger Terminals and Trains*, 214.

67. Frances Ellen Watkins Harper made a similar distinction, drawing a line between "true and false politeness." The first "is the child of the cultured heart"; the second "the offspring of the devising mind." See Frances Ellen Watkins Harper, "True and False Politeness," *African Methodist Episcopal Church Review*, 14 (1898), 339–45, reprinted in Harper, *A Brighter Coming Day*, 396–400.

68. Pennsylvania Railroad Co., *Rules and Regulations* (1874), 53; Pennsylvania Company, *Rules for the Government of the Transportation Department* (1884), 52; and Pennsylvania Company, *Rules of the Pennsylvania Lines West of Pittsburgh* (1889), 54. All in the Pennsylvania Railroad Collection, HML.

69. Pullman Palace Car Co., Car Service Rules (1888), 8.

70. *Railway Age*, 30 May 1896, 285. Julia du Pont Shubrick to Gabrielle Shubrick Crofton, 7 March [1852?], Longwood Manuscripts, HML.

71. Indianapolis and Madison Rail Road, *Instructions for Running Trains*, 21. Pennsylvania Company, *Rules for the Government of the Transportation Department* (1884), 50, in the Pennsylvania Railroad Collection, HML.

72. Droege, *Passenger Terminals and Trains*, 189.

73. "Nomadic Flirtation." For a similar story also see George, *Forty Years on the Rail*, 214–16.

74. "Convention of Railway Passenger Conductors," 6. B. B. Adams, "Every-Day Life of Railroad Men," 563.

75. *Regulations Governing Employés* (1871), 41, in the Pennsylvania Railroad Collection, HML.

76. Joseph Taylor, *A Fast Life*, 40.

77. See also Myron Bly, *Legal Hints for Travelers*, 34.

78. B. B. Adams, "Every-Day Life of Railroad Men," 563.

79. *Peck v. New York Central & H. R.R. Co.*, 70 NY 587.

80. "The Ladies' Car."

81. Cooper, *A Voice from the South*, 90.

82. Dunbar-Nelson, *Give Us Each Day*, 67.

83. Frances Ellen Watkins Harper, "We Are All Bound Up Together; Proceedings of the Eleventh Woman's Rights Convention, May 1866," reprinted in Harper, *A Brighter Coming Day*, 218.

84. Terrell, *A Colored Woman*, 296. Faced with the threat of traveling alone in the Jim Crow car at night, Terrell informed the white conductor of her fears. She recalled, "He assured me with a significant look that he himself would keep me company and remain in there with me" (297). Instead Terrell said she would get off the train, wire her father, and make arrangements for suing the railroad for denying her access to the first-class coach. The conductor relented.

85. Hopkins, *Contending Forces*, 348.

86. Ida B. Wells, *Crusade for Justice*, 19.

87. Cooper, *A Voice from the South*, 93–95.

88. Arnesen, *Brotherhoods of Color*, 2.

89. For a history that links Pullman porters and African American political activism see Bates, *Pullman Porters*. Also see Santino, *Miles of Smiles*.

90. Husband, *Story of the Pullman Car*, 155. Husband is quoted in both Arnesen, *Brotherhoods of Color*, 17; and Bates, *Pullman Porters*, 17.

91. Black porters were frequently depicted in advertisements and on sheet music attending to white women. See DeVincent Collection, "Railroad," box 24, folder D, and box 26, folder K, AC.

In my research I have not found significant concern about black porters tending to the needs of white women. The few examples I have found focus on the conduct of white women and men. Pinkerton described how the confidence woman distracted the porter by feigning a headache and playing upon his sympathy. Holderness noted with outrage that white women walked about sleeping cars in their nightgowns and "do not hesitate to treat the porter to an undress rehearsal. . . . What does it matter? . . . . The porter is nobody." Another Pullman conductor claimed that white men bribed porters in order to take advantage of white women. The porters' low wages made such a practice possible. See Allan Pinkerton, *Thirty Years a Detective*, 154; Holderness, *Reminiscences of a Pullman Conductor*, 134-35; Walbourn, *Confessions of a Pullman Conductor*, 25.

92. Even in what appears to be a minstrel song black porters are praised for their work performance. The song, in the voice of the porters, notes that the passengers are often "uneducated and overated." See Charles D. Crandall, "Porters on a Pullman Train" (New York: Hitchcock and McCargo Publishing Company, 1890) in DeVincent Collection, "Railroad," box 26, folder K, AC.

On the place of porters in the black community see Bates, *Pullman Porters*, 23-26.

93. Stephanie Shaw, *What a Woman Ought to Be*, 21-22.

94. Holderness, *Reminiscences of a Pullman Conductor*, 10. Arnesen notes that porters routinely trained new conductors. See *Brotherhoods of Color*, 17.

95. Pullman Palace Car Co., *Car Service Rules* (1888), 7.

96. See Bates, *Pullman Porters*, 43-49.

97. See Pullman Palace Car Co., *Car Service Rules* (1888), 25. Pullman rule books make no explicit mention of Jim Crow. Under the heading "Assignment of Seats and Berths" the 1888 rule book states, "If passengers, in a manner offensive to other passengers, refuse to conform to the rules of the Company, Conductors will, in exercise of discretion, assume the responsibility of refunding their full fare, and requesting them to leave the car." This seems to be a reference to Jim Crow. Pullman did distribute a volume separate from the company rule book that "contains all the Laws, Notices, and Warnings Required by law to be posted in this car." The regulations were listed alphabetically by state and included separate coach laws. See Pullman Co. Operating Department, Employee Instruction Books, 1872-1956, Pullman Collection, NL.

98. Pullman Palace Car Co., *Car Service Rules* (1888), 10. The same rules appear in the 1890, 1893, and 1899 editions of the company rule book. On concerns about intimacy between black porters and white female passengers see note 91 above.

99. Holderness, *Reminiscences of a Pullman Conductor*, 16.

100. Edward Hale, *G.T.T.*, 31.

101. Dunbar-Nelson recorded, "8:10. And the porter making down beds. So suppose I shall have to go to bed soon." Dunbar-Nelson, *Give Us Each Day*, 100.

102. Sanborn, "In the Pullman Car," 467-68. In his study of Pullman porters, Santino notes that the struggle to achieve a balance between service and control was complicated by passengers' racism: porters "had a kind of power and control over the traveling public that, because of the ambiguous nature of the position [tied to race] and the ambivalent attitudes of the public towards them, they had to be very careful in displaying." See Santino, *Miles of Smiles*, 12.

103. Reprinted as "The Sleeping Car Porter." The *Railway Age* notes that the author "seems to have been waked too early in the morning, [and] thus amusingly exaggerates the defects and ignores the virtues of that unfortunate public servant, the sleeping car porter."

104. Sanborn, "In the Pullman Car," 471.

105. Outis, *Lake Superior*, 17.

106. Dall, *My First Holiday*, 20, 424.

107. Santino, *Miles of Smiles*, 71-73.

108. Walbourn, *Confessions of a Pullman Conductor*, 121.

109. Holderness, *Reminiscences of a Pullman Conductor*, 207.

Chapter Six

1. The story is reprinted in a collection of *McClure's* railroad fiction. See Peake, "Night Run of the 'Overland.'" For the original publication see *McClure's Magazine*, June 1900, 143-49. Like many writers of railroad fiction, Peake was himself a railroad man. He worked as a railroad telegrapher and was superintendent of telegraph for the Richmond and Danville Railroad in 1893. He began writing fiction in 1896.

2. Peake, "Night Run of the 'Overland,'" 12, 15, 17.

3. Ibid., 18-19, 25.

4. Ibid., 22, 26, 29.

5. Ibid., 35-37, 39.

6. Donovan, *The Railroad in Literature*, 21. According to Donovan, women were absent from most railroad fiction: "A railroad novel is essentially one of action, adventure, and achievement with the love element of only secondary importance, if present at all. Indeed, women in short stories pertaining to the railroad are almost as scarce as they were on the frontier" (5). Recent contributions of women's historians and historians of the American West lend Donovan's observation a new irony.

7. Peake, "Night Run of the 'Overland,'" 37, 39.

8. On the New Woman in all her various guises see Ware, *Modern American Women*, Chapter 1. See also Smith-Rosenberg, *Disorderly Conduct*, especially the section "The New Woman as Androgyne: Social Disorder and Gender Crisis, 1870–1936."

9. Bederman, *Manliness and Civilization*, 14. She asserts that the New Woman "challeng[ed] past constructions of manhood" by staking claim to previously male activities and privileges.

10. Smith-Rosenberg, *Disorderly Conduct*, 258. See also Ann Douglas, "The Fashionable Diseases."

11. Nancy Cott makes such an argument about advertising images during the 1920s. See Cott, *The Grounding of Modern Feminism*, 172. According to Cott, "Modern merchandising translated the feminist proposal that women take control over their own lives into the consumerist notion of choice. . . . Advertisers hastened to package individuality and modernity for women in commodity form."

For studies that take advertising and magazine fiction seriously as sites for considering women's roles see Scanlon, *Inarticulate Longings*; and Kitch, *Girl on the Magazine Cover*.

12. See Kaplan, "Romancing the Empire" on the role of fiction in circulating images of manly heroics. For an overview of the history of manliness see Kimmel, *Manhood in America*. On the relationship between territorial and commercial expansion and the language of racial dominance see McClintock, *Imperial Leather*.

13. Kaplan's study is a notable exception. For another discussion of popular images of American women in this context see Banta, *Imaging American Women*, 531–33. Significantly, Banta notes that, beginning in the 1880s, women were often used to symbolize the new forces of technology.

14. *Railway Age*, 16 August 1901, 133.

15. For this exchange see the *Railway Age*, 16 August 1901, 133; and 30 August 1901, 189.

16. On Phoebe Snow, see Casey and Douglas, *The Lackawanna Story*, Chapter 22; and Rodney Davis "Earnest Elmo Calkins and Phoebe Snow." Both works treat the Phoebe Snow campaign as an interesting tidbit of railroad history and offer little analysis of her popular appeal.

17. For Calkins's thoughts on his creation's popularity see Calkins and Holden, *Modern Advertising*, 330–32.

18. Lynde, *A Romance in Transit*, 54.

19. Spearman, *The Daughter of a Magnate*, 145–47.

20. *Railway Age*, 1 January 1904, 18.

21. Leland, *Traveling Alone*, vii.

22. W. H. Davenport Adams, *Celebrated Women Travellers*, 216, 433, respectively. Adams also included the following quotation from Pfeiffer: "I smile when I think of those who, knowing me only through my voyages, imagine that I must be more like a man than a woman! Those who expect to see me about six feet high, of bold demeanour [*sic*], and with a pistol in my belt, will find me a woman as peaceable and as reserved as most of those who have never set foot outside their native village" (239).

23. For another take on this process of rendering exceptional women generic, one might also consider the stories that circulated about brave women who saved trains from destruction by delivering messages of washed out bridges or other dangers. The best known of these women was Kate Shelley, who saved the Northwestern's "Colorado Special." For a description of Shelley's exploits see *Railway Age*, 9 August 1901, 115.

24. "Nellie Bly" was the pen name of journalist Elizabeth Cochrane. The name was taken from a Stephen Foster song. Biographies of Bly and accounts of her globe-girdling journey can be found in Ross, *Ladies of the Press*, 48–53; *The Story of Nellie Bly*; Rittenhouse, *The Amazing Nellie Bly*; and, most recently, Kroeger, *Nellie Bly*.

25. On 8 December 1889, the *World* explained, "If [Bly] attempts any description at all of what she saw in England, it would be much the same as a man describing Broadway if he were shot out of a pneumatic tube from the Western Union Building to the Twenty-third Street Uptown Office" (1). Much of Nellie Bly's personal experiences were published after her return in both the *World* and in her own *Nellie Bly's Book*.

26. *Life*, 26 December 1889, 360. For other descriptions of Sadie McGinty's voyage see *Life*, 9 January 1890, 19; and 16 January 1890, 40. On Elizabeth Bisland's trip see Bisland, "Flying Trip Around The World."

27. Bly, "Flying Home," 2. She described the excitement for her readers: "When we had a straight piece of track I let the great machine go for all it was worth, and I am sure that nothing ever moved along the Atlantic and Pacific track in quicker time. . . . For a new engineer, the Master Mechanic said I was a rushing success."

28. Quoted in *The Story of Nellie Bly*, 34–35.

29. *New York World*, 17 November 1889, 15.

30. Ibid., 10 December 1889, 12.

31. Quoted in *The Story of Nellie Bly*, 34. It is worth noting that the daring Nellie Bly married businessman Robert L. Seaman in 1895.

32. Reprinted in the *New York World*, 17 December 1889, 2.

33. *New York World*, 17 January 1890, 2.

34. Letter and response in the *New York World*, 28 November 1889, 5.

35. Nell Nelson, "In an Engine Cab," 9.

For another reference to a woman riding in the engine cab see Prout, "Safety in Railroad Travel," 327-28. The author refers to "a lady [who] sat an hour in the cab of a locomotive hauling a fast express train over a mountain road. . . . The experience was to her magnificent, but the sense of danger was almost appalling."

36. Dress played an important role in the travels of many women. Isabella Bird, for example, was greatly offended by a rumor that she wore trousers during her travels in the United States. She was furious at the suggestion that she was less than properly clad and included the following addendum at the front of the second edition of *A Lady's Life in the Rocky Mountains*: "For the benefit of other lady travellers, I wish to explain that my 'Hawaiian riding dress' is the 'American Lady's Mountain Dress,' a half-fitting jacket, a skirt reaching to the ankles, and full Turkish trousers gathered into frills which fall over the boots, — a thoroughly serviceable and feminine costume for mountaineering and other rough traveling in any part of the world. I add this explanation to the prefatory note, together with a rough sketch of the costume, in consequence of an erroneous statement in the *Times* of November 22d." See Bird, *A Lady's Life*.

37. Lears, *No Place of Grace*; Kaplan, "Romancing the Empire"; Bederman, *Manliness and Civilization*.

38. B. B. Adams, "Every-Day Life of Railroad Men," 556. An 1886 article in the *Railway Age* likewise proclaimed "the heroes of the throttle," as a rule, "sober, steady fellows, absolutely fearless, and possessed of patience that even Job would have envied." "Heroes of the Throttle."

39. Joseph Taylor, *A Fast Life*, 220.

40. See for example George, *Forty Years on the Rail*, 131-33.

41. Busser, "Santa Fe Reading Rooms," 129.

42. Joseph Taylor, *A Fast Life*, 57.

43. George, *Forty Years on the Rail*, 175.

44. *Price Reminiscences*, unpublished manuscript (1893), 263-64, AC. Price was not the only one to use this juxtaposition. See also Warman, "A Thousand-Mile Ride," 173. After describing the work of railroad men, Warman notes, "While this was being accomplished, the one hundred and one passengers laughed, chatted, ate dinner, and went to bed." For the ob-

servation that the responsibilities of the engineer challenged class hierarchy see "Heroes of the Throttle."

45. Charles Graham, "My Dad's the Engineer," (New York: Henry J. Wechman, 1895). This song and E. Lorena Smith, "My Papa's the Engineer," (no date) can be found in the DeVincent Collection, "Railroads," box 26, folder I, AC.

46. Joseph Taylor, *A Fast Life*, 54. For fictional accounts of railroad men unnerved by railroad life see Peters, "Danger Ahead!"; and Spofford, "The Black Bess."

47. *Railway Age*, 20 May 1880, 261. For other accounts of railroad men struck ill on the job (and the dangerous consequences) see George Paine, "Railway Discipline"; "The Wreck on the Central"; and "Petit Mal Among Enginemen."

48. This passage appears in an advertisement in the *Railway Age*, 19 February 1885, 14. For other advertisements implicating the railroads in the proliferation of disease see the *New York World*, 31 December 1889, 6; and 9 January 1890, 6. Both advertisements are for Rogers's Royal Nervine. The second includes the image of a train wreck and reads, in part: "We have indeed become a very rapid and time-saving nation. We go much too fast for health, comfort, or safety in more ways than one. We drive along at top speed, neglecting full hours of sleep, proper exercise, proper time to eat or digest our food, proper time for recreation and the consequence is we are becoming a nervous, excitable and overwrought people."

49. "Influence of Railroad Traveling on Health" (1862), 137. The same study was also discussed in "Influence of Railroad Traveling on Health" (1863).

50. See, for example, "The Railway Surgeon." This article announces the publication of a new biweekly paper committed to the study of railway surgery. Presumably, such a publication was needed because "as the railway has revolutionized almost every sphere of life and human activity, so they have created new classes of injuries and lesions—even new ailments of more or less indefinite and questionable nature."

On railway spine and brain see Schivelbusch, *The Railway Journey*, 134–49. Also Drinka, *The Birth of Neurosis*, 109; and Welke, *Recasting American Liberty*, 150–56.

51. Erichsen, *Railway and Other Injuries*, 22.

52. On frailty as a feminine ideal during the Victorian era see Douglas, "The Fashionable Diseases."

53. Erichsen's study emphasizing the physical nature of railway-related diseases circulated widely in the United States and influenced medical understanding of railway diseases. By the 1880s, many American doctors felt so confident in their ability to diagnose nervous injury that they often testified in court and identified "malingers" who brought illegitimate claims against the railroad companies. One doctor contended that Erichsen's earlier works enumerating the symptoms of railway injuries "became a guide book that might lead the dishonest plaintiff, if he felt so disposed, to set out upon the broad road of imposture and dissimulation with the expectation of getting a heavy verdict." See Hamilton, *Railway and Other Accidents*, 2. For a discussion of Erichsen and his study see also Welke, *Recasting American Liberty*, 150.

In many cases, juries held railroads accountable for the trauma experienced by railroad passengers. See Drinka, *The Birth of Neurosis*, 121; and Welke, *Recasting American Liberty*, 203–34.

54. On the greater fragility of women's nerves see Rosenberg and Smith-Rosenberg, "The Female Animal," 12–13.

55. Van De Warker, "Effects of Railroad Travel," 205.

This sentiment was echoed by an 1875 article in the *New York Times* in which the author entreated husbands to travel without their wives: "If you—a strong, hearty man, with no aches or pains, or nerves—find traveling sometimes so fatiguing, such a weariness, such a pain of a pleasure, what think you is felt by the much more highly-strung creature who travels to please you. . . ?" To take your wife with you when traveling, the article concluded, was an act is of selfishness and cruelty. "The Wife As A Traveler," 4.

56. This medical interpretation, much like previous understandings of railway spine, found its way into American courts where juries frequently awarded women money to compensate them for the fright and the attendant medical problems they experienced as a result of rail travel. See Welke, *Recasting American Liberty*, 203–34.

57. On the problems of establishing legal liability for such injury see Chamallas and Kerber, "Women, Mothers, and the Law." On court rulings upholding the widely held idea that women's primary profession was the bearing and raising of children see Grossberg, "Institutionalizing Masculinity," 145–46.

58. For a similar framing of these questions see Bederman, *Manliness and Civilization*, 88.

59. "Health and Physical Habits," 747; "Health of American Women" (1882), 503; "Health of American Women" (1885), 295. "Are Americans Less Healthy," 630.

60. On this point see Bederman, *Manliness and Civilization*, 25; and Russett, *Sexual Science*, 144-48.

61. In her travel diary, Abby Woodman records an exchange in which an Englishman contends that American women endanger their domesticity when they travel. She also notes that the comment caused the women with whom she was traveling some concern. Woodman, *Picturesque Alaska*, 72-73.

62. Beard, *American Nervousness*, viii-ix, 339.

63. Giedion, "Railroad Comfort and Patent Furniture."

64. "Some Railway Literature."

65. Union Pacific Railway Passenger Department, *A Description of the Western Resorts*, 5.

66. *Vacation Gospel* (1890) in Warshaw Collection, "Railroads," box 88, AC.

67. *New York World*, 8 January 1890, 2.

68. Leland, *Traveling Alone*, viii.

69. *New York World*, 10 December 1889, 12. (Bly was actually twenty-three years old at the time of her tour around the world.)

70. Bisland, "A Flying Trip Around The World," *Cosmopolitan*, 52.

71. This particular Phoebe Snow jingle appears in Calkins and Holden, *Modern Advertising*, 331.

72. Banta, *Imaging American Women*, xxxi. See also Kitch, *Girl on the Magazine Cover*, 37. Kitch describes Charles Dana Gibson's "American Girl" as the "first visual stereotype of women in American mass media."

73. "The American Girl," 265. See also Adam, "Those American Girls in Europe"; and Davis, "The Origin of a Type." For a relatively early example of praise of the American Girl see McCarthy, "American Women and English Women," 33. Here the author argues, "There is hardly an American girl in any city of the Union who does not every day do things which society in England, to say nothing of France of Germany, would not allow her to attempt without holding up the hands and eyes of wonder and dismay."

74. Quoted in Juergens, *Joseph Pulitzer*, 140.

75. *New York World*, 17 November 1889, 4.

76. Ibid., 23 January 1890, 1.

77. Reprinted in ibid., 20 December 1889, 2.

78. Ibid., 8 January 1890, 2.

79. Calkins and Holden, *Modern Advertising*, 330.

Epilogue

1. Moshavi, "In Japan, a Grope-free Ride"; Kannapell, "Behind the Subway Trance"; Rothstein, "The Transcontinental Railroad."

2. For an example of this sensibility see Dirk Johnson, "American Romance."

3. Teachout, "The Best Part."

4. On the portrayal of the business traveler as male see "Business Class as a Way of Life."

5. Concerns about rudeness on the roads and in the air predate the events of 11 September 2001. Nonetheless, the impact of 9/11 on air travel has no doubt exacerbated the problems of incivility. Heightened security measures and passengers' anxiety have added to the stress of travel.

6. Siano, "Honk If You Think I'm Rude."

7. Quotation appears in Mansnerus, "Turbulent Manners Unsettle Fliers," 12.

8. MacGregor, "Fly the Angry Skies."

9. Both quotations are from Estabrook, "A Paycheck Weekly, Insults Daily," 12.

10. MacGregor, "Fly the Angry Skies."

BIBLIOGRAPHY

PRIMARY SOURCES

Manuscript Collections
Chicago, Ill.
  Newberry Library
    Pullman Company Collection
New Haven, Conn.
  Beinecke Rare Book and Manuscript Library, Yale University
    Western Americana Collection
Washington, D.C.
  National Museum of American History, Smithsonian Institution
    Archives Center
        Victor A. Blenkle Postcard Collection
        DeVincent Collection of Illustrated American Sheet Music
        Mr. and Mrs. Arthur D. Dubin Collection
        Photographic History Collection
        Edwin Price Reminiscences
        Pullman Palace Car Company Collection
        Warshaw Collection of Business Americana
    Transportation Division
        Pullman Photograph Collection
Wilmington, Del.
  Hagley Museum and Library
    Du Pont Coleman (Margaretta E.) Collection
    Longwood Manuscripts
    Pennsylvania Railroad Collection
    Reading Company Collection
Winterthur, Del.
  Winterthur Museum, Library, and Garden
    Columbian Exposition Collection
    Joseph Downs Collection of Manuscripts and Printed Ephemera

Newspaper and Periodicals
   Godey's Lady's Book
   New York Times
   New York World
   Railway Age (also as *Railway Age and Northwestern Railroader*
     or *Railway Age Gazette*)

Legal Cases
   Bass v. Chicago & Northwestern Railway Co., 36 Wis. 450 (1874).
   Brown v. Memphis & Charleston Railroad Co., 5 Fed 499 (1880).
   The Chicago & Northwestern Railway Co. v. Williams, 55 Ill. 185 (1870).
   Day v. Owen, 5 Mich. 520 (1858).
   Gray v. Cincinnati Southern R.R. Co., 11 Fed 683 (C.C.S.D. Ohio, 1882).
   Heard v. Georgia R.R. Co., 3 I.C.C.R. 111 (1889).
   Marquette v. The Chicago & N.W. R. Co., 33 Iowa 562 (1871).
   McDonald et ux v. The Chicago & N.W. R. Co., 26 Iowa 124 (1868).
   Peck v. New York Central & H. R.R. Co., 70 N.Y. 587 (1877).
   Smoot v. Kentucky Central Railroad, 13 Fed 337 (C.C.D. Ky., 1881).
   Texas & Pac Ry Co. v. Johnson and Wife, 2 Willson, Civ. Cas. Ct. App.
     185, 186 (1884).
   Wells v. Chesapeake, Ohio & Southwestern R.R. Co., 85 Tenn. 613 (1887).
   West Chester & Philadelphia Railroad. v. Miles, 55 Pa. 209 (1867).

Published Works
Adair, Cornelia. *My Diary, August 30th to November 5th, 1874*. Austin:
   University of Texas Press, 1965.
Adam, Juliette. "Those American Girls in Europe." *North American
   Review*, October 1890, 399–406.
"Adamless Eden on Wheels." *Chicago Tribune*, 7 May 1911.
• Adams, B. B., Jr. "The Every-Day Life of Railroad Men." *Scribner's
   Magazine*, November 1888, 546–69.
• Adams, Charles Francis. *The Railroads: Their Origin and Problems*. New
   York: G. P. Putnam's Sons, 1878.
Adams, Henry. *The Education of Henry Adams*. 1907. Reprint, New York:
   Modern Library, 1931.
Adams, W. H. Davenport. *Celebrated Women Travellers of the Nineteenth
   Century*. London: W. Swan Sonnenschein, 1883.
"Adventures of Miss Sadie McGinty." *Life Magazine*, 26 December 1889,
   360.

"The American Girl." *Nation*, 8 April 1880, 265–66.

"American Railway Traveling." *Putnam's Magazine*, February 1870, 195–205.

* Anderson, C. *A Sleeping-Car Porter's Experience. Treating in Brief Ordinary Life, Founded on Actual Experience*. Chicago: S. C. White, 1916.

Anderson, Thomas M. "Have We a National Character?" *Galaxy*, June 1876, 733–37.

* Andrews, Othello F. *A Few Tales of the Rail and Other Tales*. Chicago: Chicago Chronicle, 1899.

"Are Americans Less Healthy than Europeans?" *Galaxy*, November 1872, 630–39.

"Arms and the Chair." *New York Times*, 14 June 1876, 4.

Armstrong, Mary Frances. *On Habits and Manners*. Hampton, Va.: Normal School Press, 1888.

Athearn, F. G. "Saloons versus Railway Clubs on the Harriman Lines." *Railroad Age Gazette* 46, no. 5 (1909): 208–10.

Babcock, Louis. *Our American Resorts. For Health, Pleasure, and Recreation*. New York: National News Bureau, 1884.

Bachelder, John B. *Popular Resorts and How to Reach Them*. Boston: John B. Bachelder, 1875.

Bain, John, Jr. *Tobacco in Song and Story*. New York: Arthur Gray, 1896.

Baldwin, Simeon Eben. *American Railroad Law*. Boston: Little, Brown, 1904.

Baltimore and Ohio Railroad, Passenger Department. *Reasons Why*. Baltimore: Baltimore and Ohio Railroad, 1901.

———. *Routes and Rates for Summer Tours via Picturesque B&O*. Baltimore: Baltimore and Ohio Railroad, 1896.

Beard, George M. *American Nervousness: Its Causes and Consequences. A Supplement to Nervous Exhaustion (Neurasthenia)*. 1881. Reprint, New York: Arno Press, 1972.

———. "English and American Physique." *North American Review*, December 1879, 588–603.

Beezley, Charles F. *Our Manners and Social Customs: A Practical Guide to Deportment, Easy Manners and Social Etiquette*. Chicago: Elliott & Beezley, 1891.

* Berg, Walter G. *Buildings and Structures of American Railroads: A Reference Book for Railroad Managers, Superintendents, Master Mechanics, Engineers, Architects, and Students*. New York: John Wiley & Sons, 1893.

Bird, Isabella (Lucy). *A Lady's Life in the Rocky Mountains*. 1880. Reprint, London: Virago Press, 1983.

Bisland, Elizabth. "A Flying Trip Around The World." *Cosmopolitan*, 1889, 691-700, and 1890, 51-60, 173-84, 273-84, 401-13, 533-45, 666-77.

Bly, Myron T. *Legal Hints for Travelers*. Boston: New England Railway Publishing Company, 1887.

Bly, Nellie (Elizabeth Cochrane). "Flying Home." *New York World*, 23 January 1890. 1-2.

————. *Nellie Bly's Book: Around the World in Seventy-Two Days*. New York: Pictorial Weeklies, 1890.

Brackett, Anna C. "The Technique of Rest." *Harper's Monthly*, June 1891, 46-55.

Brightly, Schuyler. "Woman and the Weed." *Galaxy*, April 1868, 438-44.

• Brooks Brothers. *On Going Away: A Handbook for Travelers*. New York: Brooks Brothers, 1906.

Brown, Charlotte Hawkins. *"Mammy": An Appeal to the South, and The Correct Thing To Do—To Say—To Wear*. 1919 and 1940. Reprint, New York: G. K. Hall, 1995.

Bugg, Lelia Hardin. *The Correct Thing for Catholics*. New York: Benziger Brothers, 1891.

Burdette, Robert. "Rules for Travelers." *Railway Age*, 10 September 1885, 584.

Busser, S. E. "Santa Fe Reading Rooms." *Out West* 25 (1906): 125-32.

→ Byers, Charles Alma, et al. *Modern Priscilla Home Furnishing Book: A Practical Book for the Woman Who Loves Her Home*. Boston: Priscilla Publishing Company, 1925.

"C.H. & D. Railway." *Railway News*, March 1890, 603.

Calabrella, Countess De. *The Ladies' Science of Etiquette, and Hand Book of the Toilet*. Philadelphia: T. B. Peterson, 186_.

Caldwell, J. A. "Traveling Reduced to a Science." *Pittsburgh Cincinnati and St. Louis Railway*, 1879, 76-85.

Calkins, Earnest Elmo, and Ralph Holden. *Modern Advertising*. New York: D. Appleton, 1905.

Calvert, George H. *The Gentleman*. Boston: Ticknor and Fields, 1863.

Campbell, Helen. "Is American Domesticity Decreasing, and If So, Why?" *Arena*, January 1898, 86-96.

Campbell, Mrs. Rhodes. "American Girl; Her Faults and Her Virtues." *Arena*, July 1898, 254-60.

Canniff, W. H. "The Discipline and Control of Railway Employees."
    Engineering Magazine, January 1901, 753–60.

"Car for Colored People—A Colored Man's Statement." *Railway Age*,
    19 August 1887, 579.

• Carter, Charles Frederick. *When Railroads Were New*. New York:
    Simmons-Boardman Publishing, 1926.

Censor. *Don't: A Manual of Mistakes and Improprieties More or Less
    Prevalent in Conduct and Speech*. New York: D. Appleton, 1883.

"A Chaperon on the Pennsylvania Railroad." *Railway Age*, 2 March 1888,
    138.

Chapple, Joe Mitchell. "Types of Railroad Travellers." *National Magazine*,
    February 1897, 543–50.

Chicago, Rock Island and Pacific Railway. *Nellie in Dreamland. Dedicated
    to the Guardian Fairies of the Chicago, Rock Island and Pacific Railway*.
    Chicago: n.p., 1884.

Clark, Susie. *The Round Trip: From the Hub to the Golden Gate*. Boston:
    Lee and Shepard Publishers, 1890.

"A Conductor's Home." *Railway Age*, 29 November 1883, 760.

"Convention of Passenger Railway Conductors of the City of
    Philadelphia." Conference Proceedings. Philadelphia, 1871.

Cooke, Maud C. *Our Social Manual for All Occasions or Approved Etiquette*.
    Chicago: Monarch Book Company, 1896.

Cooper, Anna Julia. *A Voice from the South*. 1892. Reprint, New York:
    Oxford University Press, 1988.

"The Courteous Conductor." *Railway Age*, 11 February 1885, 81.

"Courtesy in Travel." *Railway Age*, 6 September 1883, 564.

Couthoy, Marion. "A Railway Romance." *Godey's Lady's Book*, March
    1883, 244–48.

Crane, Stephen. *The Open Boat and Other Stories*. New York: Dover
    Publications, 1993.

Crocker, Carrie Beebe. "By Telephone." *Godey's Lady's Book*, March 1883,
    256–58.

• Culver, Major Henry C. (George Farley) *The Pullman Car Detective*.
    Chicago: Laird & Lee, 1894.

Cunniff, M. G. "The Comforts of Railroad Travel." *World's Work*, June
    1903, 3576–80.

Cupid on the Rails, or Romance of A Mann Boudoir Car. New York:
    Hopcraft, Advertisers Publishing, 1885.

Dall, Caroline H. *My First Holiday; or, Letters Home From Colorado, Utah, and California*. Boston: Roberts Brothers, 1881.

Daly, James. *"For Love & Bears"; a description of a recent hunting trip with a romantic finale*. Chicago: F. S. Gray, 1886.

Davis, Richard Harding. "The Origin of a Type of the American Girl." *Quarterly Illustrator*, January 1895, 3–8.

———. *The West From a Car-Window*. New York: Harper and Brothers, 1892.

"A Decade of Railway Travel." *Nation*, 7 May 1891, 374.

Dickinson, Anna. *A Ragged Register*. New York: Harper and Brothers, 1879.

"The Disappearance of the Lunch Basket." *Railway Age and Northwestern Railroader*, 2 March 1894, 123–24.

Donan, Col. P. *The Heart of the Continent: An Historical and Descriptive Treatise for Business Men, Home Seekers, and Tourists, of the Advantages, Resources and Scenery of the Great West*. Chicago: Passenger Department, Chicago, Burlington & Quincy Railroad, 1882.

Doty, Mrs. Duane. *The Town of Pullman*. Pullman, Illinois: T. P. Struhsacker, 1893.

"Do You Remember." *Railway Age*, 11 February 1886, 80.

Dreiser, Theodore. *Sister Carrie*. New York: Harper and Brothers, 1900.

• Droege, John A. *Passenger Terminals and Trains*. New York: McGraw-Hill, 1916.

Dunbar-Nelson, Alice. *Give Us Each Day: The Diary of Alice Dunbar-Nelson*. Edited by Gloria T. Hull. New York: W. W. Norton, 1984.

Earle, Mary Tracy. "'On the Night Train'." *Atlantic Monthly*, June 1900, 748–56.

Emery, Isaiah S. "Railroad Passenger Service." *Cosmopolitan*, 1889, 67–72.

"English and American Railroads." *American*, 1 May 1886, 23–24.

"English and American Railroads Compared." *Van Nostrand's Engineering Magazine*, 34 (1885/6): 151–53.

"English and American Railways." *Harper's New Monthly Magazine* 71, no. 423 (1886): 375–89.

? Erichsen, John Eric. *Railway and Other Injuries of the Nervous System*. Philadelphia: Henry C. Lea, 1867.

Etiquette for Americans. New York: Herbert S. Stone, 1898.

Everett, Marshall. *The Etiquette of Today*. Chicago: Henry Neil, 1902.

• Fagan, James O. *Confessions of a Railroad Signalman*. Boston: Houghton Mifflin, 1908.

Faithfull, Emily. *Three Visits to America*. Edinburgh: David Douglas, 1884.

"The Family Car." *Godey's Lady's Book*, June 1874, 563.

Farnham, Eliza Woodson. *Life In Prairie Land*. [c. 1846] Reprint, New York: Arno Press, 1972.

"A Female Deadbeat." *Railway Age*, 23 September 1880, 499.

"Floy's Journey and What Came of It." *Godey's Lady's Book*, June 1870, 557-58.

• Forney, Matthias N. *The Car-Builders Dictionary: An Illustrated Vocabulary of Terms Which Designate American Railroad Cars, Their Parts, and Attachments*. New York: Railroad Gazette, 1879.

Francis, Harriet Elizabeth. *By Land and Sea*. Troy, New York: Nims and Knight, 1891.

Frost, Sarah Annie. *Frost's Laws and By-laws of American Society*. New York: Dick & Fitzgerald, 1869.

Gardiner, Paul. *A Drummer's Parlor Stories*. New York: A. P. Gardiner, 1898.

General Passenger Department, St. Louis, Kansas City & Northern Railway. *The Famous Rocky Mountain Resorts in Colorado and How to Reach Them*. St. Louis: St. Louis, Kansas City & Northern Railway, 1875.

• George, Charles B. *Forty Years on the Rail*. New York: Belford, Clarke, 1888.

→ Gilman, Charlotte Perkins. *The Home: Its Work and Influence*. 1903. Reprint, Urbana: University of Illinois Press, 1972.

Good Manners. New York: Butterick Publishing Company, 1888.

"Good Manners as a Factor in Railway Management." *Railway Age*, 4 September 1884, 554.

Gordon, Reginald. "Gilded Stairs and Marble Halls." *Engineering Magazine*, February 1916, 708-21.

Gorren, Aline, "American Popularity." *Scribner's Magazine*, October 1898, 497-500.

———. "Womanliness as a Profession." *Scribner's Magazine*, 5 May 1894, 610-15.

Graves, John Temple. *The Winter Resorts of Florida, South Georgia, Louisiana, Texas, California, Mexico and Cuba . . . and How to Reach Them*. N.p.: Passenger Department, Savannah, Florida, and Western Railway Co., 1883.

Hale, Edward Everett. *G.T.T., or The Wonderful Adventures of a Pullman*. Boston: Roberts Brothers, 1877.

———. "The Modern Sinbad. Thirty-one States in Thirty Days." *Atlantic Almanac*, 1870, 3–12.

Hall, Florence Marion. *The Correct Thing in Good Society*. Boston: Estes and Lauriat, 1888.

Hamilton, Allan McLane, M.D., F.R.S.E. *Railway and Other Accidents with Relation to Injury and Disease of the Nervous System, A Book for Court Use*. New York: William Wood, 1904.

"Handicapped." *New York Times*, 23 June 1885, 4.

Hanford, Thomas W. *The Home Instructor: A Guide to Life in Private and Public*. Chicago: Donohue & Henneberry, 1885.

"Hardships on the Rails." *New York Times*, 16 July 1875.

→ Harland, Marion. *House and Home: A Complete Housewife's Guide*. Philadelphia: Franklin New Company, 1889.

Harper, Frances Ellen Watkins. *A Brighter Coming Day: A Frances Ellen Watkins Harper Reader*. Edited by Frances Smith Foster. New York: Feminist Press, 1990.

Hart, Alfred A. *The Traveler's Own Book, A Souvenir of Overland Travel, via The Great and Attractive Route, Chicago, Burlington & Quincy to Burlington. Burlington & Missouri River R.R. to Omaha. Union Pacific Railroad to Ogden. Utah Central Railroad to Salt Lake City. Central Pacific Railroad to Sacramento. Western Pacific Railroad to San Francisco*. N.p., 1870.

Hartley, Cecil B. *The Gentleman's Book of Etiquette, and Manual of Politeness; being a Complete Guide for a Gentleman's Conduct in All His Relations towards Society*. Boston: G. W. Cottrell, 1860.

Hartley, Florence. *The Ladies' Book of Etiquette, and Manual of Politeness. A Complete Hand Book for the Use of the Lady in Polite Society*. Boston: G. W. Cottrell, 1860.

Harvey & Co. *Harvey & Co.'s Popular California Excursions*. N.p., 1888.

"The Health and Physical Habits of English and American Women." *Scribner's Magazine*, 1873, 747–55.

"The Health of American Women." *Nation*, 8 October 1885, 295–96.

"The Health of American Women." *North American Review*, December 1882, 503–24.

"Heroes of the Throttle." *Railway Age*, 29 July 1886, 417.

Hill, Thomas E. *Hill's Manual of Social and Business Forms*. Chicago: Hill Standard Book Company, 1882.

• Holderness, Herbert O. *The Reminiscences of a Pullman Conductor, or Character Sketches of Life in a Pullman Car*. Chicago: n.p., 1901.

→ Holloway, Laura C. *The Hearthstone; or, Life at Home. A Household Manual*. Philadelphia: Bradley, Garretson, 1883.

Holt, Emily. *Encyclopædia of Etiquette*. New York: Syndicate Publishing Company, 1915.

Hopkins, Pauline E. *Contending Forces: A Romance Illustrative of Negro Life North and South*. 1900. Reprint, New York: Oxford University Press, 1988.

Houghton, Walter, et al. *American Etiquette and Rules of Politeness*. Indianapolis: A. E. Davis, 1882.

• Howells, William Dean. *The Sleeping-Car and Other Farces*. New York: Houghton, Mifflin, 1876.

————. *Their Wedding Journey*. Boston: James R. Osgood, 1872.

Howland, David B. "Making Stations Attractive." *World's Work*, March 1901, 517-27.

"How to Tell a Lady." *American Phrenological Journal and Life Illustrated*, March 1865, 77.

How to Make Home Happy: A Housekeeper's Hand Book. New York: John W. Lovell, 1884.

Hull, Jessie Howell. "A Pullman Car Wooing." *Overland Monthly*, March 1891, 288-91.

• Husband, Joseph. *The Story of the Pullman Car*. Chicago: A. C. McClurg, 1917.

Hutchinson, Robert. *A Treatise on the Law of Carriers as Administered in the Courts of the United States, Canada and England*. Chicago: Callaghan, 1906.

Iddings, Lewis Morris. "The Art of Travel." *Scribner's Magazine*, March 1897, 351-67.

The Illustrated Manners Book. A Manual of Good Behavior and Polite Accomplishments. New York: Leland Clay, 1855.

"Improvement in Character of Railway Men." *Railway Age*, 15 February 1889, 112.

Indianapolis and Madison Rail Road. *Instructions for Running Trains on the Indianapolis and Madison Rail Road*. New Albany: Norman & Matthews, 1864.

"Influence of Railroad Traveling on Health." *Eclectic Magazine*, December 1863, 424-26.

"Influence of Railroad Traveling on Health." *Littell's Living Age*, October 1862, 136-38.

Jackson, James C., M.D. *Tobacco; and Its Effect Upon the Health and Character of Those Who Use It*. Dansville, N.Y.: Sanitorium Publishing Company, 1886.

Jenkins, H. D. "Railway Stations." *Overland Monthly*, October 1871, 312-17.

———. "Those Americans." *Overland Monthly*, December 1869, 534-38.

"The 'Jim Crow Car'—Defense of the Georgia Railway Company." *Railway Age*, 19 August 1887, 591.

Johnson, James Weldon. *The Autobiography of an Ex-Coloured Man*. 1912. Reprint, New York: Alfred A. Knopf, 1961.

Jones, Mary Cadwalader. "American Mothers and Daughters." *Delineator*, December 1896, 799-800.

———. *European Travel for Women*. New York: Macmillan, 1900.

Knox, Thomas W. *How to Travel: Hints, Advice, and Suggestions to Travellers by Land and Sea all over the Globe*. New York: C. T. Dillingham, 1881.

"The Ladies' Car." *New York Times*, 1 February 1879, 4.

"Ladies on the Horse Cars." *New York Times*, 2 June 1878, 5.

"Lady Travellers." *Living Age*, August 1896, 279-94.

• Laut, Agnes C. *The Romance of the Rails*. New York: R. M. McBride, 1929.

Leland, Lilian. *Traveling Alone. A Woman's Journey Around the World*. New York: American News Company, 1890.

Leslie, Eliza. *The Behavior Book: A Manual for Ladies*. 4th ed. Philadelphia: Wilis P. Hazard, 1854.

Leslie, Miriam Florence. *California; A Pleasure Trip from Gotham to the Golden Gate*. New York: G. W. Carleton, 1877.

Lloyd, Charles. *Travels at Home and Voyages by the Fire-side for the Instruction and Entertainment of Young Persons*. Vol. 2. Philadelphia: Edward Earle, 1816.

Lynde, Francis. *A Romance in Transit*. New York: Charles Scribner's Sons, 1897.

"Making Railway Journeys Pleasant." *Railway Age*, 26 March 1885, 200.

"The Manners of Railway Officers—Some Popular Ideas on the Subject." *Railway Age*, 1 October 1885, 636.

Martine, Arthur. *Martine's Hand-Book of Etiquette and Guide to True Politeness*. New York: Dick & Fitzgerald, 1866.

Mathews, Victoria Earle. "The Awakening of the Afro-American Woman." In *With Pen and Voice: A Critical Anthology of Nineteenth-*

Century African American Women, edited by Shirley Wilson Logan,
150–55, Carbondale: Southern Illinois University Press, 1995.

McCabe, James D. *National Encyclopædia of Business and Social Forms.
The Laws of Etiquette & c., &c.* New York and Boston: M. R. Gately,
187–.

McCarthy, Justin. "American Women and English Women." *Galaxy*, July
1870, 25–36.

McClary, Ben, and LeRoy P. Graf, eds. "'Vineland' in Tennessee, 1852:
The Journal of Rosine Parmentier." *East Tennessee Historical Society* 31
(1959): 95–111.

Melville, Herman. *The Confidence Man.* 1857. Reprint, New York:
Airmont Publishing Company, 1966.

The Middle States: A Handbook for Travellers. Boston: James R. Osgood,
1877.

• Minot, Robert S. *Railway Travel in Europe and America.* Boston:
A. Williams, 1882.

Mitchell, Maria. *Maria Mitchell: Life, Letters, and Journals.* Edited by
Phoebe Mitchell Kendall. Freeport, New York: Books for Libraries
Press, 1971.

"A Model Employes' Library." *Railway Age*, 28 April 1899, 316.

Moss, Tetia, "A Ride to Stroudsbourg." *Godey's Lady's Book*, June,
1873, 44.

Napheys, George H. *The Physical Life of Women: Advice to the Maiden, Wife,
and Mother.* Philadelphia: H. C. Watts, 1884.

Nelson, Nell. "In an Engine Cab; Nell Nelson's Midnight Ride on the
Washington Express." *New York World*, 5 January 1890, 9.

*Nelson's Pictorial Guide-Books. The Central Pacific Railroad: A Trip across the
North American Continent from Ogden to San Francisco.* New York:
T. Nelson and Sons, n.d.

*Nelson's Pictorial Guide-Books. The Union Pacific Railroad: A Trip across the
North American Continent from Omaha to Ogden.* New York: T. Nelson
and Sons, n.d.

"Nerves and Discipline." *New York Times*, 18 May 1877, 4.

Nixon, James L. "A Chase for an Heiress." In *Mountain and Lake Resorts.*
N.p.: Lackawanna Railroad, 1907.

"Nomadic Flirtation." *New York Times*, 11 September 1877, 4.

Northrop, Henry Davenport. *The Household Encyclopædia of Business and
Social Forms Containing the Rules of Etiquette for all Occasions. . . .*
Boston: Desmond Publishing, 189–.

"Not So Very Hoggish After All." *Railway Age*, 8 October 1885, 646.

"Other Types of the 'American Girl.'" *Nation*, 3 June 1880, 417-18.

"Our Railway Reforms." *Godey's Lady's Book*, January 1874, 88.

Outis. *Lake Superior, The Overland Railroad and The Isthmus*. Buffalo: Warren Johnson, 1872.

"The Pacific Railroad." *Godey's Lady's Book*, August 1869, 174-75.

• Paine, Charles. *The Art of Railroading: A Series of Short Essays from The Railroad Gazette, 1884*. Chevy Chase, Maryland: Claycomb Press, 1987.

Paine, George Hebrad. "Railway Discipline." *Munsey's Magazine*, April 1900, 396-400.

"Pants Pressed for Plebeians." *Railroad Age Gazette*, May 1909, 950.

"Parlor-Car Manners." *New York Times*, 10 July 1892, 4.

Peake, Elmore Elliott. "The Night Run of the 'Overland,' A Story of Domestic Life Among the Railroad People." In *The Railroad*, 11-39. New York: McClure, Phillips, 1901.

Pennsylvania Company. *Rules for the Government of the Transportation Department of the Line of Railroad Operated by the Pennsylvania Company*. Pittsburgh: Jos. Eichbaum, 1884.

————. *Rules of the Pennsylvania Lines West of Pittsburgh, for the Government of the Transportation Department*. Pittsburgh: Wm. G. Johnson, 1889.

"The Pennsylvania Railroad." *Railway News*, January 1890, 541-51, 555-56.

Pennsylvania Railroad Co. *Rules and Regulations for the Government of the Transportation Department of the Pennsylvania Railroad*. Altoona, Pa.: McCrum & Dern, 1864.

————. *Rules and Regulations for the Government of the Transportation Department of the Pennsylvania Railroad Company*. Philadelphia: E. C. Markley & Son, 1874.

————. *Rules for the Government of the Transportation Department*. N.p., 1910.

————. *Tour to the Mardi Gras, Mexico and Grand Canyon*. Philadelphia: Allen, Land & Scott, 1910.

Peters, Mrs. M. Sheffy. "Danger Ahead!" *Godey's Lady's Book*, November 1884, 470-75.

"Petit Mal Among Enginemen." *Railway Age*, 13 March 1903, 359.

Phelps, Egbert. "'Ladies' Car' Humbug." *Lakeside Monthly*, March 1872, 253-54.

Philadelphia & Reading Railway Co. and Affiliated Lines. *Rules of the Operating Department*. N.p., 1903.

Pinkerton, Allan. *Tests on Passenger Conductors made by the National Detective Agency*. Chicago: Beach & Barnard Steam Printers, 1870.

———. *Tests on Passenger Conductors made by the National Detective Agency*. Chicago: Beach, Barnard, 1876.

———. *Thirty Years a Detective. A Thorough and Comprehensive Expose of Criminal Practices of all Grades and Classes. Containing Numerous Episodes of Personal Experience in the Detection of Criminals, and Covering a Period of Thirty Years' Active Detective Life*. New York: G. W. Dillingham, 1886.

Pinkerton, William A[llan]. *Train Robberies, Train Robbers and The 'Holdup' Men*. 1907. Reprint, New York: Arno Press, 1974.

Pohanka, Brian, ed. *A Summer on the Plains, 1870: From the Diary of Annie Gibson Roberts*. Mattituck, NY: J. M. Carroll & Co., 1983.

Porter, Horace. "Railway Passenger Travel." *Scribner's Magazine*, September 1888, 296–318.

Pritchett, Henry S. "The Politics of a Pullman Car." *Atlantic Monthly*, August 1909, 195–98.

Prout, H. G. "Luxury as a Stimulus to Railroad Travel." *Engineering Magazine*, 1896/97, 213–19.

———. "Safety in Railroad Travel." *Scribner's Magazine*, September 1889, 327–50.

Pullman Company. *Instructions for Employes on Cars of the Pullman Company*. Chicago: Roger & Company, 1903.

———. *Instructions for Employes on Cars of the Pullman Company*. Chicago: Roger & Company, 1905.

———. *Instructions for Employes on Cars of the Pullman Company*. Chicago: Roger & Company, 1906.

———. *Instructions for Employes on Cars of the Pullman Company*. Chicago: Gunthorp-Warren Printing Company, 1911.

———. *The Story of Pullman*. N.p., 1893.

"Pullman Conductors and Porters—Their Pay and Penalties." *Railway Age*, 8 April 1886, 190.

Pullman Palace Car Co. *Car Service Rules of the Operating Department of Pullman's Palace Car Company*. Chicago: C. H. Blakely, 1888.

———. *Car Service Rules of the Operating Department of Pullman's Palace Car Company*. Chicago: Columbia Printing Co., 1890.

● ———. *Car Service Rules of the Operating Department of Pullman's Palace Car Company*. Chicago: W. H. Pottinger, 1893.

● ———. *Regulations for Employees*. Chicago: F. Munson, 1872.

Putnam, Emily James. *The Lady: Studies of Certain Significant Phases of Her History*. 1910. Reprint, Chicago: University of Chicago Press, 1970.

"A Queer Mixture." *Railway Age*, 8 July 1886, 375.

"Railroad Manners." *New York Times*, 23 July 1887, 4.

"The Railroad Record." *New York Times*, 12 September 1895, 4.

"Railroad Travel in England and America." *Scribner's Magazine*, October 1894, 399–419.

"Railroads and the People." *Scribner's Monthly*, November 1880, 258–65.

"Railway Advertising in Newspapers." *Railway Age*, 17 March 1905, 358.

● *The Railway Anecdote Book: A Collection of Anecdotes and Incidents of Travel by River and Rail*. New York: D. Appleton, 1871.

"Railway Conductors Defended." *Railway Age*, 22 December 1881, 725.

"Railway Literature." *Living Age*, 17 May 1845, 333–37.

"Railway Manners." *Railway Age*, 6 May 1880, 237.

"Railway-Stations." *Lippincott's Magazine of Popular Literature and Science*, January 1882, 63–69.

"The Railway Surgeon." *Railway Age*, 1 June 1894, 305.

"Railway Travel." *New York Times*, 15 September 1895, 4.

● Ray, Clarence Everly. *The Railroad Spotter; An Expose of the Methods Employed by Detective Agencies and Bonding Companies; The Personal Experiences and Observations of Fifteen Years as a Railway "Spotter."* St. Paul: Virtue Printing Co., 1916.

"Reading Rooms for Employes on the Santa Fe Road," *Railway Age*, 4 March 1887, 156.

Regulations Governing Employés Upon the Main and Branch Lines of the Philadelphia, Wilmington and Baltimore Rail Road Company. Philadelphia: Bryson & Sons, 1871.

Rhodes, Albert. "Shall the American Girl Be Chaperoned?" *Galaxy*, October 1877, 451–58.

Richards, Cornelia. *At Home and Abroad*. New York: Evans and Dickinson, 1854.

"Right Up and Down Woman." *Spice Mill*, June 1881, 173–74.

Riviere, Marguerite. "Experiences at the Sea Shore." *Godey's Lady's Book*, October 1862, 343–45.

———. "The Vertical Railway." *Godey's Lady's Book*, October 1863, 348–53.

Rogers, Robert Vashon. *Wrongs and Rights of a Traveller By Boat—By Stage—By Rail*. Toronto: R. Carswell, 1875.

Russell, Marion B. "Our Trip to Mount Hood, 1893." *Oregon Historical Quarterly* 79 (1978): 203-10.

Ruth, John A. *Decorum: A Practical Treatise on Etiquette and Dress of the Best American Society*. New York: Union Publishing House, 1880.

Rutledge, Belle. "A Railway Journey: And What Came of It." *Godey's Lady's Book*, May 1863, 446-49.

Sanborn, E. W. "In the Pullman Car." *New England Magazine*, June 1895, 467-72.

Sangster, Margaret E. *The Art of Home-Making in City and Country—in Mansion and Cottage*. New York: Christian Herald Bible House, 1898.

"Santa Claus on the Cars." *Railway Age*, 8 January 1880, 19.

Sayings and Writings about the Railways, by those who have Managed them and those who have Studied their Problems. New York: Railway Age Gazette, 1913.

Shaw, M. M. *Nine Thousand Miles on a Pullman Train: An Account of a Tour of Railroad Conductors from Philadelphia to the Pacific Coast and Return*. Philadelphia: Allen, Lane & Scott, 1898.

Shearer, Frederick E. *The Pacific Tourist and Guide of Travel Across the Continent*. New York: J. R. Bowman, 1882.

Sherwood, M. E. W. "American Girls in Europe." *North American Review*, June 1890, 681-91.

"The Sleeping Car Porter." *Railway Age*, 26 August 1880, 449.

"Sleeping Car Progress." *Railway Age*, 5 October 1882, 548.

Smith, Stephe R., ed. *Romance and Humor of the Rail. A book for railway men and travellers, representing everyday life on the railroad in every department of the railway service, with sketches and rhymes of romance, and numerous anecdotes and incidents*. New York: G. W. Carleton, 1873.

Snell, Joseph W., ed. "Roughing It on Her Kansas Claim: The Diary of Abbie Bright, 1870-1871." *Kansas Historical Quarterly* 37 (1971): 233-428.

Socolofsky, Homer, ed. "The Private Journals of Florence Crawford and Arthur Capper." *Kansas Historical Quarterly* 30 (1964): 15-61, 163-208.

"Some Railway Literature." *Railway Age*, 19 February 1880, 82.

Spearman, Frank H. *The Daughter of a Magnate*. New York: Charles Scribner's Sons, 1903.

"Speed on Railroads; American Run that Breaks the World's Record."
North American Review, December 1893, 75–80.

Spofford, Harriet Prescott. "The Black Bess." *Galaxy*, May 1868, 517–28.

Still, William.*The Underground Railroad*. 1872. Reprint, New York: Arno Press, 1968.

Streeter, N. R., ed. *Gems from an Old Drummers Grip*. Groton, N.Y.: N. R. Streeter, 1889.

"The Substitution of Iron and Steel for Wood in Railway Sleepers." *American Architect and Building News*, 11 October 1884, 177–78.

Taylor, Benjamin F. *The World on Wheels and Other Sketches*. Chicago: S. C. Griggs, 1874.

• Taylor, Joseph. *A Fast Life on the Modern Highway; Being A Glance into the Railroad World From a New Point of View*. New York: Harper and Brothers, 1874.

"Teamwork on the Road." *Pullman Porters' Review*, August 1921, 372–73.

Terrell, Mary Church. *A Colored Woman in a White World*. Washington, D.C.: Ransdell, 1940.

"That Dreadful and Ridiculous Thing, The Railroad." *Railway News*, April 1890, 625.

• Thomas, G. F., ed. *Anecdotes and Incidents of Travel, Appleton's Illustrated Railway and Steam Navigation Guide*. N.p., 1859.

• Thomas, John J. *Fifty Years on the Rail*. New York: Knickerbocker Press, 1912.

Thompson, Joseph P. "America as Seen from Europe." *Every Saturday*, 21 February 1874, 201–5.

Thompson, Seymour D. *The Law of Carriers of Passengers*. St. Louis: F. H. Thomas, 1880.

Thomson, Estelle. "Romance on Wheels." *Godey's Lady's Book*, October 1882, 315–47.

Thornwell, Emily. *The Lady's Guide to Perfect Gentility*. New York: Derby and Jackson, 1857.

Tocqueville, Alexis de. *Democracy in America*. 1835 and 1840. Reprint, New York: Modern Library, 1981.

Tournier, Wilton. "Entirely by Rail." *Godey's Lady's Book*, May 1894, 599–609.

"Train Girls." *New York Times*, 19 October 1882, 4.

Transcontinental. Published aboard the Pullman Hotel Express between Boston and San Francisco, 23 May–4 July 1870.

Union Pacific Railway Passenger Department. *A Description of the Western*

Resorts for Health and Pleasure reached via Union Pacific Railway, "The Overland Route." Chicago: Rand, McNally, 1889.

Uzanne, Octave. "The End of Books." *Scribner's Magazine*, August 1894, 221–31.

Van De Warker, Ely. "Effects of Railroad Travel on the Health of Women." *Georgia Medical Companion*, April 1872, 193–206.

"A Vegetable Engine." *Railway Age*, 12 October 1894, 575.

Victor, Metta Victoria. "In the Erie Tunnel." *Godey's Lady's Book*, November 1869, 431–37.

Vose, George L. "Safety in Railway Travel." *North American Review*, October 1882, 374–85.

• Walbourn, Charles H. *Confessions of a Pullman Conductor*. San Francisco: H. S. Crocker, 1913.

Warman, Cy. "A Thousand-Mile Ride on the Engine of the Swiftest Train in the World." *McClure's Magazine*, December 1893, 164–84.

Wayne, Edgar. "My Valise and I." *Godey's Lady's Book*, January 1870, 77–81.

Weld, Charles Richard. *A Vacation Tour in the United States and Canada*. London: Longman, Brown, Green, and Longmans, 1855.

Wells, Ida B. *Crusade for Justice: The Autobiography of Ida B. Wells*. Edited by Alfreda M. Duster. Chicago: University of Chicago Press, 1970.

———. *The Memphis Diary of Ida B. Wells*. Edited by Miriam DeCosta-Willis. Boston: Beacon Press, 1991.

Wells, Richard A., A.M. *Manners, Culture and Dress of the Best American Society*. Springfield, Mass.: King, Richardson, 1890.

Wharton, Edith. *The House of Mirth*. 1905. Reprint, New York: New American Library, 2000.

White, Annie R. *Polite Society at Home and Abroad*. Chicago: Monarch Book Company, 1891.

Whitman, Walt. *Leaves of Grass*. 1892. Reprint, New York: Modern Library, 2001.

"The Wife as a Traveler." *New York Times*, 28 November 1875, 4.

Williams, Fannie Barrier. "Vacation Values." *Voice of the Negro*, December 1905, 863–66.

Williams, Henry T. *The Pacific Tourist*. New York: Henry T. Williams, 1879.

Williams, Samuel. "Some Americans Who Travel." *Overland Monthly*, May 1869, 418–24.

Wilson, Edward L. *Wilson's Lantern Journeys: A Series of Descriptions of*

Journeys at Home and Abroad. Including the Centennial Exhibition and the Paris Exposition for Use with Views in the Magic Lantern or the Stereoscope. 6th ed. Philadelphia: Edward L. Wilson, 1879.

"Woman and the Sleeping Car." *Railway Age*, 11 October 1889, 677.

"Womanhood and American Chivalry." *Lippincott's Magazine of Literature, Science and Education*, April 1868, 417–21.

"Women and Children in America." *Godey's Lady's Book*, May 1867, 467–68.

"Women and Street Cars." *Godey's Lady's Book*, March 1864, 312.

"Women's Complaints about Car Seats." *Railway Age*, 12 November 1885, 722.

• Wood, Stanley. *An Unattended Journey, or Ten Thousand Miles by Rail. A Tour by Four Young Ladies*. Chicago: White City Art Company, 1895.

Woodlock, Thomas F. "Increased Confidence in American Railroad Securities." *Engineering Magazine*, May 1897, 165–71.

Woodman, Abby. *Picturesque Alaska: A Journal of a Tour Among the Mountains, Seas and Islands of the Northwest, from San Francisco to Sitka*. New York: Houghton Mifflin, 1889.

Woods, E. M. *The Negro in Etiquette: A Novelty*. St Louis: Buxton & Skinner, 1899.

"A Word for the Traveling Public." *New York Times*, 23 August 1865, 2.

"The Wreck on the Central of New Jersey." *Railway Age*, 6 March 1903, 322.

• Wright, Julia MacNair. *On a Snow-Bound Train. A Winter's Tale*. New York: American Tract Society, 1893.

Wright, Roy V. "Are You Making Friends for Your Railroad? An Appeal to Every Employee Concerning the Vital Necessity of Directing His Efforts Toward This End." *Railway Age Gazette*, 22 January 1915, 129–31.

———. *The Complete Home: An Encyclopædia of Domestic Life and Affairs*. Philadelphia: Bradley, Garretson, 1879.

"Y.M.C.A. Influence in Railroad Work." *International Ticket Agent and Traffic Revue*, February 1898, 10–11.

Young, Nellie May. *An Oregon Idyl*. Glendale, Calif.: Arthur H. Clark Company, 1961.

Abelson, Elaine. *When Ladies Go A-Thieving: Middle-Class Shoplifters in the Victorian Department Store*. New York: Oxford University Press, 1989.

Alexander, Edwin P. *Down at the Depot; American Railroad Stations from 1831 to 1920*. New York: C. N. Potter, 1970.

Alvarez, Eugene. *Travel on Southern Antebellum Railroads, 1828–1860*. University, Ala.: University of Alabama Press, 1974.

Anderson, Benedict. *Imagined Communities*. New York: Verso, 1991.

Arnesen, Eric. *Brotherhoods of Color: Black Railroad Workers and the Struggle for Equality*. Cambridge: Harvard University Press, 2002.

Aron, Cindy Sondik. *Ladies and Gentlemen of the Civil Service: Middle-Class Workers in Victorian America*. New York: Oxford University Press, 1987.

———. *Working at Play: A History of Vacations in the United States*. New York: Oxford University Press, 1999.

Ayers, Edward. *Promise of the New South: Life After Reconstruction*. New York: Oxford University Press, 1992.

Bain, David Haward. *Empire Express: Building the First Transcontinental Railroad*. New York: Viking, 1999.

Baker, Paula. "The Domestication of Politics: Women and American Political Society, 1780–1920." *American Historical Review* 89, no. 3 (1984): 620–47.

Banta, Martha. *Imaging American Women: Idea and Ideals in Cultural History*. New York: Columbia University Press, 1987.

Bates, Beth Tomkins. *Pullman Porters and the Rise of Protest Politics in Black America, 1925–1945*. Chapel Hill: University of North Carolina Press, 2001.

Bederman, Gail. *Manliness and Civilization: A Cultural History of Gender and Race in the United States, 1880–1917*. Chicago: University of Chicago Press, 1995.

Beebe, Lucius. *Mr. Pullman's Elegant Palace Car*. Garden City, N.Y.: Doubleday, 1961.

Bender, Thomas. *Community and Social Change in America*. Baltimore: Johns Hopkins University Press, 1978.

———. "Metropolitan Life and the Making of Public Culture." In *Power, Culture, and Place: Essays on New York City*, edited by John Hull Mollenkopf, 261–71. New York: Russell Sage Foundation, 1988.

————. *New York Intellect: A History of Intellectual Life in New York City, from 1750 to the Beginning of Our Own Time*. Baltimore: Johns Hopkins University Press, 1987.

————. *Toward an Urban Vision*. Baltimore: Johns Hopkins University Press, 1975.

————. "Wholes and Parts: The Need for Synthesis in American History." *Journal of American History* 73 (June 1986): 120-36.

Benson, Susan Porter. *Counter Cultures: Saleswomen, Managers, and Customers in American Department Stores, 1890-1940*. Urbana: University of Illinois Press, 1986.

Berman, Marshall. *All That Is Solid Melts into Air: The Experience of Modernity*. New York: Penguin, 1982.

Birkett, Dea. *Spinsters Abroad*. New York: Basil Blackwell, 1989.

Blackmar, Elizabeth. *Manhattan for Rent, 1785-1850*. Ithaca: Cornell University Press, 1989.

Blewett, Mary H. *Men, Women, and Work: Class, Gender, and Protest in the New England Shoe Industry, 1780-1910*. Urbana: University of Illinois Press, 1988.

Bloom, Lisa. *Gender on Ice: American Ideologies of Polar Expeditions*. Minneapolis: University of Minnesota Press, 1994.

Blumin, Stuart M. *The Emergence of the Middle Class: Social Experience in the American City, 1760-1900*. New York: Cambridge University Press, 1989.

Blunt, Alison. *Travel, Gender, and Imperialism: Mary Kingsley and West Africa*. New York: Guilford Press, 1994.

Blunt, Alison, and Gillian Rose, ed. *Writing Women and Space: Colonial and Postcolonial Geographies*. New York: Guilford Press, 1994.

Boris, Eileen. "From Parlor to Politics: Women and Reform in America, 1890-1925." *Radical History Review* 5 (Spring 1991): 191-203.

Botkin, B. A., and Alvin H. Harlow, eds. *A Treasury of Railroad Folklore: The Stories, Tall Tales, Traditions, Ballads and Songs of the American Railroad Man*. New York: Crown Publishers, 1953.

Brand, Dana. *The Spectator and the City in Nineteenth-Century American Literature*. New York: Cambridge University Press, 1991.

Brandimarte, Cynthia A. "'To Make the World More Homelike': Gender, Space, and America's Tea Room Movement." *Winterthur Portfolio* 30, no. 1 (1995): 1-19.

Brody, Jennifer Devere. "Rereading Race and Gender: When White Women Matter." *American Quarterly* 48, no. 1 (March 1996): 153-60.

Bronner, Simon J., ed. *Consuming Visions: Accumulation and Display of Goods in America: 1880-1920*. Winterthur, Del.: Henry Francis du Pont Winterthur Museum, 1989.

Brown, Elsa Barkley. "Polyrhythm and Improvization: Lessons for Women's History." *History Workshop* 31 (1991): 85-90.

———. "'What Has Happened Here': The Politics of Difference in Women's History and Feminist Politics." *Feminist Studies* 18 (Summer 1992): 295-312.

Brucken, Carolyn. "In the Public Eye: Women and the American Luxury Hotel." 31, no. 4 (Winter 1996): 203-20.

Buder, Stanley. *Pullman: An Experiment in Industrial Order and Community Planning, 1880-1930*. New York: Oxford University Press, 1967.

Burman, Shirley. "Women and the American Railroad." *Journal of the West* 33, no. 2 (1994): 36-41.

Bushman, Richard. *The Refinement of America: Persons, Houses, Cities*. New York: Vintage, 1992.

"Business Class as a Way of Life." *New York Times Magazine*, special issue, 8 March 1998.

Casey, Robert J., and W. A. S. Douglas. *The Lackawanna Story: The First Hundred Years of the Delaware, Lackawanna, and Western Railroad*. New York: McGraw-Hill, 1951.

Cell, John W. *The Highest Stage of White Supremacy: The Origins of Segregation in South Africa and the American South*. New York: Cambridge University Press, 1982.

Certeau, Michel de. *The Practice of Everyday Life*. Berkeley: University of California Press, 1984.

Chamallas, Martha, and Linda Kerber. "Women, Mothers, and the Law of Fright: A History." *Michigan Law Review* 88, no. 4 (1990): 814-63.

Chandler, Alfred. *Visible Hand: The Managerial Revolution in American Business*. Cambridge: Harvard University Press, 1977.

Chateavert, Melinda. *Marching Together: Women of the Brotherhood of Sleeping Car Porters*. Urbana: University of Illinois Press, 1998.

Chauncey, George. *Gay New York: Gender, Urban Culture, and the Making of the Gay Male World 1890-1940*. New York: Basic Books, 1994.

Chudacoff, Howard P. *The Age of the Bachelor: Creating an American Subculture*. Princeton: Princeton University Press, 1999.

Clark, Clifford Edward, Jr. *The American Family Home*. Chapel Hill: University of North Carolina, 1986.

Cocks, Catherine. *Doing the Town: The Rise of Urban Tourism in the United States, 1850–1915*. Berkeley: University of California Press, 2001.

Cohen, Patricia Cline. "Safety and Danger: Women on American Public Transport, 1750–1850." In *Gendered Domains: Rethinking Public and Private in Women's History*, edited by Dorothy O. Helly and Susan M. Reverby, 109–22. Ithaca: Cornell University Press, 1992.

Cohen, William. *At Freedom's Edge: Black Mobility and the Southern White Quest for Racial Control, 1861–1915*. Baton Rouge: Louisiana State University Press, 1991.

Cohn, Carol. "Wars, Wimps, and Women: Talking Gender and Thinking War." In *Gendering War Talk*, edited by Miriam Cooke and Angela Woollacott, 227–46. Princeton: Princeton University Press, 1993.

Condit, Carl W. *The Railroad and the City*. Columbus: Ohio State University, 1977.

Corn, Joseph. "Making Flying 'Thinkable': Women Pilots and the Selling of Aviation, 1927–1940." *American Quarterly* 31 (1979): 556–71.

Cott, Nancy. *The Bonds of Womanhood: "Women's Sphere" in New England, 1780–1835*. New Haven: Yale University Press, 1977.

———. *The Grounding of Modern Feminism*. New Haven: Yale University Press, 1987.

———. "Of Men's History and Women's History." In *Meanings for Manhood: Constructions of Masculinity in Victorian America*, edited by Mark C. Carnes and Clyde Griffen, 205–11. Chicago: University of Chicago Press, 1990.

Cronon, William. *Nature's Metropolis: Chicago and the Great West*. New York: W. W. Norton, 1991.

Danly, Susan, and Leo Marx, ed. *The Railroad in American Art: Representations of Technological Change*. Cambridge: MIT Press, 1988.

Davies, Margery. *Woman's Place Is at the Typewriter*. Philadelphia: Temple University Press, 1982.

Davin, Anna. "Imperialism and Motherhood." *History Workshop* 5 (Spring 1978): 9–65.

Davis, Rodney O. "Earnest Elmo Calkins and Phoebe Snow." *Railroad History* 163 (1990): 89–92.

D'Emilio, John, and Estelle B. Freedman. *Intimate Matters: A History of Sexuality in America*. New York: Perennial Library, 1989.

"Dinner in the Diner: A History of Railway Catering." *Railroad History* 159 (Fall 1988) 98–99.

Donovan, Frank P., Jr. *The Railroad in Literature: A Brief Survey of Railroad*

Fiction, Poetry, Songs, Biography, Essays, Travel and Drama in the English Language, Particularly Emphasizing Its Place in American Literature. Boston: Railway & Locomotive Historical Society, 1940.

Douglas, Ann. "The Fashionable Diseases: Women's Complaints and Their Treatment in Nineteenth-Century America." In *Women and Health in America*, edited by Judith Walzer Leavitt, 222-38. Madison: University of Wisconsin Press, 1984.

————. *The "Feminization" of American Culture.* New York: Knopf, 1977.

Drinka, George Frederick. *The Birth of Neurosis: Myth, Malady, and the Victorians.* New York: Simon and Schuster, 1984.

Duggan, Lisa. "Theory in Practice: The Theory Wars, or Who's Afraid of Judith Butler." *Journal of Women's History* 10, no. 1 (Spring 1998): 9-19.

Earle, Edward W., ed. *Points of View: The Sterograph in America—A Cultural History.* Rochester, N.Y.: Visual Studies Workshop Press, 1979.

Elshtain, Jean Bethke. *Public Man, Private Woman: Women in Social and Political Thought.* Princeton: Princeton University Press, 1981.

Enloe, Cynthia. *Bananas, Beaches, and Bases: Making Feminist Sense of International Politics.* Berkeley: University of California Press, 1990.

Enstad, Nan. "Dressed for Adventure: Working Women and Silent Movie Serials in the 1910s." *Feminist Studies* 21 (1995): 67-90.

————. *Ladies of Labor, Girls of Adventure: Working Women, Popular Culture, and Labor Politics at the Turn of the Twentieth Century.* New York: Columbia University Press, 1999.

Erenberg, Lewis A. *Steppin' Out: New York Nightlife and the Transformation of American Culture, 1890-1930.* Chicago: University of Chicago Press, 1981.

Estabrook, Barry. "A Paycheck Weekly, Insults Daily." *New York Times,* 15 February 2004, 10-12.

Ethington, Philip J. *The Public City: The Political Construction of Urban Life in San Francisco, 1850-1900.* New York: Cambridge University Press, 1994.

Fabian, Ann. *Card Sharps, Dream Books and Bucket Shops: Gambling in Nineteenth-Century America.* Ithaca: Cornell University Press, 1990.

Faust, Drew Gilpin. *Mothers of Invention: Women of the Slaveholding South in the American Civil War.* Chapel Hill: University of North Carolina Press, 1996.

Federhen, Deborah Anne, et al. *Accumulation and Display: Mass*

Marketing Household Goods in America, 1880–1920. Winterthur, Del.:
Henry Francis du Pont Winterthur Museum, 1986.

Felski, Rita. *The Gender of Modernity*. Cambridge: Harvard University
Press, 1995.

Finley, Ruth E. *The Lady of Godey's, Sarah Josepha Hale*. Philadelphia:
J. B. Lippincott Company, 1931.

Fischer, Claude S. *America Calling: A Social History of the Telephone to
1940*. Berkeley: University of California Press, 1992.

Fogel, Robert William. *Railroads and American Economic Growth: Essays
in Econometric History*. Baltimore: Johns Hopkins University Press,
1964.

Foucault, Michel. "Of Other Spaces." *Diacritics* 16, no. 1 (Spring 1986):
22–27.

Fox, Richard Wightman, and T. J. Jackson Lears, eds. *The Culture of
Consumption: Critical Essays in American History, 1880–1980*. New York:
Pantheon, 1983.

Fraser, Nancy. "Rethinking the Public Sphere: A Contribution to the
Critique of Actually Existing Democracy." In *Habermas and the Public
Sphere*, edited by Craig Calhoun, 109–42. Cambridge: MIT Press,
1992.

Frederick, Bonnie, and Susan H. McLeod, eds. *Women and the Journey:
The Female Travel Experience*. Pullman: Washington State University
Press, 1993.

Freeman, Michael. *Railways and the British Imagination*. New Haven:
Yale University Press, 1999.

Garvey, Ellen Gruber. *The Adman in the Parlor: Magazines and the
Gendering of Consumer Culture, 1880s to 1910s*. New York: Oxford
University Press, 1996.

———. "Reframing the Bicycle: Advertising-Supported Magazines and
Scorching Women." *American Quarterly* 47 (1995): 66–101.

Giddings, Paula. *When and Where I Enter: The Impact of Black Women on
Race and Sex in America*. New York: William Morrow, 1984.

Giedion, Sigfried. "Railroad Comfort and Patent Furniture." *Technology
Review* (1944): 25–31, 97–103.

Gilfoyle, Timothy. *City of Eros: New York City, Prostitution, and the
Commercialization of Sex, 1790–1920*. New York, W. W. Norton, 1992.

Gilmore, Glenda. *Gender and Jim Crow: Women and the Politics of White
Supremacy in North Carolina, 1896–1920*. Chapel Hill: University of
North Carolina Press, 1996.

Gordon, Sarah Herbert. "A Society of Travelers: Rail Travel 1865–1910." Ph.D. diss., University of Chicago, 1981.

Grant, H. Roger, ed. *We Took the Train*. Dekalb: Northern Illinois University Press, 1990.

Grave, Kathleen De. *Swindler, Spy, Rebel: The Confidence Woman in Nineteenth-Century America*. Columbia: University of Missouri Press, 1995.

Green, Leon. "'Fright' Cases." *Illinois Law Review* 27 (1933): 761–886.

Grier, Katherine. *Culture and Comfort: People, Parlors, and Upholstery*. Rochester, N.Y.: Strong Museum, 1988.

Grossberg, Michael. "Institutionalizing Masculinity: The Law as a Masculine Profession." In *Meanings for Manhood: Constructions of Masculinity in Victorian America*, edited by Mark C. Carnes and Clyde Griffen, 133–51. Chicago: University of Chicago Press, 1990.

Habermas, Jürgen. *The Structural Transformation of the Public Sphere: An Inquiry into a Category of Bourgeois Society*. Cambridge: MIT Press, 1989.

Hale, Grace Elizabeth. *Making Whiteness: The Culture of Segregation in the South, 1890–1940*. New York: Pantheon, 1998.

Haley, Bruce. *The Healthy Body and Victorian Culture*. Cambridge: Harvard University Press, 1978.

Hall, Jacquelyn Dowd. *Revolt against Chivalry: Jesse Daniel Ames and the Women's Campaign against Lynching*. Revised edition. New York: Columbia University, 1993.

Halttunen, Karen. *Confidence Men and Painted Women: A Study of Middle-Class Culture in America, 1830–1870*. New Haven: Yale University Press, 1982.

———. "From Parlor to Living Room: Domestic Space, Interior Decoration, and the Culture of Personality." In *Consuming Visions: Accumulation and Display of Goods in America: 1880–1920*, edited by Simon J. Bronner, 157–89. Winterthur, Del.: Henry Francis du Pont Winterthur Museum, 1989.

Hamalian, Leo. *Ladies on the Loose*. New York: Dodd, Mead, 1981.

Harding, Carroll R. *George M. Pullman (1831–1897) and the Pullman Company*. New York: Newcomen Society in North America, 1951.

Harris, Cheryl I. "Whiteness as Property." *Harvard Law Review* 106 (June 1993): 1709–91.

Harris, Neil. *Cultural Excursions: Marketing Appetites and Cultural Tastes in Modern America*. Chicago: University of Chicago Press, 1990.

Hayden, Dolores. *The Grand Domestic Revolution: A History of Feminist Designs for American Homes, Neighborhoods, and Cities*. Cambridge: MIT Press, 1981.

———. *Redesigning the American Dream: The Future of Housing, Work, and Family Life*. New York: W. W. Norton, 1984.

Hemphill, Christina Dallett. "Manners for Americans: Interaction Ritual and the Social Order." Ph.D. diss., Brandeis University, 1988.

Higginbotham, Evelyn Brooks. "African-American Women's History and the Metalanguage of Race." *Signs* 17 (Winter 1992): 251–74.

———. "Beyond the Sound of Silence: Afro-American Women in History." *Gender and History* 1, no. 1 (Spring 1989): 50–67.

Higham, John. "The Reorientation of American Culture in the 1890s." In *The Origins of Modern Consciousness*, edited by John Weiss, 25–48. Detroit: Wayne State University Press, 1965.

Hine, Darlene Clark, ed. *Black Women in America: An Historical Encyclopedia*. New York: Carlson Publishing, 1993.

Hodes, Martha. "The Sexualization of Reconstruction Politics: White Women and Black Men in the South after Reconstruction." *Journal of the History of Sexuality* 3, no. 3 (January 1993): 402–17.

Holbrook, Stewart H. *The Story of American Railroads*. New York: Bonanza Books, 1947.

Hollander, Ron. *All Aboard: The Story of Joshua Lionel Cowen and His Lionel Train Company*. New York: Workman Publishing, 2000.

Horowitz, Daniel. "Frugality or Comfort: Middle-Class Styles of Life in the Early 20th Century." *American Quarterly* 37, no. 2 (Summer 1985): 239–59.

Horowitz, Helen Lefkowitz. *Alma Mater: Design and Experience in the Women's Colleges from Their Nineteenth-Century Beginnings to the 1930s*. New York: Alfred A. Knopf, 1984.

Howe, Daniel Walker, ed. *Victorian America*. Philadelphia: University of Pennsylvania Press, 1976.

Huff, Cynthia A., and Suzanne L. Bunkers, ed. *Inscribing the Daily: Critical Essays on Women's Diaries*. Amherst: University of Massachusetts Press, 1996.

Hughes, Jonathan. *American Economic History*. 2nd ed. Glenview, Ill.: Scott, Foresman, 1987.

Hunter, Tera. *To 'Joy My Freedom: Southern Black Women's Lives and Labors after the Civil War*. Cambridge: Harvard University Press, 1997.

Ingemanson, Birgitta Maria. "Under Cover: The Paradox of Victorian

Women's Travel Costume." In *Women and the Journey: The Female Travel Experience*, edited by Bonnie Frederick and Susan H. McLeod, 5–23. Pullman, Wash.: Washington State University Press, 1993.

Jackson, Kenneth. *Crabgrass Frontiers: The Suburbanization of the United States*. New York: Oxford University Press, 1985.

Jacobson, Matthew Frye. *Whiteness of a Different Color: European Immigrants and the Alchemy of Race*. Cambridge: Harvard University Press, 1998.

Johnson, Dirk. "American Romance: A Journey on Rails." *New York Times*, 20 August 1995, 20.

Johnson, Walter. *Soul by Soul: Life Inside the Antebellum Slave Market*. Cambridge: Harvard University Press, 2000.

Juergens, George. *Joseph Pulitzer and "The New York World"*. Princeton: Princeton University Press, 1966.

Kannapell, Andrea. "Behind the Subway Trance." *New York Times*, 16 July 1995, sec. 13, p. 1.

Kaplan, Amy. "Manifest Domesticity." *American Literature* 70, no. 3 (September 1998): 581–605.

———. "Romancing the Empire: The Embodiment of American Masculinity in the Popular Historical Novel of the 1890s." *American Literary History* 2, no. 4 (Winter 1990): 659–90.

———. *The Social Construction of American Realism*. Chicago: University of Chicago Press, 1988.

Kardish, Laurence. *Junction and Journey: Trains and Film*. New York: Museum of Modern Art, 1991.

Kasson, John F. *Amusing the Million: Coney Island at the Turn of the Century*. New York: Hill and Wang, 1978.

———. *Civilizing the Machine: Technology and Republican Values in America, 1776–1900*. New York: Viking Press, 1976.

———. *Rudeness and Civility: Manners in Nineteenth-Century Urban America*. New York: Hill and Wang, 1990.

Kelley, Mary. *Private Woman, Public Stage: Literary Domesticity in Nineteenth-Century America*. New York: Oxford University Press, 1984.

Kelley, Robin D. G. "Congested Terrain: Resistance on Public Transportation." In *Race Rebels: Culture, Politics, and the Black Working Class*, 55–75. New York: Free Press, 1994.

Kerber, Linda. *No Constitutional Right To Be Ladies: Women and the Obligations of Citizenship*. New York: Hill and Wang, 1998.

———. "Separate Spheres, Female Worlds, Woman's Place: The

Rhetoric of Women's History." *Journal of American History* 75, no. 1 (June 1988): 9-39.

Kimmel, Michael. *Manhood in America: A Cultural History*. New York: Free Press, 1996.

Kirby, Lynne Elizabeth. "The Railroad and the Cinema, 1895-1929: Institutions, Aesthetics and Gender." Ph.D. diss., University of California, Los Angeles, 1989.

Kitch, Carolyn. *The Girl on the Magazine Cover: The Origins of Visual Stereotypes in American Mass Media*. Chapel Hill: University of North Carolina Press, 2001.

Kraditor, Aileen S. *The Ideas of the Woman Suffrage Movement, 1890-1920*. New York: W. W. Norton, 1981.

Kroeger, Brooke. *Nellie Bly: Daredevil, Reporter, Feminist*. New York: Times Books, 1994.

Kwolek-Folland, Angel. "The Elegant Dugout: Domesticity and Moveable Culture in the United States, 1870-1900." *American Studies* 25, no. 2 (Summer 1984): 21-37.

————. *Engendering Business: Men and Women in the Corporate Office, 1870-1930*. Baltimore: Johns Hopkins University Press, 1994.

Leach, William. *Land of Desire: Merchants, Power, and the Rise of a New American Culture*. New York: Vintage Books, 1993.

————. "Transformations in a Culture of Consumption: Women and Department Stores, 1890-1925." *Journal of American History* 71, no. 2 (September 1984): 319-42.

Lears, T. J. Jackson. *Fables of Abundance: A Cultural History of Advertising in America*. New York: Basic Books, 1994.

————. *No Place of Grace, Antimodernism and the Transformation of American Culture, 1880-1920*. New York: Pantheon Books, 1981.

Leavitt, Sarah A. *From Catherine Beecher to Martha Stewart: A Cultural History of Domestic Advice*. Chapel Hill: University of North Carolina Press, 2002.

Levine, Lawrence. *Highbrow/Lowbrow: The Emergence of Cultural Hierarchy in America*. Cambridge: Harvard University Press, 1988.

Leyendecker, Liston E. *Palace Car Prince: A Biography of George Mortimer Pullman*. Niwot, Colo.: University Press of Colorado, 1992.

Licht, Walter. *Working for the Railroad; The Organization of Work in the Nineteenth Century*. Princeton: Princeton University Press, 1983.

Loeb, Lori Anne. *Consuming Angels: Advertising and Victorian Women*. New York: Oxford University Press, 1994.

Lofgren, Charles. *The Plessy Case: A Legal-Historical Interpretation*. New York: Oxford University Press, 1987.

Lomazzi, Brad S. *Railroad Timetables, Travel Brochures and Posters*. Spencertown, N.Y.: Golden Hill Press, 1995.

Lutz, Tom. *American Nervousness 1903, An Anecdotal History*. Ithaca: Cornell University Press, 1991.

MacCannell, Dean. *The Tourist*. New York: Schocken Books, 1989.

MacGregor, Jeff. "Fly the Angry Skies." *New York Times Magazine*, 24 September 2000, 21.

Mack, Arien, ed. *Home: A Place in the World*. New York: New York University Press, 1993.

Mansnerus, Laura. "Turbulent Manners Unsettle Flyers." *New York Times*, 15 February 2004, 11-12.

Marchand, Roland. *Advertising the American Dream: Making Way for Modernity, 1920-1940*. Berkeley: University of California Press, 1985.

Marsh, Margaret. "Suburban Men and Masculine Domesticity, 1870-1915." *American Quarterly* 40, no. 2 (June 1988): 165-86.

Martin, Albro. *Railroads Triumphant: The Growth, Rejection, and Rebirth of a Vital American Force*. New York: Oxford University Press, 1992.

Martin, Michele. *"Hello Central?" Gender, Technology, and Culture in the Formation of Telephone Systems*. Buffalo: McGill-Queen's University Press, 1991.

Marx, Leo. *The Machine in the Garden: Technology and the Pastoral Ideal in America*. New York: Oxford University Press, 1964.

McClintock, Anne. *Imperial Leather: Race, Gender, and Sexuality in the Imperial Contest*. New York: Routledge, 1995.

McCraw, Thomas K. *Prophets of Regulation*. Cambridge: Harvard University Press, 1984.

McGaw, Judith. "Women and the History of American Technology." *Signs* 7 (Summer 1982): 798-828.

McLuhan, T. C. *Dream Tracks: The Railroad and the American Indian 1890-1930*. New York: Harry N. Abrams, 1985.

McMillen, Neil. *Dark Journey: Black Mississippians in the Age of Jim Crow*. Urbana: University of Illinois Press, 1989.

Meeks, Carol Louis Vanderslice. *The Railroad Station: An Architectural History*. New Haven: Yale University Press, 1956.

Meikle, Jeffrey. *Twentieth Century Limited: Industrial Design in America*. Philadelphia: Temple University Press, 1979.

Menken, August. *The Railroad Passenger Car; An Illustrated History of the*

First Hundred Years with Accounts by Contemporary Passengers.
Baltimore: Johns Hopkins University Press 1957.

Meyerowitz, Joanne. *Women Adrift: Independent Wage Earners in Chicago, 1880–1930*. Chicago: Chicago University Press, 1988.

Middleton, Philip Harvey. *Railways and Public Opinion, Eleven Decades*. Chicago: Railway Business Association, 1941.

Minter, Patricia Hagler. "The Codification of Jim Crow: The Origins of Segregated Railroad Transit in the South, 1865–1910." Ph.D. diss., University of Virginia, 1994.

Molella, Arthur. "Mr. Fisher and Mr. Mumford." *Railroad History* 161 (Fall 1989): 5–8.

Montrose, Louis. "The Work of Gender in the Discourse of Discovery." *Representations* 33 (Winter 1991): 1–41.

Moshavi, Sharon. "In Japan, a Grope-Free Ride." *Boston Globe*, 4 July 2001.

Motz, Marilyn Ferris, and Pat Browne, eds. *Making the American Home: Middle-Class Women and Domestic Material Culture, 1840–1940*. Bowling Green, Ohio: Bowling Green State University Popular Press, 1988.

Nasaw, David. *Going Out: The Rise and Fall of Public Amusements*. New York: Basic Books, 1993.

Nash, Roderick. *Wilderness and the American Mind*. New Haven: Yale University Press, 1982.

Nissenbaum, Stephen. *The Battle for Christmas*. New York: Alfred A. Knopf, 1996.

"No More Separate Spheres!" *American Literature* 70, no. 3 (September 1998).

Nord, Deborah Epstein. *Walking the Victorian Streets: Women, Representation, and the City*. Ithaca: Cornell University Press, 1995.

Nye, David E. *American Technological Sublime*. Cambridge: MIT Press, 1994.

Ohmann, Richard. *Selling Culture: Magazines, Markets, and Class at the Turn of the Century*. New York: Verso, 1996.

O'Malley, Michael. *Keeping Watch, A History of American Time*. New York: Penguin Books, 1990.

Page, Martin. *The Lost Pleasures of the Great Trains*. London: Wiedenfeld and Nicolson, 1975.

Peiss, Kathy. *Cheap Amusements: Working Women and Leisure in Turn-of-the-Century New York*. Philadelphia: Temple University Press, 1986.

————. *Hope in a Jar: The Making of America's Beauty Culture*. New York: Metropolitan Books, 1998.

Perata, David D. *Those Pullman Blues: An Oral History of the African American Railroad Attendant*. New York: Twayne Publishers, 1996.

Persons, Stow. *The Decline of American Gentility*. New York: Columbia University Press, 1973.

Pesavento, Wilma J. "Sport and Recreation in the Pullman Experiment, 1880-1900." *Journal of Sport History* 9, no. 2 (Summer 1982): 38-62.

Poling-Kempes, Lesley. *The Harvey Girls: Women Who Opened the West*. New York: Paragon House, 1989.

Poovey, Mary. *Uneven Developments: The Ideological Work of Gender in Mid-Victorian England*. Chicago: University of Chicago Press, 1988.

Pratt, Mary Louise. *Imperial Eyes: Travel Writing and Transculturation*. London: Routledge, 1992.

Railroad Historical Research; A Fascinating and Valuable Avocation. What to Write and How to Write It. New York: Railroadians of America, 1946.

Rapson, Richard L., ed. *Britons View America: Travel Commentary, 1860-1935*. Seattle: University of Washington Press, 1971.

Rawls, Walton. *The Great Book of Currier & Ives' America*. New York: Abbeville Press, 1979.

Reed, Robert C. *Train Wrecks, A Pictorial History of Accidents on the Main Line*. New York: Bonanza Books, 1968.

Reinhardt, Richard. *Workin' on the Railroad, Reminiscences from the Age of Steam*. Palo Alto: American West Publishing Co., 1970.

Reynolds, David. *Walt Whitman's America: A Cultural Biography*. New York: Alfred A. Knopf, 1995.

Richards, Jeffrey, and John M. MacKenzie. *The Railway Station: A Social History*. Oxford: Clarendon, 1986.

Riegel, Stephen J. "The Persistent Career of Jim Crow: Lower Federal Courts and the 'Separate but Equal' Doctrine, 1865-1896." *American Journal of Legal History* 28 (January 1984): 17-40.

Rittenhouse, Mignon. *The Amazing Nellie Bly*. New York: E. P. Dutton, 1956.

Robinson, Jane. *Unsuitable for Ladies: An Anthology of Women Travellers*. New York: Oxford University Press, 1994.

————. *Wayward Women*. New York: Oxford University Press, 1991.

Rosenberg, Charles, and Carroll Smith-Rosenberg. "The Female Animal: Medical and Biological Views of Woman and Her Role in Nineteenth-Century America." In *Women and Health in America*, edited by Judith Walzer Leavitt, 12–27. Madison: University of Wisconsin Press, 1984.

Rosenzweig, Roy, and Elizabeth Blackmar. *The Park and the People: A History of Central Park*. Ithaca: Cornell University Press, 1992.

Ross, Ishbel. *Ladies of the Press: The Story of Women in Journalism by an Insider*. New York: Harper Brothers, 1936.

Rostow, W. W. *The Process of Economic Growth*. Oxford: Oxford University Press, 1953.

———. *The Stages of Economic Growth*. Cambridge: Cambridge University Press, 1960.

Rothstein, Edward. "The Transcontinental Railroad as the Internet of 1869." *New York Times*, 11 December 1999, B11.

Ruchames, Louis. "Jim Crow Railroads in Massachusetts." *American Quarterly* 8, no. 1 (Spring 1956): 61–75.

Russett, Cynthia Eagle. *Sexual Science: The Victorian Construction of Womanhood*. Cambridge: Harvard University Press, 1989.

Ryan, Mary P. *Civic Wars: Democracy and Public Life in the American City during the Nineteenth Century*. Berkeley: University of California Press, 1997.

———. *Cradle of the Middle Class: The Family in Oneida County, New York, 1790–1865*. New York: Cambridge University Press, 1981.

———. "Gender and Public Access: Women's Politics in Nineteenth-Century America." In *Habermas and the Public Sphere*, edited by Craig Calhoun, 259–88. Cambridge: MIT Press, 1992.

———. *Women in Public: Between Banners and Ballots, 1825–1880*. Baltimore: Johns Hopkins University Press, 1990.

Santino, Jack. *Miles of Smiles, Years of Struggle: Stories of Black Pullman Porters*. Urbana: University of Illinois Press, 1989.

Scanlon, Jennifer. *Inarticulate Longings: "The Ladies' Home Journal," Gender, and the Promises of Consumer Culture*. New York: Routledge, 1995.

Scharff, Virginia. *Taking the Wheel: Women and the Coming of the Motor Age*. New York: Free Press, 1991.

Schivelbusch, Wolfgang. *The Railway Journey: The Industrialization of Time and Space in the 19th Century*. Berkeley: University of California Press, 1986.

Schlichting, Kurt C. *Grand Central Terminal: Railroads, Engineering, and Architecture in New York City*. Baltimore: Johns Hopkins University Press, 2001.

Schneider, Dorothy, and Carl J. Schneider. *American Women in the Progressive Era*. New York: Facts on File, 1993.

Schriber, Mary Suzanne, ed. *Telling Travels: Selected Writings By Nineteenth-Century American Women Abroad*. Dekalb: Northern Illinois University Press, 1995.

Scott, Anne Firor. *The Southern Lady: From Pedestal to Politics, 1830-1930*. Chicago: University of Chicago Press, 1970.

Scott, Joan. "The Evidence of Experience." *Critical Inquiry* 17, no. 4 (1991): 773-97.

———. *Gender and the Politics of History*. New York: Columbia University Press, 1988.

Seale, William. *The Tasteful Interlude: American Interiors through the Camera's Eye, 1860-1917*. Nashville: American Association for State and Local History, 1981.

Sears, John F. *Sacred Places: American Tourist Attractions in the Nineteenth Century*. New York: Oxford University Press, 1989.

Sennett, Richard. *The Fall of Public Man*. New York: Vintage Books, 1978.

———, ed. *Classic Essays on the Culture of Cities*. Englewood Cliffs, N.J.: Prentice Hall, 1969.

Shaw, Stephanie J. *What a Woman Ought To Be and To Do: Black Professional Women Workers during the Jim Crow Era*. Chicago: University of Chicago Press, 1996.

Siano, Joseph. "Honk If You Think I'm Rude." *New York Times*, 15 February 2004, 11.

Sklar, Kathryn Kish. *Catharine Beecher: A Study in American Domesticity*. New Haven: Yale University Press, 1973.

Smith, Carl. *Chicago and the American Literary Imagination, 1880-1920*. Chicago: University of Chicago Press, 1984.

———. *Urban Disorder and the Shape of Belief: The Great Chicago Fire, the Haymarket Bomb, and the Model Town of Pullman*. Chicago: University of Chicago Press, 1995.

Smith-Rosenberg, Carroll. *Disorderly Conduct: Visions of Gender in Victorian America*. New York: Oxford University Press, 1985.

Spain, Daphne. *Gendered Spaces*. Chapel Hill: University of North Carolina Press, 1992.

———. *How Women Saved the City*. Minneapolis: University of Minnesota, Press, 2001.

Stanley, Amy Dru. "Home Life and the Morality of the Market." In *The Market Revolution in America: Social, Political, and Religious*

Expressions, edited by Melvyn Stokes and Stephen Conway, 74–96. Charlottesville: University Press of Virginia, 1996.

Stansell, Christine. *City of Women: Sex and Class in New York, 1789–1860*. Chicago: University of Illinois Press, 1987.

Stevenson, Louise L. *The Victorian Homefront: American Thought and Culture, 1860–1880*. New York: Twayne Publishers, 1991.

Stilgoe, John. *Metropolitan Corridor: Railroads and the American Scene*. New Haven: Yale University Press, 1983.

Stimpson, Catharine R. *Where the Meanings Are: Feminism and Cultural Spaces*. New York: Methuen, 1988.

The Story of Nellie Bly, American Flange Manufacturing Company, 1951.

Stover, John F. *The Life and Decline of the American Railroad*. New York: Oxford University Press, 1970.

Stowe, William W. *Going Abroad: European Travel in Nineteenth-Century American Culture*. Princeton: Princeton University Press, 1994.

Sutton, Horace. *Travellers: The American Tourist from Stagecoach to Space Shuttle*. New York: William Morrow, 1980.

Swiencicki, Mark A. "Consuming Brotherhood: Men's Culture, Style, and Recreation as Consumer Culture." *Journal of Social History* 31, no. 4 (Summer 1998): 773–808.

Taylor, William R. "The Evolution of Public Space in New York City: The Commercial Showcase of America." In *Consuming Visions: Accumulation and Display of Goods in America, 1880–1920*, edited by Simon Bronner, 287–309. New York: W. W. Norton, 1989.

Teachout, Terry. "The Best Part of the Rail Journey Was Found Outside My Window." *Wall Street Journal*, 28 January 2004, D6.

Thompson, E. P. *Making of the English Working Class*. London: V. Gollancz, 1963.

Tichi, Cecelia. *Shifting Gears: Technology, Literature, Culture in Modernist America*. Chapel Hill: University of North Carolina Press, 1987.

Tinling, Marion. *Women into the Unknown: A Sourcebook on Women Explorers and Travelers*. New York: Greenwood Press, 1989.

Vance, James E., Jr. *The North American Railroad: Its Origin, Evolution, and Geography*. Baltimore: Johns Hopkins University Press, 1995.

Wajcman, Judy. *Feminism Confronts Technology*. University Park: Pennsylvania State University Press, 1991.

Walkowitz, Judith. *City of Dreadful Delight: Narratives of Sexual Danger in Late-Victorian London*. Chicago: University of Chicago Press, 1992.

Wall, Diana diZerega. *The Archaeology of Gender: Separating the Spheres in Urban America*. New York: Plenum Press, 1994.

Ward, James A. *Railroads and the Character of America, 1820-1887*. Knoxville: University of Tennessee Press, 1986.

Ware, Susan, ed. *Modern American Women: A Documentary History*. 2nd ed. New York: McGraw-Hill, 1997.

————. *Still Missing: Amelia Earhart and the Search for Modern Feminism*. New York: W. W. Norton, 1999.

Welke, Barbara Y. *Recasting American Liberty: Gender, Race, Law, and the Railroad Revolution, 1865-1920*. New York: Cambridge University Press, 2001.

————. "When All the Women Were White, and All the Blacks Were Men: Gender, Class, Race, and the Road to Plessy, 1855-1914." *Law and History Review* 13, no. 2 (Fall 1995), 261-316.

Welter, Barbara. "The Cult of True Womanhood, 1820-1860." *American Quarterly* 18 (Summer 1966): 151-75.

White, John H., Jr. *The American Railroad Passenger Car*. Baltimore: Johns Hopkins University Press, 1978.

Wiebe, Robert. *The Search for Order, 1877-1920*. New York: Hill and Wang, 1967.

Wolff, Janet. "The Invisible Flaneuse: Women and the Literature of Modernity." *Theory, Culture and Society* 2, no. 3 (1985): 37-46.

Woodward, C. Vann. *Origins of the New South, 1877-1913*. Baton Rouge: Louisiana State University Press, 1951.

————. *The Strange Career of Jim Crow*. 2nd ed., rev. New York: Oxford University Press, 1966.

Wright, Gwendolyn. *Building the Dream: A Social History of Housing in America*. Cambridge: MIT Press, 1983.

————. *Moralism and the Model Home*. Chicago: University of Chicago Press, 1980.

Zunz, Olivier. *Making America Corporate, 1870-1920*. Chicago: University of Chicago Press, 1990.

INDEX

Dickens, Charles, 94

Dickinson, Anna, 49, 50, 55–56, 72

Discomfort of railroad travel, 42, 44, 60–61, 65–66, 183 (n. 36); devices to alleviate, 66

Domesticity: and armchair travel, 64–65, 188–89 (n. 26); consumerism, advertising, and, 213 (n. 11); consumerism vs. moral self-restraint in, 7, 61–62, 78–80, 82, 85, 87, 187 (n. 15), 213 (n. 11); contemporary forms of, in traveling situations, 162; extended to railway stations, 70–71, 190 (n. 47); and model trains, 63–64, 188 (n. 21); and morality of Victorian home, 61, 62, 71–72, 73–74, 77–78, 85, 192 (nn. 68, 69, 71), 194 (n. 84); and the parlor, 61, 63, 64, 65, 187 (n. 15), 188 (n. 19); parlor cars, as expressions of, 68, 69, 70, 79–80, 81, 82, 196 (n. 97); public spaces, as places of, 78–79, 187 (n. 2), 194–95 (n. 87); railroad cars as men's spaces of, 108–10, 205 (n. 100); railroad cars as places of, 4, 57, 59–61, 63, 169 (n. 26), 186 (n. 1), 187 (n. 17), 189–90 (n. 36); railroad cars as women's moral spaces of, 7–8, 71–72, 74–75, 80, 88; railroad cars' furnishings reflecting, 67–70, 71–72, 156, 190 (nn. 41, 53); railroad cars' uneven progress towards, 60–61, 187

(n. 9); values of, in Victorian homes, 61–62, 63–64, 65, 187 (nn. 14, 15), 188 (nn. 19, 20), 189 (n. 28); Victorian women and ideals of, 32–34, 37–39, 40, 74, 114, 193 (n. 73); women traveling to escape, 37, 181 (nn. 14, 15)

Dreiser, Theodore, 14, 19, 39

Dressing rooms/lavatories on trains, 44–45, 61, 67–68, 69, 70, 80, 183 (n. 36)

Droege, John, 71, 116, 124

Du Bois, W. E. B., 5

Dunbar-Nelson, Alice, 53, 56, 113, 127

du Pont, Louisa d'Andelot, 50, 52

Elliott, Howard, 116

Emigrant cars, 81–82, 83, 86, 108, 196 (nn. 98, 99), 201 (n. 48)

Engineers, 36; and dangers of railway life, 149–51, 216 (nn. 48, 50), 217 (n. 53); psychological strains on, 136, 151–53, 216 (nn. 46, 47); qualities and duties, 149–51, 215–16 (nn. 38, 44)

Englishwoman in America, An (Bird), 86

Erichsen, John Eric, 152, 153, 154

Etiquette books: for African Americans to follow for train travel, 48, 101–2, 202–3 (n. 66); on dressing room use, 44–45; on gentlemanliness, 101–2, 199 (n. 23); on honeymoon trips, 35; on ladies' car use, 93, 95; on ladyhood,

as American version of first-
class, 81; influence of furnishings on home tastes, 79–80,
192 (n. 67), 195 (nn. 90, 91);
limiting speed of trains, 71;
luxurious décor of, 68, 73–
74, 78–80, 187 (n. 9), 188–89
(n. 26), 191 (nn. 55, 61), 192
(n. 67). *See also* Sleeping cars
Pullman Car Tea Shop, 194–95
(n. 87)
Pullman Palace Car Company:
advertising luxury of cars, 68,
79–80, 188–89 (n. 26); company town of, 208 (n. 39);
company treatment of women
passengers, 93, 200 (n. 31);
detectives checking workers of,
121; dressing rooms, 45; and
expectations of service, 124,
177 (n. 66); and honeymoon
accommodations, 180 (n. 8);
and Jim Crow segregation, 131,
211 (n. 97); and politeness,
as company policy, 119–20,
124, 133, 208 (n. 41); poor pay
of workers, 122–23, 133; rule
books of, 124, 131, 211 (nn. 97,
98); service standards of, 177
(nn. 66, 67)
Pullman porters, 128–33; and
African American passengers,
129; duties of, 129, 131–32,
211 (n. 94); enforcing Jim
Crow segregation, 131, 211
(n. 97); hardworking reputation of, 129, 131, 207 (n. 19),
211 (n. 92); and intimacy with
white women, 131, 210–11

(n. 91); passenger perception of, 115, 129, 131–33, 178
(n. 74), 212 (nn. 101–3); and
politeness, 26, 112–13, 207
(n. 19); and politeness as job
vs. gentlemanliness, 115, 119–
20, 124–25, 133, 207 (n. 21),
208 (n. 41); significance of
being African American, 25,
128–29, 177 (n. 67), 210–11 (nn.
89, 91); songs about, 129, 211
(n. 92); subsidized leisure activities for, 131; and tipping,
47, 132–33; union organizing
of, 178 (n. 74), 207 (n. 20); vs.
maids, 206 (n. 10)
Pullman Porters' Review, 115
Putnam, Emily, 90, 90–91, 92,
198 (n. 8)
Putnam's Magazine, 22, 96

Racism on trains: black porters experiencing, 132–33,
212 (n. 102); men experiencing, 111, 128, 202 (n. 60), 203
(n. 67); women experiencing,
47, 83–84, 100–102, 185–86
(n. 79), 203 (n. 67); women
legally challenging, 99–100,
102–4, 111, 203–4 (n. 71);
women reacting to, 54–55, 100,
127–28, 210 (n. 84)
Rail gauge, 14, 171 (n. 11)
Railroad cars: dressing rooms/
lavatories in, 44–45, 61, 67–
68, 69, 70, 80, 183 (n. 36);
furnishings reflecting domesticity, 67–70, 71–72, 156, 190
(n. 41), 190–91 (n. 53); lack of

privacy in open, 17, 21, 44, 66–67, 80–81; luxury of, compared with rugged scenery, 72–73, 191 (n. 61); as men's spaces of domesticity, 108–10, 205 (n. 100); open cars as symbol of classless society, 17–18, 66–67, 195–96 (n. 92); open cars as symbol of classless society, challenges to, 80–81, 97, 196 (n. 96); as public places of domesticity, 4, 57, 59–61, 63, 169 (n. 26), 186 (n. 1), 187 (n. 17), 189–90 (n. 36); uneven progress towards domesticity, 60–61, 187 (n. 9); vestibules, 68, 189–90 (n. 36); as women's moral spaces of domesticity, 7–8, 71–72, 74–75, 80, 88. *See also* Jim Crow railcars; Ladies' cars; Privacy, lack of in railroad cars; Public culture; Pullman cars; Sleeping cars; Smoking cars; Specialty cars

Railroad companies: accommodating more passengers, 13–14, 170 (n. 9); administration of, 11, 14, 169–70 (n. 1); control of commercial nature of, 23–25, 175–76 (nn. 55, 56); increase in amenities offered by, 25–26, 67–68, 177 (nn. 66, 67); and legal liability for passengers, 24, 126–27, 176 (n. 58); and libraries and reading rooms for employees, 118–19, 208 (n. 39); politeness of railway workers as policy of, 112–23, 125–27, 207 (nn. 19, 27), 208

(n. 41); promoting for vacations, 156–57; promoting image as cure for modern stress, 155–57; rule books of, 119–21, 124, 125–27, 131, 211 (nn. 97, 98); rule books of, for passengers, 177 (n. 61); treatment of women passengers by, 93, 107, 199–200 (nn. 28, 31). *See also* Railway workers; Victorian advertising; *individual companies*

Railroad Division of the Young Men's Christian Association, 118

Railroad literature. *See* Narratives of railroads

Railroads, The: Their Origin and Problems (Adams), 11

Railway Age, 77, 108, 142; on conductors' quarters, 118; on death of engineer, 151–52; on Jim Crow cars, 85, 111; on politeness on railroads, 87, 106, 116; promoting railroads as cure for modern stress, 156; on Pullman cars, 79; on women in railway advertising, 75; on women railway workers, 139; and women's rights, 105, 107

Railway Age and Northwestern Railroader, 81, 111

Railway News, 80

"Railway spine," 66, 152

Railway stations, 70–71, 190 (n. 47)

Railway workers: and dangers of railway life, 149–51, 216 (nn. 48, 50), 217 (n. 53); and detectives checking work of, 121–22; as gentlemen, 47, 112, 113–14, 115–23, 127, 206 (n. 2); home-like quarters provided for, 118–19, 208 (n. 34); libraries and reading rooms provided for, 118–19, 208 (n. 39); politeness of, required by railroad companies, 112–23, 125–27, 207 (nn. 19, 27), 208 (n. 41); politeness of vs. freely given gentlemanliness, 47, 115, 124–25, 128, 133, 207 (nn. 19, 21), 209 (n. 67); poor pay of, 122–23, 133; psychological strain on, 136, 151–53, 216 (nn. 46, 47); and unruly passengers, 125–27; women as, 139–40. *See also* Conductors; Engineers; Pullman porters

Respectability: and accommodation for men on trains, 95–98, 108–9, 204 (n. 81); and African American men, 101–2, 111, 128, 202 (n. 60), 203 (n. 67); and African American women, 45, 46, 47, 53–54, 92, 99–104, 199 (n. 26), 202–3 (nn. 58, 65, 66, 67); etiquette on, 33, 106–7, 182–83 (n. 32), 188 (n. 20), 191 (n. 57), 198 (n. 11); and exposure of private life on trains, 6, 21, 28–30, 42, 44, 72, 75; and Jim Crow railcars, 85, 102, 111, 127, 198 (n. 11); and ladyhood, 46, 53–54, 90–93, 198 (n. 14), 199 (nn. 24, 26), 202 (nn. 58, 65, 66); and outfits for traveling, 41–42, 43, 45, 182–

83 (n. 32); and possibility of being kissed in a tunnel, 22–23, 175 (n. 52), 185–86 (n. 79); and social class, 32–33, 92–93, 165 (n. 1), 179 (n. 3), 199 (n. 24); as Victorian value, 4, 7, 27, 114, 165 (n. 1); and women accepting service of strange men, 23, 45–46, 48–52, 86–88, 89–90; and women travelers maintaining, 6, 32–34, 35, 37, 44, 148–49, 179–80 (n. 4)

Rhodes, Albert, 105

Rock Island Railroad, 44

Romance in Transit, A (Lynde), 141

Rules for the Government of the Transportation Department (Pennsylvania Railroad), 120

Ruth, John A., 45

Rutland & Burlington Railroad, 121

Sanborn, E. W., 26, 132, 133

"Santa Claus' New Team" (story), 15, 16

Santa Fe Railroad, 119

Saturday Evening Post, 136

Savannah, Florida and Western Railway Company, 70

Scenery, from trains: celebrated by railroad company advertising, 20, 172 (n. 28), 173 (n. 39), 174 (n. 40); compared with luxury of trains, 72–73, 191 (n. 61); creating American consciousness by travel through it, 18–19, 20, 56; inspiring women's imaginations, 55–56, 57

201 (n. 48); Wagner Palace Car, 59, 61. *See also* Emigrant cars; Ladies' cars; Pullman cars; Railroad cars; Sleeping cars; Smoking cars

Speed of trains, 56–57, 71, 190 (n. 52)

Spice Mill, 38

Spotters, railway, 121–22

Standard time, 14, 171 (n. 11)

Stereographs, 64, 65

Stevens, John, 13

Stevenson, Louise, 64

Taylor, Benjamin Franklin, 30, 42, 44, 60, 96, 112

Taylor, Joseph, 115, 116, 126, 150

Teachout, Terry, 162

Technology of railroads, 12–15, 31, 56–57, 67, 68–70; anxiety about, 20, 174 (n. 41); creating mobility, 19–20; equipment standardization, 14, 171 (n. 11); first locomotives, 12, 13; from individual short lines to integrated system, 13–14, 20; and innovations throughout nineteenth century, 12–13, 25, 67, 170 (n. 5), 191 (n. 55)

Terrell, Mary Church, 54, 55, 83, 92, 127

Texas Railroad, 84

Their Wedding Journey (Howells), 16

Thomas, John J., 36

Tour guides, 114

Transcontinental railroad, 1–2, 19; Boston Board of Trade excursion to San Francisco, 36,

73, 173 (n. 35), 193 (n. 76); changes in, according to social class, 81–83; "golden spike" ceremony for, 13–14; and transforming power of travel, 57–58

Travel books. *See* Guidebooks

Traveling salesmen, 39–40, 182 (n. 25)

Traveller's Tour (parlor game), 65

Travels at Home and Voyages by the Fire-side for the Instruction of Young Persons (Lloyd), 64

"Types of Railroad Travelers" (article), 27

Union Pacific Railroad, 11, 13, 156, 169–70 (n. 1)

Vacation Gospel (railroad publication), 156

Vacations, trains for, 26, 53, 156–57, 185 (n. 76)

Vanderbilt, Cornelius, 118

Van De Warker, Ely, 153–54, 155

Vermont & Massachusetts Railway, 25

Vestibules in railroad cars, 68, 189–90 (n. 36)

Victorian advertising: and board games using Phoebe Snow and Nellie Bly, 144, 145; and Dr. Morse's Indian Root Pills, using Nellie Bly, 144, 146; and Pennsylvania Railroad poster girl, 1, 2; women and railroad imagery in, 63; women used in, 138, 144–46

—for railroads: addressed to

women, 80, 93, 140; and luxurious amenities, 25, 68, 70, 80, 108-9; Phoebe Snow as fictional spokesperson for, 140-41, 157, 159-60; scenery celebrated in, 20, 172 (n. 28), 173 (n. 39), 174 (n. 40); using images of women, 75, 76, 139. *See also* Fashion and railroad imagery

Victorian values, 4, 166 (n. 9); consumerism vs. self-restraint, 7, 61-62, 78-80, 82, 85, 87, 187 (n. 15), 213 (n. 11); freely given gentlemanliness vs. impersonal service, 47, 115, 124-25, 128, 133, 207 (nn. 19, 21), 209 (n. 67); and gender differences, 103-4, 155, 193 (n. 73); gentlemanliness vs. consumerism, 86-87, 107-8; manliness, 138, 149, 150-52, 213 (n. 12); progress, 1, 4-5, 18-19, 20, 63, 71, 72, 155, 167 (n. 12), 173 (nn. 30, 31); self-restraint vs. consumerism, 24-25, 80, 81, 176-77 (n. 60); separate spheres of men and women, 6-8, 9, 32-34, 94; white supremacy, 52, 173 (n. 37); and women, changes brought about by railroads, 5-6, 137-39, 140-42, 147-49. *See also* Domesticity; Respectability

Voice of the Negro, 53

Wagner Palace Car, 59, 61
Walbourn, Charles, 133
Warman, Cy, 136

Welke, Barbara, 99
Wells, Ida B., 45, 54-55, 100, 127
Whitman, Walt, 13, 15
Williams, Anna, 102
Williams, Fannie Barrier, 53
Wilson, Edward, 64
"Womanhood and American Chivalry" (article), 105-6, 110
Women: admiring railroads as male endeavor, 56-57; "American Girl" of late nineteenth century, 158-60, 218 (n. 73); American vs. British, health of, 154; as civilizers of men, 90-91, 96, 198 (nn. 8-10); as civilizers of men, challenges to, 104-7, 110-11, 204 (n. 83), 205 (n. 98); locomotives compared with, 32, 33, 34, 179 (nn. 1, 2); new models of, in railway literature, 134-39, 212 (n. 6); and New Woman of late nineteenth century, 9, 57, 137-39, 141-42, 144, 147, 154-55, 158, 213 (nn. 9, 13); public address of, 107, 205 (n. 97); and public conduct, 5-6, 168 (nn. 18, 20), 169 (n. 24); as railway workers, 139-40; role played in quarters provided for railway workers, 118, 208 (n. 34). *See also* African American passengers; Domesticity; Women passengers
Women passengers: actresses and suffragists, 181-82 (n. 16); asserting rights, 105-7; with bouquets, 75, 193 (n. 76); as chaperones, 114; as confi-

dence women, 23, 91; creating railcars as moral spaces of domesticity, 7–8, 71–72, 74–75, 80, 88; enjoying speed and adventure of train travel, 56–57, 186 (n. 91); heroic women travelers, 142–44, 158–59, 180 (n. 5), 214 (nn. 22, 23, 25, 27); as ill-suited for commercial life, 38–40, 47; inconveniences of train travel, 42, 44, 60–61, 65–66, 183 (n. 36); locomotive driving/riding, real and fictional, 134–36, 141–42, 144, 147, 148, 157, 158, 214 (n. 27), 215 (n. 35); maintaining family ties while traveling alone, 36–37, 181 (n. 12); maintaining respectability despite lack of privacy, 6, 32–34, 35, 37, 44, 179–80 (n. 4); and nervous strain of train travel, 153–56, 217 (nn. 55–57); as observers of strangers, 48–51, 184 (n. 53); packing for train travel, 40–41, 42, 182 (nn. 27, 28); receiving gentlemanly help, 40, 45–47, 50–51, 86–92, 157, 197–98 (nn. 1, 2, 7); talking with strangers unlike themselves, 51–52; and travel as identity-changing, 53–54, 55, 186 (n. 83); traveling alone, 36, 38, 39–40, 42, 45–47, 51; traveling for extended family reasons, 36–37; traveling outfit of, 41–42, 43, 148, 182–83 (n. 32), 215 (n. 36); traveling skills of, 47–48; traveling to escape domesticity, 37, 181 (nn. 14, 15); traveling with husbands, 35–36, 44. *See also* African American passengers; Domesticity; Ladies' cars; Women

Woodman, Abby, 56

World's Work, 19, 71

Youth's Companion, 136

GENDER & AMERICAN CULTURE

Too Much to Ask: Black Women in the Era of Integration, by Elizabeth Higginbotham (2001).

Imagining Medea: Rhodessa Jones and Theater for Incarcerated Women, by Rena Fraden (2001).

Painting Professionals: Women Artists and the Development of Modern American Art, 1870–1920, by Kirsten Swinth (2001).

Remaking Respectability: African American Women in Interwar Detroit, by Victoria W. Wolcott (2001).

Ida B. Wells-Barnett and American Reform, 1880–1930, by Patricia A. Schechter (2001).

Taking Haiti: Military Occupation and the Culture of U.S. Imperialism, 1915–1940, by Mary A. Renda (2001).

Before Jim Crow: The Politics of Race in Postemancipation Virginia, by Jane Dailey (2000).

Captain Ahab Had a Wife: New England Women and the Whalefishery, 1720–1870, by Lisa Norling (2000).

Civilizing Capitalism: The National Consumers' League, Women's Activism, and Labor Standards in the New Deal Era, by Landon R. Y. Storrs (2000).

Rank Ladies: Gender and Cultural Hierarchy in American Vaudeville, by M. Alison Kibler (1999).

Strangers and Pilgrims: Female Preaching in America, 1740–1845, by Catherine A. Brekus (1998).

Sex and Citizenship in Antebellum America, by Nancy Isenberg (1998).

Yours in Sisterhood: Ms. Magazine and the Promise of Popular Feminism, by Amy Erdman Farrell (1998).

We Mean to Be Counted: White Women and Politics in Antebellum Virginia, by Elizabeth R. Varon (1998).

Women Against the Good War: Conscientious Objection and Gender on the American Home Front, 1941–1947, by Rachel Waltner Goossen (1997).

Toward an Intellectual History of Women: Essays by Linda K. Kerber (1997).

Gender and Jim Crow: Women and the Politics of White Supremacy in North Carolina, 1896–1920, by Glenda Elizabeth Gilmore (1996).

Delinquent Daughters: Protecting and Policing Adolescent Female Sexuality in the United States, 1885–1920, by Mary E. Odem (1995).

U.S. History as Women's History: New Feminist Essays, edited by Linda K. Kerber, Alice Kessler-Harris, and Kathryn Kish Sklar (1995).

Common Sense and a Little Fire: Women and Working-Class Politics in the United States, 1900–1965, by Annelise Orleck (1995).

How Am I to Be Heard?: Letters of Lillian Smith, edited by Margaret Rose Gladney (1993).

Entitled to Power: Farm Women and Technology, 1913–1963, by Katherine Jellison (1993).

Revising Life: Sylvia Plath's Ariel Poems, by Susan R. Van Dyne (1993).

Made From This Earth: American Women and Nature, by Vera Norwood (1993).

Unruly Women: The Politics of Social and Sexual Control in the Old South, by Victoria E. Bynum (1992).

The Work of Self-Representation: Lyric Poetry in Colonial New England, by Ivy Schweitzer (1991).

Labor and Desire: Women's Revolutionary Fiction in Depression America, by Paula Rabinowitz (1991).

Community of Suffering and Struggle: Women, Men, and the Labor Movement in Minneapolis, 1915–1945, by Elizabeth Faue (1991).

All That Hollywood Allows: Re-reading Gender in 1950s Melodrama, by Jackie Byars (1991).

Doing Literary Business: American Women Writers in the Nineteenth Century, by Susan Coultrap-McQuin (1990).

Ladies, Women, and Wenches: Choice and Constraint in Antebellum Charleston and Boston, by Jane H. Pease and William H. Pease (1990).

The Secret Eye: The Journal of Ella Gertrude Clanton Thomas, 1848–1889, edited by Virginia Ingraham Burr, with an introduction by Nell Irvin Painter (1990).

Second Stories: The Politics of Language, Form, and Gender in Early American Fictions, by Cynthia S. Jordan (1989).

Within the Plantation Household: Black and White Women of the Old South, by Elizabeth Fox-Genovese (1988).

The Limits of Sisterhood: The Beecher Sisters on Women's Rights and Woman's Sphere, by Jeanne Boydston, Mary Kelley, and Anne Margolis (1988).